D0908515

GEORGE WASHINGTON JULIAN
RADICAL REPUBLICAN

Indiana Historical Collections
Volume XLV

GEORGE WASHINGTON JULIAN

GEORGE WASHINGTON JULIAN

Radical Republican

A Study in Nineteenth-Century Politics and Reform

By

Patrick W. Riddleberger

INDIANA HISTORICAL BUREAU

1966

To

Anne and Francis

PREFACE ⟨◇⟩◇⟨◇⟩◇⟨◇⟩◇⟨◇⟩◇⟨◇⟩◇⟨◇⟩◇⟨◇⟩

GEORGE WASHINGTON JULIAN was not in the first rank of American leaders of his generation. Schoolboys would not have heard of him from their teachers or read about him in their textbooks. The highest elective office he held was that of Congressman from his Indiana district, hardly an elevated position. But his name has a way of cropping up in more specialized works on such diverse subjects as public land policy, woman's rights, antislavery, Free Soilism, the labor movement, the Radical Republicans, the Liberal Republican Movement, the settlement of the West, the Quakers, and the Unitarians. In short, Julian's life and career touched many of the nerve-endings of his era. From 1840 to 1890 he was a member of five different political parties and was active in most of the important reform movements of these years. But the major theme that emerges as one deepens his research on Julian is the combination of reformer and politician. He was a man deeply involved in mid-nineteenth-century reform and at the same time driven on by personal political ambition. When conditions were right he was rewarded with political office which abetted his reformism. When they were not right Julian's life was one of frustration, or even tragedy.

Julian's personal story is in some measure enmeshed in the larger tragedy of the Civil War itself, especially since he was a public man both before and after the war. Everybody knows now of the profound changes ushered in by the Civil War, but our minds may be refreshed as to the poignancy of these changes by examining the career of an active participant, like Julian, for whom both the nature and magnitude of change were unexpected and harsh.

My original interest in Julian was aroused by the fact that he was one of the Radical Republicans, whose role during the years of Civil War and Reconstruction has been so intriguing and baffling to historians. Questions about the Radicals, especially their motivations, are as alive today as they have been throughout nearly a century of historical dialectics on the subject. Indeed, it may well be that I have placed Julian in the broader framework of political reform throughout five or six decades of the nineteenth century because this became necessary to an understanding of his radical Republicanism. I have found the abandonment of the Negro by Julian and some other Radicals during Reconstruction to be an engrossing and a most significant aspect of Reconstruction history. Although my personal biases have made the task more difficult, I have tried to understand these men rather than sit in judgment on them from the vantage point of a century.

It is no longer possible, I believe, to avoid the psychological problems that confront the biographer, for they are inherent in this kind of historical writing. And where the subject of the biography is a "true believer" the probability of psychic questions arising is increased. In attempting to handle these problems, which I submit in Julian's case must be dealt with if the book is to be valid, I have sought and received professional advice. Even so, those portions of the book treating psychological explanations remain the most tenuous, and I hope that the reader will find in them suggestions which may make for clearer insights rather than conclusive evidence or fixed ideas.

The debts that one owes in the writing of a book—even a little book such as this one—are many and varied, and the author himself may not be consciously aware of all of them. In the list of creditors are teachers, friends, colleagues, and loved ones who in some way have had an effect on the tone and quality of the book. But there are those to whom we know we are indebted and without whose help the book could not have been written.

I am especially indebted to Professor Kenneth M. Stampp of the University of California, Berkeley, in whose seminar I was introduced, so to speak, to the Radical Republicans. His unflagging interest and support during a busy and productive period of his life has been a constant source of encouragement to me.

The Indiana Historical Bureau has been co-operative in every way. I am indeed fortunate in having as editors Miss Gayle Thornbrough and Miss Dorothy Riker. Their keen editorial eye and their intimate knowledge of Indiana history have made this a better book than it otherwise could have been.

During my sojourn in the Indiana State Library Mrs. Hazel Hopper and Mr. Harold Burton, as well as other members of the Library staff, were always helpful. Mr. Luther Feeger, publisher and editor of the Richmond (Indiana) *Palladium-Item,* generously made available to me the back files of the Richmond *Palladium.* I am equally indebted to the staff of the Manuscript Division, Library of Congress, where much of the research was carried on.

I am grateful to Dr. Roger Bardsley of Livermore, California, for suggestions concerning the psychological aspects of Julian's life.

Southern Illinois University has made my task easier by giving me released time from teaching duties as well as a financial grant for typing. I am indebted to Miss Joan Zilinski for typing the last seven chapters of the manuscript, under the pressure of time and circumstances.

The manuscript has been read in whole or in part by Earl S. Beard, Director, University of Wisconsin County Center, Sheboygan; Frank Otto Gatell, Stanford University; Harold M. Hyman, University of Illinois; and Donald Dolton, English Department, Washington University, St. Louis. I am grateful to all of them for criticism and suggestions. Of course, I am alone responsible for errors and other deficiencies.

PATRICK W. RIDDLEBERGER

SOUTHERN ILLINOIS UNIVERSITY
EDWARDSVILLE CAMPUS
February, 1966

CONTENTS

ILLUSTRATIONS

THE
WHITEWATER
VALLEY

CHAPTER 1

ON a day in the autumn of 1823 Isaac Julian packed his wife, Rebecca, and six small children into a covered wagon and moved them from Centreville, a town in Wayne County near the eastern border of Indiana, to an area farther west known as the New Purchase. He had already visited here and built a cabin on a site near Lafayette, where he hoped to start a new life. The fourth child of the family was George Washington Julian, born May 5, 1817, and six years old at the time of the New Purchase venture.[1]

Isaac Julian had migrated to Indiana Territory in 1808, and had soon risen to a position of some prominence for a young man. He courted and won the hand of Rebecca Hoover, a daughter of one of Wayne County's most respected families. After military service in the War of 1812, he began a career as a public servant and became successively justice of the peace, county commissioner, and trustee of the town of Centreville. In 1822 he launched what appeared to be a promising political career by winning election to the state legislature at Corydon.[2]

---

1 Grace Julian Clarke, *George W. Julian (Indiana Historical Collections,* Vol. 11, Indianapolis, 1923), 1, 27-30.

2 *Ibid.,* 28-29; Stephen B. Weeks, *Southern Quakers and Slavery . . .* (Baltimore, 1896), 283.

The reasons for his decision to move away from Centreville are not altogether clear. One of them might have been that while in the legislature he had signed several notes for a friend who had defaulted. Called on to make good the notes, Isaac may have seen that the quickest way to secure the needed funds was to sell his home. With the proceeds he would be able to pay off the debt and move to a more unsettled area where land was cheaper.[3] However, the move also may have resulted from an argument between Isaac and his brother-in-law, Henry Hoover, over the location of the county seat in Wayne County. They were contestants in a larger controversy between Salisbury and Centreville which ended in 1817 with the removal of the county government from Salisbury to Centreville; but enmities remained, and the breech between Isaac and Henry was one of those that never healed.[4] It is also conceivable that a man like Isaac, full of pride and confidence and intent on making his own way in the world, was embarrassed and annoyed by his marital ties with the Hoovers, whose prestige in the community exceeded his own. Nor was migration westward strange to a Julian, in whose family it had become almost a tradition since the arrival in Maryland of René St. Julien from France early in the eighteenth century. Succeeding generations of Julians (the adopted American name of the family) moved to Virginia and later to North Carolina, whence Isaac came to Indiana in the great Quaker migration of the early nineteenth century.[5]

3 Clarke, *Julian*, 29.

4 Henry Clay Fox, *Memoirs of Wayne County and the City of Richmond Indiana* (2 vols. Madison, Wis., 1912), 1:37-38.

5 Grace Julian Clarke, "Isaac Hoover Julian," in *Indiana Magazine of History*, 28 (1932):9-12.

Whatever the reasons for Isaac's decision to move, the subsequent events were tragic. Shortly before the departure Isaac had contracted a fever. During the journey his illness grew more severe, and within a month after arriving at the new home he was dead. Fortunately the widow, courageous and resourceful, was ready and able to assume her new responsibilities. Her first step was to dispose of the new homestead and to take her children back to Wayne County, among her own people. There was little money, but enough to purchase a fifty-acre farm near Centreville. Here she entered into the arduous undertaking of raising her family.[6]

Rebecca Hoover Julian belonged to the third generation of her family in America. Her German grandfather, Andrew Hoover, settled originally in Maryland. After a sojourn in Pennsylvania the family migrated, around 1750, to North Carolina, where they joined a Quaker settlement in Randolph County. Later Rebecca's father led the family to Ohio, but not satisfied there, he sent his sons scouting for a new location suitable for a permanent home. Thus it was that in 1806 David Hoover chose for the family home the area in the northern sector of the Whitewater Valley that would later become Wayne County, Indiana. The following year the Hoover family moved in along with a few other Ohio families, the advance guard of a general Quaker migration into the area.[7]

The chief geographical feature of the fertile and bucolic region into which they came was the Whitewater River, which flowed south generally parallel to the Ohio border and eventually changed its direction to the southeast

6 Clarke, *Julian*, 30-31.
7 Fox, *Memoirs of Wayne County*, 1:17-18, 56-57, 541-49.

before emptying into the Ohio River at Lawrenceburg.
The triangle of land, known as "the Gore," containing
the Whitewater and its East Fork, was part of the land
ceded by the Indians under the terms of the Treaty of
Greenville in 1795 and in 1803 became part of Indiana
Territory. A number of emigrants from North Carolina,
many of them Quakers, soon established themselves in
the area comprising present Franklin and Union counties
lying south of the present Wayne County, which came
to be known as the "Carolina Settlement."[8] In 1809 the
Indians ceded a strip of land lying west of the Gore
through which the West Fork of the Whitewater flowed.
Into this area and into the present Fayette and Wayne
counties there came more Quakers, who by this time
were joined by Methodists and Baptists.[9]

By the time Rebecca returned with her brood from
Lafayette the upper Whitewater Valley was in the throes
of a virulent contest for control between Quakers and
Methodists. The Quakers, jealous of their initial hold,
bitterly resented Methodist inroads, barred their schools
and meeting places to the itinerant preachers of the opposition, refused them the shelter of their homes, and
sought in every way to check the Wesleyan advance. Only
late in the decade, after the Methodists had entrenched
themselves beyond hope of expulsion, did the contest
subside.[10] Although there was no final victor in this
contest, the region, especially Wayne County, maintained
a strong Quaker flavor.

8 Chelsea L. Lawlis, "Settlement of the Whitewater Valley, 1790-1810,"
in *Indiana Magazine of History*, 43 (1947):23-35.
9 *Ibid.*, 43:36-37,
10 Chelsea L. Lawlis, "Migration to the Whitewater Valley, 1820-1830,"
in *Indiana Magazine of History*, 43 (1947):235-36.

Cincinnati was the entrepôt of the area. Through that city most of the immigrants came, and over the quaggy roads leading to it pioneer farmers hauled their wheat and bacon and drove their herds of cattle; occassionally a stagecoach made its way over the hazardous seventy-five miles between Cincinnati and Cambridge City, on the western fringe of Wayne County.[11]

Whitewater Valley people had another outlet to the east along the National Road, which was completed as far as Richmond on the eastern border of Indiana when George Julian was ten years of age. But their commercial orientation at this stage of their history was toward rivers and canals rather than turnpikes, and they looked forward to a day in the not distant future when they would have easy access to the great Ohio. Thus the "canal fever" that spread throughout America during the third and fourth decades of the nineteenth century was indigenous to this developing western region.[12]

In 1836, after nearly fifteen years of debate on the subject, provision for a canal to parallel the Whitewater River from the National Road to the Ohio River was included in the Internal Improvement Act passed by the state legislature.[13] But the canal was never finished by the state. The internal improvements question was one of the most difficult in Indiana during the Jacksonian era, and the people of the Whitewater Valley were still aroused over it in 1845, the year Wayne County sent youthful George Julian to the state legislature. Indeed, it was Julian's stand on a bill involving the state debt, contracted

---

11 Fox, *Memoirs of Wayne County*, 1:119-20.

12 Chelsea L. Lawlis, "Prosperity and Hard Times in the Whitewater Valley, 1830-1840," in *Indiana Magazine of History*, 43 (1947):369-70.

13 *Ibid.*; *Laws of Indiana*, 1835-36 (general), p. 7.

as the result of a canal-building program, that would give him his first political prominence in the Hoosier state.

The antislavery movement also commanded the attention of Whitewater Valley people. Many of the Quaker migrants from the South had come to escape the incubus of the "peculiar institution," and although the Quakers themselves were divided on the question of abolition, their presence in Wayne County made it the center of the antislavery movement in Indiana. As a locale it was made to order for such action, and nearly a decade before William Lloyd Garrison organized the American Anti-Slavery Society, Levi Coffin had made the village of Newport a station, perhaps the first one, in the Underground Railroad. Then in 1836 the Indiana Yearly Meeting of Friends provided the leadership in the formation of the Indiana Anti-Slavery Society.[14]

II

It was to this region, not far removed from the pioneer stage, that George Julian at age seven returned with his mother and his brothers and sisters. John, an attractive and affectionate boy of twelve, was the oldest son on whose shoulders fell responsibilities beyond his years. He was more like a father than anybody else in the Julian household. From speeches of favorite politicians, especially Henry Clay, and from the works of Tom Paine and Robert Burns, he read to the family in the evening around the fireside. Somewhat later, Garrison's *Liberator* was included in the reading material. The Bible, which was an

14 William Henry Smith, *A Political History of Slavery* . . . (2 vols. New York and London, 1903), 1:9; Carl R. Fish, *The Rise of the Common Man, 1830-1850* (New York, 1927), 276-77; Lawlis, "Prosperity and Hard Times in the Whitewater Valley," in *Indiana Magazine of History*, 43:373.

essential in this orthodox Quaker family, Rebecca herself read to the children.[15]

After John came ten-year-old Sarah, then Jacob, who was two years older than George. Elizabeth and Isaac, an infant of six months at the time of the Lafayette move, were the two children younger than George.[16] From this large family circle it was Isaac, a romantic and a poet who was never able to adjust to the practical realities of life, to whom George was most attached. The warm friendship that developed between them in their childhood ripened as they grew through adolescence and into manhood.

The year 1823 was a traumatic one for George Julian. Shortly before the departure for Lafayette his two-year-old brother, Henry, had died. Then there was the uprooting of the family from Centreville, followed by the death of the father and then the return to Centreville to a different house from the one he had left. The timidity and shyness that characterized him in his early years are understandable in these circumstances. That he did not stray often or far from his mother's side is natural enough. Rebecca Julian was no ordinary woman, and she lent her faith and her strength to her children and dedicated her life to them. At age seven or eight George was a witness to a proposal of marriage to her and heard her refusal on the ground that her life was not hers but her children's.[17] Accepting adversity as something to be expected, Rebecca organized the family into a co-operative and functioning unit. Although she received some help from her brother, Henry Hoover, whose house they shared for a time during the winter of 1823 and 1824, the Julian family was soon essentially on its own. Each child had his assigned chores

15 Clarke, *Julian,* 32.
16 *Ibid.,* 29n-30n.
17 *Ibid.,* 32-36.

to do, and as the children grew older responsibilities were
increased. To Rebecca's way of thinking one must meet
and overcome adversity almost as a test of the right to
live. If one would use his talents and energies to the
utmost, live clean and work hard, God would do the rest.
Her unquestioning orthodox Quaker faith undoubtedly
served her well, and without it the difficulties she faced
after her husband's death might have been overwhelming.[18] Her strong personality and character left their im-
print on her son, George, who at the time also shared her
religious zeal. Later, however, both the mother's character
and her religion led to problems, the solutions of which
brought decisions that would shape George's life and
career.

In this household, in which the mother was the dominant figure, George experienced both warmth and auster-
ity. He liked to lie on the floor at his mother's feet listen-
ing to her conversation with friends who would call. The
favorite visitor seems to have been Mrs. Martha Sackett,
wife of the county recorder, who engaged Rebecca in just
the sort of conversation George liked to hear.[19] They
talked of the pioneer days, the development of the Valley,
events in the lives of friends and relatives, and the usual
gossip of rural family life. And there may have been talk
of George's father, his election to the legislature at Corydon, and the great future he seemed to have had before
him. Outside the home there were rudimentary amuse-
ments common to rural America in the nineteenth cen-

18 Grace Julian Clarke, daughter of George, states that "his family
connections were with Hicksite Quakers" (Clarke, *Julian*, 41), while his
own writings about the religious environment of his childhood and youth
clearly indicate that during this time his mother was an orthodox
Quaker. Since Julian wrote extensively on the subject of religion and
was concerned with it, his version has been accepted by the author.
19 Clarke, *Julian*, 40.

tury—house raisings and warmings, husking bees and spelling bees. But if there was warmth in Julian's childhood there was hardly gaiety. Later he recalled these years as a virtual "battle for life."[20] His mother's religion was not conducive to lightheartedness, and he was to discover with some surprise when later he saw life beyond the Whitewater Valley that it was common among the more libertarian Hicksite Quakers "to have a piano and also regular dancing parties among the young and newly married. How different," he recalled, "is such Quakerism from that to which we have been accustomed!"[21]

The intense shyness from which George suffered as a child did not diminish as he grew into adolescence, and he developed a seriousness in demeanor and action that became a permanent part of his personality. The timidity that afflicted him in childhood forced his withdrawal from the company of others of his own age and made it almost impossible for him to face strangers. More and more he turned for companionship to his dogs and horses, whose names and habits he remembered all his life.[22] And when he learned to read he was able to remove himself more effectively from the company of other children. The evidence of Julian's early scholarliness, or bookishness, is found in his own written memoirs and, considering his desire to be viewed as an intellectual, must be assessed with some skepticism. But even when we allow for exaggeration, it is clear that before his fifteenth birthday he had begun a program of self-education that was remarkably successful.

20 G[eorge] C. C[ottman], "Mr. Julian's Autobiography," in *Indiana Magazine of History*, 2 (1906):70-72; Fox, *Memoirs of Wayne County*, 1:239.

21 Grace Julian Clarke (ed.), "Home Letters of George W. Julian, 1850-1851," in *Indiana Magazine of History*, 29 (1933):136.

22 Clarke, *Julian*, 37-38.

Between ages twelve and fifteen he conducted boyhood business enterprises the proceeds of which were used to purchase books and other reading materials. One of those enterprises was an annual gathering of walnuts which he sold to a local merchant for six cents a bushel. The books that he acquired he read at night and on Sunday. Since candles and lamp oil were so dear, he read by the light of little fires made of "kindlings" that he had gathered for that express purpose.[23] Occasionally his scholarly predilections came to the attention of acquaintances who supplemented his library. One of these was an old man who prided himself on his freedom of thought and his knowledge of unusual books. He liked to have George read to him, and together they investigated such "infidel" works as Volney's *Ruins,* the *Lectures* of Frances Wright, and the works of David Hume and Rousseau.[24]

The religious life of the Valley, including the conflict among several sects, also aroused Julian's interest and influenced his thinking and reading. As a Quaker, he was concerned for a time by the inroads the Methodists were making in the area, religious zealots whom he later described as "primitive" and "volcanic." But his first contact with Universalism aroused him even more and had more lasting effects. This resulted from his friendship with Jonathan Kidwell, an old itinerant Universalist minister, a "master at invective," who fascinated George even though he was anathema to the orthodox of the community. But fearing that he might be subjecting himself to too many heretical influences, Julian sought opposing argument in Richard Watson's *Apology for the Bible,*

23 C[ottman], "Mr. Julian's Autobiography," in *Indiana Magazine of History,* 2:70-71.

24 George W. Julian, "A Search after Truth," in *Unitarian Review,* 29 (1888):48-57, reprinted in *Indiana Magazine of History,* 32 (1936):250-58. See p. 251.

David Simpson's *Plea for Religion,* and Joseph Butler's *Analogy of Religion.*[25] This search for religious truth continued as Julian grew into manhood, and he was still deeply involved in it when, around 1846, he read the works of William Ellery Channing. This experience not only led him into Unitarianism, it also took him into the front ranks of the antislavery movement.[26]

Julian's scholarly inclinations and his introspective tendencies did not hinder his physical development. At sixteen he was an expert swimmer and could hold his own at foot racing and weight lifting. In that year, too, he reached his full height of six feet two inches.[27] His face, regular in its features, could be described as handsome, but the sternness that dominates the expression in later photographs may already have been noticeable. His forehead was high, his mouth sensitive yet firm, his eyes, set deep under dark brows, were sharp and penetrating. This combination of physical strength, good looks, and scholarly interests was enough to give him a position of some prestige in the Centreville area as he approached that age when he would have to determine upon a career.

His decision, at eighteen, to become a schoolteacher, was a logical one. Not only was he the best-educated young man of the community, but he was also following a precedent set by both his father and older brother John, who had also been teachers. The recent death of the latter, to whom George had been particularly attached, had given the family another stunning blow.[28]

---

25 *Ibid.,* 252; Clarke, *Julian,* 41-42.

26 Julian, "A Search after Truth," in *Indiana Magazine of History,* 32:252-53.

27 Clarke, *Julian,* 37-39.

28 As an old man Julian recalled his brother. On August 21, 1889, he wrote in his Journal, "This is the anniversary of my brother's death—just fifty-five years ago. I remember almost as vividly as if it had been

George's first teaching job, which began in 1835, was in the Harvey district, about two miles west of the Centreville home. The next year he taught at Milton. Determined to use the best professional methods, Julian tried for a time to follow the suggestions of Dr. Jacob Abbott's book on pedagogy only to abandon them in favor of flogging, which he discovered was more effective with unresponsive students.[29] The inability of Julian's elderly predecessor in the Harvey school to discipline his students was notorious, and the young teacher was determined to keep the upper hand. The first real test came when the students insisted that Julian follow the custom of providing a treat for them at Christmas. Formerly the custom had resulted in misconduct of which Julian did not approve; also, he could not afford the treat. When he announced that there would be none, a group of recalcitrant students decided to teach him a lesson. Exactly what they planned to do is not clear, but it was rumored that they would seize him and throw him into the icy waters of a nearby stream, as they had done his predecessor. To carry out their scheme, these ruffians, who were nearly as large as Julian, enlisted the aid of some men working on the National Road. Julian's known physical strength, together with the proffered aid from some of the students, prevented the carrying out of the plan—whatever it was. Before this episode ended people for miles around had heard of it. Julian's successful stand seems to have enhanced his reputation in the community.[30]

yesterday his charming traits of character, his devotion to his mother and the children so like a father . . . his love of me as manifested in so many ways . . . ." Julian's Journal, Indiana Division, Indiana State Library.

29 Clarke, *Julian*, 45-47.

30 *Ibid.*, 44-45; Fox, *Memoirs of Wayne County*, 1:200.

III

During his teaching years Julian continued to broaden the scope of his studies; his reading now included the histories of Goldsmith, Gibbon, and Hume, the writings of John Locke, *Don Quixote,* the novels of Sterne and Fielding, Godwin's *Political Justice,* Combe's *Constitution of Man,* and Spurzheim's works on phrenology and education. He also undertook a brief investigation of astronomy.[31] It is hardly strange, therefore, that he began to outgrow, intellectually, the life of a country schoolteacher and to question the wisdom of remaining in a profession that could satisfy neither his intellect nor his growing ambition.

A summer stint as a surveyor on the Whitewater Canal aroused his enthusiasm for a time, perhaps owing to his fascination with mathematics, but a disagreement with his employer helped him to decide against surveying as a career.[32] He was twenty-one years old, uncertain and confused about his future, when in the spring of 1839 some friends invited him to accompany them on a trip to Iowa. They planned to visit former neighbors who had migrated there. A journey away from Centreville, George thought, might help him to come to some conclusion about a career. The possibility of purchasing a farm in the West was in his mind as he set out for Iowa, and hoping to find a suitable plot of land, he carried with him the savings he had accumulated during the past four or five years. His indecision was not resolved by his visit to Iowa, and instead of returning home he made a visit to Dr. Thomas Willetts, a former resident of Wayne County and friend of the Julian family, then living in Mercer County, Illinois. The hospitable doctor was a sympa-

31 Clarke, *Julian,* 47.
32 *Ibid.,* 46.

thetic listener, and Julian soon poured out to him his
anxieties about his future. Dr. Willetts' advice to him,
apparently given without hesitation, was for Julian to
study law and to start immediately.[33]

The contact with Dr. Willetts, with the decision to study
law that resulted from it, shows how wanting in self-
confidence Julian was at this age. The account of this
episode, written by Julian's daughter, whose information
presumably came from her father's lips, says that Julian
was flattered by the doctor's advice, "for he had not supposed that any person could entertain so favorable an
opinion of his capacity," and that prior to this time the
idea of studying law had never entered his mind. In
proffering his advice, Willetts pointed out that the only
obstacle that might keep Julian from a legal career was
his self-distrust, which he was sure Julian could overcome
if he made the effort.[34] He needed little persuasion and
began at once to read Blackstone's *Commentaries*. His
introduction to the study of law, then, occurred in the
Mississippi River town of New Boston, Illinois, where he
took another teaching job to support himself. Only to his
brother, Isaac, did he disclose what he was doing, and
even to Isaac he apologized by explaining that he was
studying law merely for general knowledge rather than
because of any intention of entering the legal profession.

After six months in New Boston nostalgia drove him
back to Centreville where, again, he became a schoolteacher, but this time he entered openly into a more
formal legal study and let it be known that he intended
to become a lawyer. A cousin, John S. Newman, took
George into his law office and tutored him through the
rest of his training. In the fall of 1840 he was licensed to

33 Clarke, *Julian*, 47-49.
34 *Ibid.*

practice. Once more he left Centreville, this time for
New Castle, a village in Henry County to the west of
"Old Wayne." Here, where he again taught for a time,
he began the practice of his profession.[35] Although he
could hardly have been aware of it, he had entered the
second phase of his training for a career in politics. Like
so many politicians of his generation, especially in the
Old Northwest, he had first been a teacher, and then a
lawyer. Politics was the logical next step.

[35] *Ibid.,* 52.

METAMORPHOSIS
OF A WHIG

⬦◇⬦◇⬦◇⬦◇⬦◇⬦◇⬦◇⬦◇⬦◇⬦

IN 1840 Julian voted for the first time in a presidential election, casting his vote for the Whig candidate, William Henry Harrison. The ebullient "hard cider" campaign provided an opportunity for a rollicking good time of a sort that he had not experienced before, and he made the most of it. But this was also the beginning of a serious eight-year period that was perhaps the most critical in Julian's life. During that time he would decide where he stood politically and would begin a political career that would last most of his life. He would become involved in the reform movement that swept America in the 1840's, and, to his own satisfaction at least, he would find solutions to intellectual and emotional problems the early phase of which we have already noted. By 1848 he was committed to the party and the program of the political antislavery men, who gave a new direction and a new meaning to American politics during the two decades preceding the Civil War. In its ranks were such men as John Quincy Adams and Joshua R. Giddings, "conscience Whigs" who fought the antislavery battles in Congress; James G. Birney, leader of the Liberty party; Charles Francis Adams and Charles Sumner, Massachusetts Free Soilers; and Salmon P. Chase of Ohio. Julian's interest and participation in the antislavery movement was an experience whereby, for the first time in his life, he transcended the limited world in which he had grown up and the personal problems, such as religion and his career, in which he had been immersed.

Julian's vote for the Whig candidate in 1840 and his membership in the Whig party stemmed from "the influence of early associations" and the preponderance of the party of John Quincy Adams and Henry Clay in the "Burnt District," the Whitewater region where the Democrats had been burned out, leaving it the principal Whig stronghold in Indiana.[1] If he was aware of the differences between the two major parties over issues such as public land policy, the national bank, internal improvements, and pre-emption, he did not concern himself with them. The existence of the Liberty party, if he knew about it, did not impress him. At twenty-three Julian was much more taken with the gaiety and spirit of the election, which he later called a "grand national frolic."[2] He attended the mass meetings and joined in the enthusiasm for the old Hero of Tippecanoe and was beguiled by the representation of Harrison as a log-cabin frontiersman who stood for the rights of the poor and the oppressed against the aristocrat, Martin Van Buren. One of the mass meetings Julian attended was held at the Tippecanoe Battleground late in May. To get there, he wrote, "I rode on horseback through the mud and swamps one hundred and fifty miles," a journey for which he felt well compensated by the spirit of the crowd and the abundance of hard cider. In September he went to another rally in Dayton, Ohio, where he actually saw the old hero. "He

1 George W. Julian, *Politicial Recollections 1840 to 1872* (Chicago, 1884), 11; Grace Julian Clarke, "The Burnt District," in *Indiana Magazine of History*, 27 (1931):119-24.

2 Julian, *Political Recollections*, 12.

was the first 'great man' I had seen," Julian recalled, "and
I succeeded in getting quite near him; and . . . gazing
into his face with an awe which I have never since felt
for any mortal. . . ."[3]

Even though the politicians of 1840 succeeded in ob-
scuring the issues from Julian and others, significant
changes were taking place and important problems were
awaiting solution. The very nomination of General Harrison, who could have had no valid claim to the Presidency in the pre-Jacksonian days, and the nature of the
campaign were manifestations of the changes that led a
prominent social historian of the era to give his study
the title, *The Rise of the Common Man.*[4] The reform
movements that flourished until the Civil War—prison
reform, labor reform, the common school movement,
woman's rights, land reform—were well under way. Also,
the nation was in the throes of the worst economic depression it had experienced up to that time.

In the area of reform the most profound effects were to
be found in the antislavery movement. First organized as
a nonpolitical crusade under the leadership of William
Lloyd Garrison, by the middle of the 1830's it made its
way into Congress in the form of a contest over appropriate action to be taken on antislavery petitions. Representatives John Quincy Adams of Massachusetts and
Joshua R. Giddings of Ohio, in their fight against the
"gag rule," dramatized the connection between antislavery
and civil liberties. Outside Congress leadership was passing from the Garrisonians to politically oriented men
such as Theodore Dwight Weld and James G. Birney. In
1840 Birney became the presidential candidate of a new

[3] *Political Recollections*, 16-17.
[4] Carl R. Fish, *The Rise of the Common Man, 1830-1850 (A History of
American Life*, vol. 6, New York, 1927).

political party dedicated to the abolition of slavery. The scant seven thousand votes that he received did not accurately reflect the importance of the Liberty party, for slavery was in politics to stay until the ultimate tragic settlement of 1861-65.[5]

Julian's own state had its peculiar problems, too, challenging enough for a young man who would soon be beginning a career in politics. The incompleted internal improvements program had left the state saddled with a thirteen million dollar debt, at a time when tax revenues were decreasing in the aftermath of the Panic of 1837.[6] Other important issues were river and harbor legislation, public land policy, banking, and the tariff. Indiana's location on the Ohio River meant that there were continuing commercial ties with the South; yet at the same time the Old Northwest was coming into more direct contact with the East. The increasing emphasis on slavery aggravated the race question and made it imperative that Hoosiers determine the status of the Negro within their borders. Indeed, Indiana's location in the Old Northwest made her increasingly the balance of power between North and South. Which way she would finally throw her weight was not fully determined until the Civil War. The Whigs, who were in control as these problems grew critical, found their hold on the state weakening. They were especially embarrassed by their inability to pay off the mounting debt. In 1843 the Democrats won a stunning victory, electing their candidate for governor, eight

[5] Gilbert H. Barnes, *The Antislavery Impulse, 1830-1844* (New York and London, 1933), 176; Dwight L. Dumond, *Antislavery Origins of the Civil War in the United States* (University of Michigan Press, 1939), 5, 91; Etta Reeves French, "Stephen S. Harding: A Hoosier Abolitionist," in *Indiana Magazine of History,* 27 (1931):220-21.

[6] Logan Esarey, *A History of Indiana . . .* (2 vols. Fort Wayne, 1924), 1:425.

of the ten Congressmen, and majorities in both houses of the General Assembly.[7]

Julian's native Upper Whitewater Valley was involved in all these developments. On the eve of commercial expansion, financial depression began, and the Valley people were concerned about the acute currency shortage and more than ever about the means of transporting their products to markets in Cincinnati and elsewhere. The Whigs continued to maintain their control of the "Burnt District," but were fearful lest the depression and the increasing number of German and Irish immigrants, many of them laborers on the canal, might mean the strengthening of the Democratic vote.[8]

II

Meanwhile, Julian went about establishing himself in the practice of law. In New Castle, where he moved in 1840, he experienced merely an introduction to the legal profession, forced as he was by economic necessity to teach school again. But after six months there he moved farther west to the town of Greenfield, where he began the practice of his profession in earnest. Here he got off to a good start and might have remained had he not become involved in a controversy with one of the town's leading lawyers. This conflict was so acrimonious and so painful

[7] Dorothy Riker and Gayle Thornbrough (comps.), *Indiana Election Returns, 1816-1851 (Indiana Historical Collections,* vol. 40, Indianapolis, 1960), 105-9, 150-53, 272-78; Esarey, *History of Indiana,* 1:530-31; Henry C. Hubbart, " 'Pro-Southern' Influences in the Free West 1840-1865," in *Mississippi Valley Historical Review,* 20 (1933-34):48-52; Kenneth M. Stampp, *Indiana Politics during the Civil War (Indiana Historical Collections,* vol. 31, Indianapolis, 1949), 1-4.

[8] Chelsea L. Lawlis, "Changes in the Whitewater Valley, 1840-1850," in *Indiana Magazine of History,* 44 (1948):69-77; Lawlis, "Prosperity and Hard Times in the Whitewater Valley," in *Indiana Magazine of History,* 43 (1947):363-66, 377.

for Julian that his stay in Greenfield, too, was of short duration.[9]

It is worth noting here that as a very young man a habit of contentiousness had developed in Julian. He had left his job on the Whitewater Canal in a huff after a disagreement with his employer; as a teacher, although he proved himself a good disciplinarian, he did not enjoy amicable relations with his students; later a conflict with his brother Jacob would bring the dissolution of their law partnership. And controversy of an unusually bitter nature would characterize Julian's political career from beginning to end.

In Greenfield, however, Julian developed one of his first strong friendships, with George Pattison, another young lawyer. Both of them were timid and wanting in self-confidence, and both were determined to do something about it. Their efforts led to the organization of an exchange club which they called the "Dark Lyceum" of which Julian and Pattison were the only members. The purpose of the club was to improve their public speaking and to make them more effective in the courtroom. Meetings were held in total darkness where, not intimidated by probing human eyes, the young men orated to one another on legal questions and current topics of national and local interest.[10]

Relief from the troubles of Greenfield was not too long in coming, and again it came from a member of Julian's family. In 1843 his older brother, Jacob, proposed that the two of them form a law partnership in Centreville,

9 Clarke, *Julian*, 55.

10 *Ibid.*, 52-55. In a letter to a friend Julian referred to Greenfield as a place of "moral outrage and rebellion against God." Pattison apparently escaped from Greenfield before Julian, leaving the latter alone in the friendless village. Julian to Monomia Bunnell, April 27, 1843, Samuel S. Boyd Papers, Bancroft Library, University of California, Berkeley.

and without hesitation George decided to accept; here was an opportunity not only to escape Greenfield but to return to his native village, for which he had a strong and lasting attachment.[11]

Centreville was more than a native village; it was the cultural center of Wayne County, if not of the whole of eastern Indiana. Located there was a seminary and an active literary society, which gave the town more intellectual and cultural life than was usually found in semi-frontier communities. Some of the lawyers at the bar there were prominent beyond the borders of Wayne County; many had been to the state legislature, some had been to Congress, and still others were to be active, in 1850 and 1851, in the framing of a new state constitution. James Rariden, perhaps the most successful of these men, eschewed "book learning" and conducted his law practice through "intuition" and "inspiration." John S. Newman, Julian's relative and mentor, left politics alone so as to concentrate on the law and was thought to be the "strongest lawyer" in the area. The shrewd William W. Wick had been Indiana's secretary of state under his friend Governor James B. Ray. Judge Charles H. Test, a future Indiana secretary of state, reputed to be the ugliest man in Indiana, had been reared to the law as the son of a judge and had practiced in various towns throughout the Whitewater Valley. Oliver P. Morton was destined to be Indiana's Civil War governor and Julian's most powerful and bitter political antagonist.[12]

In this elite professional company some feeling of inadequacy in a young lawyer would have been natural, but Julian suffered unduly from it. Although he had been

---

11 Clarke, *Julian*, 55.

12 Fox, *Memoirs of Wayne County*, 1:256-67; Richmond *Palladium-Item*, September 29. 1941.

practicing law for three years, his first public appearance
in the Centreville court, at which he was called on to make
the opening speech, was a painful experience. "I well
remember," he later wrote of it, "what I suffered from
the dread of doing this in the presence of old lawyers and
the curious crowd of acquaintances who had come to
hear me."[13]

Once again Julian tried to overcome his affliction with
the aid of a "Dark Lyceum." The society that he organized in Centreville was larger than the one in Greenfield, and the range of subjects was broader; but the basic
purposes were the same.[14] In his autobiography Julian
described it:

Desiring to consult the ornamental as well as the useful in this
enterprise, we created three offices in addition to that of Premier, namely, Prelate, Inductor and Sponsor, the duties of
which were particularly defined. The origin of our secret
order, as we now styled it, was traced back to Demosthenes,
who made it the instrument of his wonderful triumphs of
oratory; and its history was solemnly set forth by the Premier
on the initiation of a candidate. We allowed the public to
know enough of our proceedings to excite curiosity, while
the exclusiveness of the body awakened some opposition and
jealousy among outsiders. . . .

   Its controlling purpose was intellectual improvement, and
the discussions were earnest, always creditable and sometimes
able . . . and I feel sure that every surviving member would
acknowledge his indebtedness to it for valuable training and
real improvement in the art of public speaking.[15]

The "Dark Lyceum" may have served another purpose
that was as vital for Julian as intellectual development or

[13] Clarke, *Julian*, 57.
[14] William Dudley Foulke, *Life of Oliver P. Morton* . . . (2 vols. Indianapolis, 1899), 1:31-32.
[15] Quoted in Clarke, *Julian*, 53-54.

oratorical improvement. It was an organization that must have given him a sense of belonging that was otherwise missing at this time in his life. If Julian had been more of an extrovert than he was, he might have shared the camaraderie of the legal fraternity in Centreville; but this he did not do. Although he sometimes rode the Whitewater circuit with the other lawyers, he did not join in their frolic at the taverns or participate in their practical jokes and story telling around the camp fire.[16] Julian could make a living from his law practice, but it was soon apparent that it held no particular fascination for him professionally or socially. Rather, it was an instrument that would help to launch him on a political career, and it was in politics and not in the law as such that he would find his life's work.

III

By 1844 Julian had gained enough confidence to enable him to enter actively, as a speaker, into the forthcoming national political campaign. He had developed a keen interest in national and local issues, but he was undecided as to which of the political parties to support. The time had passed when he could simply vote for the Whig ticket because of his family connections. Indeed, he was beginning to have doubts about the wisdom of Whig leaders and the soundness of Whig policies. He was convinced that the Whigs were wrong in advocating high tariffs. Their "pet dogma of 'the higher the duty the lower the price of the protected article,' " was specious, he believed; and their arguments on the necessity of a national bank

16 Leander J. Monks, *et al., Courts and Lawyers of Indiana* (3 vols. Indianapolis, 1916), 1:94. For "incidents and anecdotes" relating to life on the circuit see *ibid.,* 148-73.

he regarded as obsolete.[17] Finally, however, Julian decided to work for a Whig victory. As he explained it in his *Political Recollections,* the decision resulted from the convincing arguments of "conscience Whigs," especially Adams and Giddings whose speeches in Congress Julian had been reading with avid interest. All other questions were overshadowed by slavery and annexation, and Julian was convinced, with good reason, that if Polk were elected the annexation of Texas would inevitably follow. He never forgot the emotional shock of Polk's victory or how he brooded over it and that "for nearly a week sleep was impossible." Toward the Liberty party, for its part in throwing the election to Polk, he felt only indignation.[18]

Julian's account of his political thinking and his ultimate decision in 1844 is valid enough as far as it goes. Although Clay was equivocal on the annexation question, many annexation men of good conscience voted for him as the lesser of two evils. But for men sharing Julian's views the Liberty party did present an alternative that deserved more credence than he gave it. Indeed, it was an alternative similar to the one Julian chose four years later in joining the Free Soilers. What Julian did not reveal in his account was the imminence of his own initial campaign for political office and its relation to his 1844 decision. In a Whig stronghold like Wayne County it would have been extremely difficult, if not impossible, for a young Liberty heretic from the Whig ranks to win elec-

[17] Although immediate local problems and the failure of the Whig party to solve them undoubtedly influenced Julian's thinking on economic questions, he was probably also influenced by his reading of the economic theories of Jean-Baptiste Say, nineteenth-century interpreter of Adam Smith. Clarke, *Julian,* 58-59.

[18] Julian, *Political Recollections,* 38; Julian, "Autobiography," quoted in Clarke, *Julian,* 59.

tion to the General Assembly. Julian could not have been unaware of this. His role in politics in 1844 and his explanation of it are both significant, in that they show a genuine awareness of the moral aspects of national issues together with a capacity for rationalization that would reappear again and again throughout his political career.

With the experience of 1844 behind him, the time had come for Julian to make his first bid for political office, and on March 12, 1845, the Richmond *Palladium,* the leading newspaper of Wayne County, announced his candidacy for one of the three Wayne County seats in the lower house of the General Assembly. He successfully overcame an insurgent effort by a few fellow Whigs to block his nomination and went on to win in the election. Although the Whig opposition to Julian stemmed from personality differences and was of no great immediate consequence, it is interesting that in his first campaign he was faced with opposition from within his own party. Such internecine contests became a regular pattern of his political life. In this election, the importance of Julian's loyalty to the Whigs is seen in the summary of it that appeared in one of the county newspapers. The defeat of Julian and Caleb B. Smith, Whig candidate for Congress, this paper stated, had been the "watch-word of the Democrats . . . warmly aided by a few disorganizing, pretended Whigs," but against this "combined and mongrel opposition" the Whigs of Old Wayne had "done their duty" and had been rewarded with the victory. Although Julian won rather handily, he ran somewhat behind the other Whig candidates in the county.[19] In electing their

19 Clipping of letter from Julian, dated July 26, 1845, to Centreville *Wayne County Record,* Grace Julian Clarke Scrapbooks, 1:[30], in Indiana Division, Indiana State Library; Centreville *Wayne County Record,* August 6, 1845.

entire slate in 1845 Wayne County Whigs were, as usual, bucking the political trend in Indiana, for in that year the Democratic dominance of 1843 continued. The election brought an equal division in the state Senate, but the Democrats maintained undisputed control of the House and again elected all but two Congressmen.

The breakdown in the Whig ranks can be attributed to several factors. With a mounting state debt and only unfinished canals to show for it, Whigs could no longer campaign effectively on a program of internal improvements. Democratic candidates also made an effective appeal to Hoosier voters against the Whigs' high tariff policy. Where was the logic, they asked, in the Whig argument that farmers gained from selling in an unproctected market and buying in one where prices were held artificially high behind tariff walls? Where, indeed, was the market for Hoosier agricultural products? It lay, they argued, down the Ohio and Mississippi rivers. And if protection hurt the South—as Southerners claimed—it also hurt Indiana. Also, the Liberty party vote, although not substantial, augmented Democratic political power by cutting into the Whig vote. Hence, in 1843 the Democrats not only took over the state government, the next year James K. Polk carried Indiana by a substantial majority.[20]

On Monday, December 1, 1845, Julian was in Indianapolis to be sworn in as a member of the thirtieth session of the Indiana General Assembly.[21] Some of his colleagues there were old friends from the Whitewater Valley, among them Joseph Morrow, one of Julian's former teachers, Dennis Pennington, an old pioneer who

---

[20] Esarey, *History of Indiana,* 1:528-39; Richmond *Palladium,* August 27, 1845.

[21] Indiana *House Journal,* 1845-46, p. 5.

had served in the legislature with George's father, and
Reuben A. Riley, father of the Hoosier poet. Among the
men whom Julian met for the first time were two who
would come into prominence within and beyond Indiana
during the next two or three decades: Conrad Baker
would one day be governor of Indiana, and Joseph Lane,
who later migrated to Oregon, was to become United
States Senator from that state and vice-presidential candidate in 1860 on the ticket with John C. Breckinridge.[22]

Abjuring the customary practice of freshmen members
of legislative bodies to play passive roles while they
learned from their political elders how to conduct the
affairs of state, Julian entered immediately into the debates in the General Assembly and wrote forcefully on
current issues to various newspapers throughout the state.
These articles and letters to the press are notable for the
clarity with which they state the author's position on current legislative measures. The first was a bill providing
for the abolition of capital punishment. Through his
work in committee and on the House floor, Julian was
credited with having a major part in the adoption of
the bill.[23] The number of petitions to the Assembly for
divorce apparently was another concern of Julian's. A
long letter to the *Indiana State Journal*, dated December
23, 1845, and signed "A Lobby Member," was written by
him. In it the writer argued that by its very nature a
legislature was an improper body to render decisions on
divorce and frequently acted without making a thorough
investigation; "thus the institution of marriage is dese-
crated and scoffed at, by a set of unreflecting and uncon-
scientious politicians." But more important, he argued, the
legislature did not have the constitutional authority to

22 Clarke, *Julian*, 63-64.
23 Fox, *Memoirs of Wayne County*, 1:202; Indiana *House Journal*,
1845-46, pp. 373-74; Richmond *Palladium*, January 7, 1846.

grant divorce because it was a judicial matter.[24] Although Julian's plea did not bring an immediate change in the statutes, the new constitution of 1851 did change the divorce procedures in line with Julian's recommendations.

The Butler bill, which dealt with the question of internal improvements and the state debt, was by far the most important legislation of the session, and Julian's part in pushing this measure through the General Assembly had a direct bearing on his political future. For an appreciation of the debate on the bill and Julian's role in it, a brief review of developments leading up to it is necessary. The history of the internal improvements and debt question dated from 1828, when Indiana accepted a Federal land grant the proceeds of which were to be used in aid of the construction of a canal to connect the Wabash River with Lake Erie. For a time regional jealousy delayed the passage of legislation necessary to implement the grant. The Whitewater Valley, which sought appropriations for projects of its own, was particularly adamant in its opposition. (David Hoover, Julian's uncle, was the leader of the delaying faction in the legislature.) Construction of the Wabash and Erie Canal finally got under way in 1832, while other regions continued their clamor for projects of their own. Then in 1836 a grand scheme for a statewide system of roads, canals, and railroads was adopted, accompanied by a huge appropriation of $10,000,000. Among the projects was a Whitewater Canal extending from Cambridge City to Lawrenceburg on the Ohio.[25]

So great was the optimism about the future of these improvements that no adequate plan was devised for pay-

24 Clipping from Indianapolis *Indiana State Journal* in Grace Julian Clarke Scrapbooks, 1:[28-30]; Clarke, *Julian*, 61-62.
25 Esarey, *History of Indiana*, 1:402-14.

ment of the resulting debt. Jubilant political leaders and
proponents of internal improvements were convinced that
tolls would cover construction and maintenance; hence
no tax funds were set aside even for payment of interest
charges. After 1836, depression, mismanagement, and
floods combined to disrupt the system, and in 1839, amidst
a general financial and engineering breakdown, all work
stopped. Corruption also took its toll; from the bond issues, which ultimately reached approximately $15,000,000,
the state received only $8,600,000 in cash, while state offi-
cials and agents made off with an estimated $2,000,000.[26]

Soon many Hoosiers became fearful that the outcome
of the internal improvements fiasco would be repudiation of the debt, and they protested that it must never be
allowed to happen in Indiana. The General Assembly
concurred in these views when, in January, 1845, it
adopted a resolution that repudiation would be a blot on
the honor of the state.[27] It was easy to denounce repudiation, but quite another matter to take positive action to
prevent it, and as the election of 1845 approached nothing
had been done about it. Then in the summer of 1845
Charles Butler, an agent of the bondholders, appeared in
Indiana with instructions to find a way to salvage at least
part of the investment in the internal improvements system. After speaking in several localities, he met with a
joint committee of the General Assembly, from which
emerged the first Butler bill. The long, complex measure
which was finally passed in January, 1846, could not be
executed and was amended in 1847. The effect of this
bill was to divide the outstanding bonds of the state into
two equal parts, one of which with accumulated interest
was assumed by the state and the other made a debt on

26 Esarey, *History of Indiana*, 1:427.
27 *Ibid.*, 1:430; *Laws of Indiana*, 1844-45 (general), p. 92.

the Wabash and Erie Canal. For the latter the state assumed no further responsibility. The canal was deeded to the bondholders.[28]

The passage of the bill in 1846 provoked a great debate. Those who opposed it accused its proponents of outright repudiation and of sacrificing the honor of the state. Although both Whigs and Democrats had voted for it, the Democrats, in control of the legislature, were held responsible. In no quarter was the cry of repudiation more bitter than from the Whigs of Wayne County. Not only had the honor of the state been ruined, they lamented, but the bill was altogether impracticable. The Richmond *Palladium* took the lead in opposing the measure, asserting that there was not the slightest possibility that the bondholders would advance the amount called for or that the revenues from the canal would approach paying half the debt.[29]

Julian, as a Whig who voted for the bill, could not escape the scorn of men in his own party. The most telling attack on him was made by David P. Holloway, proprietor of the Richmond *Palladium* and senator from Wayne County, who impugned Julian's character with the statement that no honorable man could have voted for the Butler bill.[30] Although Julian's answer was restrained and dealt with the specific provisions of the bill rather than in personalities, the feelings that developed between

[28] Esarey, *History of Indiana,* 1:432-35; Indianapolis *Indiana State Sentinel* (weekly), January 22, 1846; Logan Esarey, *Internal Improvements in Early Indiana* (Indiana Historical Society *Publications,* vol. 5, no. 2, Indianapolis, 1912), 137-39. Julian also approved the amended bill. See clippings of letters to the Centreville *Wayne County Record,* signed "Caveat," and dated February 22 and 27, 1847, Grace Julian Clarke Scrapbooks, 1:[57-59].

[29] Clarke, *Julian,* 63; Richmond *Palladium,* July 7, 1846.

[30] Richmond *Palladium,* February 18, 1846.

the two men were hostile. From that time on Holloway was an intransigent political foe.

In the press and in the General Assembly Julian defended his stand in a detailed way that demonstrated a good understanding of a complex subject. He admitted that a grave error had been made in not providing for payment of all the interest on the debt but argued that it was too late to correct the error by outright taxation; a compromise was essential, and speedy action was paramount because the interest was accruing so rapidly that the debt was outdistancing the ability of the state to pay it. Payment of half was far better than nothing at all and the other half had not necessarily been forfeited, because a plan had been devised to meet it. Julian cast aside as irrelevant the contention of his opponents that Charles Butler's connection with the bill made it odious. Whether or not Butler was a corrupt Wall Street broker and an infamous "black leg," as his traducers claimed, made little or no difference; internal improvements and the state debt were the important considerations. Julian placed his greatest emphasis on the tax that would have been necessary to pay off the whole debt. Indeed, sympathy with the common taxpayer may have been the determining factor in Julian's decision to support the bill. The current property and poll taxes, he asserted, were a burden that could not be increased. Moreover, as he said, "the people in large portions of the State have been scourged with sickness, and a failure of crops, and a heavy Delinquent List is already hanging over their heads."[31]

The Butler bill controversy also gave Julian an opportunity to voice some ideas about the conduct of repre-

[31] Clipping of letter from Julian to Centreville *Wayne County Record*, dated February 11, 1846, Grace Julian Clarke Scrapbooks, 1:[31-32].

sentative government. One group in the legislature proposed, as a solution, that the whole question of internal
improvements and state debts be referred to the people
at the next election. On the floor of the House Julian
firmly opposed this proposal. He believed it was the duty
of the General Assembly to "decide the question upon
its *merits,* leaving the consequences to take care of themselves. . . . No man should ask the people to perform a
duty which he is employed and sworn to do *for* them; no
man, holding any office from the people, should ever
shrink from any responsibility incident to that office."[32]
Throughout his political career Julian usually acted in
accordance with these principles. However much he may
have tried to rationalize his motives as a legislator, he was
usually informed on measures to be decided and was able
to take a stand.

In 1847 Julian was again a candidate for political office,
when he sought the Whig nomination for state senator
from Wayne County. This time his opponent was the
incumbent David P. Holloway, and the Butler bill was,
of course, an issue in the campaign; but perhaps more
significant was the introduction of the slavery question
in a bid for political office. Recent antislavery letters of
Julian's, published in a Centreville newspaper, irritated
men of more conservative views. In these he made two
main points: first, that the constitutional right of freedom
of speech was no longer accorded to abolitionists and,
second, that colonization as a scheme for solving the
slavery question was unworkable and morally wrong. In
attacking colonization Julian was striking at a popular
plan for abolishing slavery and simultaneously removing
the race problem from America. Its support came from
conservatives who were concerned about slavery but

32 Indianapolis *Indiana State Journal,* January 28, 1846.

wanted to avoid being branded as abolitionists.[33] It is natural that these men would resent Julian's remarks, and that they would charge him with being an abolitionist. In such a contest his defeat could hardly have been unexpected, and Holloway was nominated.

Thus ended a phase of Julian's political life that had begun in 1844. Since then he had tasted both victory and defeat; he had tested himself in an arena bigger than the local courtroom or lyceum, and the result had not been altogether bad. As a legislator and candidate he had dealt with major issues of his era, and his name was no longer unknown throughout the land of the Hoosiers.

V

In May, 1845, Julian had married Anne Elizabeth Finch, a light-hearted, pretty, eighteen-year-old girl, who added a welcome touch of gaiety to his life. A graduate of the local seminary and daughter of a lawyer, Anne had a better education than the average girl of her era in the Old Northwest. She shared her husband's intellectual interests, though she lacked his intensity, and together they read the antislavery and religious literature that so fascinated George. In April, 1846, a son, Edward Channing, arrived to enliven further the little one-story brick house they occupied.[34]

Beneath Julian's efforts during these years to determine his political stand on such problems as slavery was the

---

33 Richmond *Palladium,* February 2, March 16, 23, August 17, 1847; Clarke, *Julian,* 67-68; clipping of letter from Julian to Centreville *News-Letter* in the spring of 1846, Grace Julian Clarke Scrapbooks, 1:[55-57]; Early Lee Fox, *The American Colonization Society 1817-1840* (Johns Hopkins University *Studies in Historical and Political Science,* vol. 37, no. 3, Baltimore, 1919), 79-80; John D. Barnhart and Donald F. Carmony, *Indiana. From Frontier to Industrial Commonwealth* (4 vols. New York, 1954), 2:89-90.

34 Clarke, *Julian,* 59-61.

continuing struggle to solve his religious perplexities. Although unable to break away from the orthodox indoctrination of his childhood and youth, he persisted in his investigation of religious questions. While becoming more and more skeptical of orthodox views, which seemed to be mere folklore and fantasy, he was left uneasy by the absence of a set of beliefs to take their place. In this disturbed emotional condition Julian discovered in the writings of William Ellery Channing some satisfying answers. Here he found a reasonable faith supported by logical arguments, and soon had consumed the six volumes of Channing's writings with magnificent effect. "I felt," he wrote of the experience, "like one coming out of a fearful darkness into the full light of day." Doctrines like the trinity, total depravity, and vicarious atonement, which Julian could no longer accept, Channing treated as "revolting corruptions" of the Bible. From the religious works of the great Unitarian Julian turned to the antislavery tracts, and they became his "constant companions . . . [and] ceaseless trumpet-call to battle against oppression." Apparently a doctrine of good works was resolving some of Julian's difficulties. When he "espoused the anti-slavery cause and unselfishly gave [his] whole heart to its service, . . . doctrinal doubts and anxieties . . . seemed unworthy of one who loved his neighbors and believed in the brotherhood of man."[35]

It was not through Channing alone that Julian was shown the connection between religion and antislavery. Additional help came from the writings of Harriet Martineau who, along with Channing, gave him more "tranquility of mind," even though he could not accept her positivism and the denial of the future life. Also, Miss

[35] Julian, "A Search after Truth," in *Indiana Magazine of History* 32:252-57; Julian, "Autobiography," in Clarke, *Julian*, 72-73.

Martineau's *Society in America* acquainted Julian with the woman's rights movement, of which he became an advocate. He also sought the advice of Lucretia Mott, who, with her husband, was a guest of the Julians during a tour through the West. Mrs. Mott took an immediate interest in him and referred his case to William Henry Furness, another Unitarian minister in the antislavery movement, who encouraged him not to be fearful of his reform proclivities. Mrs. Mott, who shared some of Julian's skepticism, suggested to him that "free-thinkers may go to the other extreme, and fail to award to the Scriptures all the beautiful and blessed instruction they contain." Lucretia Mott remained a close and influential friend until her death.[36]

It is evident that while Julian was becoming involved in the antislavery movement and participating in Indiana politics he was making a gradual break with the Whig party—a break that began with his vote on the Butler bill and was completed with the Free Soil campaign of 1848. It was a part of the whole wrenching experience of this critical period in his life. The decision to leave the Whig party was not simple or easy. He belonged to a Whig family, and his brother Jacob, who was also his law partner, was a party stalwart; also, most of his clients were Whigs. However, both local and national issues made his decision easier. As we have noted, the Butler bill controversy had an attenuating effect on his Whig ties. Nationally, the Mexican War and the Wilmot Proviso had made the slavery issue more conspicuous and more

---

[36] Anna Davis Hallowell (ed.), *James and Lucretia Mott. Life and Letters* (Boston and New York, 1884), 305-8; Clarke, *Julian,* 69-73. Mrs. Mott was only one of a number of women whose friendship Julian cherished. As a child he had found it easier to make friends with girls than with boys, and as a mature man he had an easier rapport with women than with men.

pressing than it had been; slavery was now, inextricably, a political question. The paramount concern of the "Conscience" (antislavery) Whigs as the campaign of 1848 approached was whether they or the compromise "Cotton" Whigs could control the party. The nomination of Gen. Zachary Taylor, Mississippi slaveholder and hero of the Mexican War, was a shock that forced the antislavery Whigs to consider alternatives. Late in June they met in convention in Columbus, Ohio, where they issued a call for a national convention to meet in Buffalo in August.[37]

Meanwhile, developments in the Democratic party gave more hope for a successful third party movement than had existed at any time since the formation of the Liberty party in 1840. In New York the Democratic ranks were split between the Hunkers, who followed the lead of Polk, and the Barnburners, Van Buren's henchmen. When the Barnburners met at Utica, in June, and nominated Van Buren for the Presidency, the division in New York became irreparable. Moreover, the Democrats, in nominating the "doughface" Lewis Cass for the Presidency, alienated the antislavery wing of their party. It was these insurgent elements in the two major parties, together with the Liberty party, that combined in Buffalo to form the Free Soil party and to nominate Martin Van Buren for President.[38]

Hoosier Free Soilers had met in convention in Indianapolis late in July and selected Julian as one of the dele-

[37] William H. Smith, *A Political History of Slavery*, 1:96-97; Alto Lee Whitehurst, *Martin Van Buren and the Free Soil Movement* (Chicago, 1935), 159-60. The Whigs, according to the wishes of their candidate, did not adopt a platform at their Philadelphia convention. Theodore C. Smith, *The Liberty and Free-Soil Parties in the Northwest* . . . (New York, 1897), 126-30.

[38] William H. Smith, *A Political History of Slavery*, 1:86; Theodore C. Smith, *The Liberty and Free-Soil Parties*, 124-26.

gates to the Buffalo convention.[39] Before the convention
Julian was skeptical of Van Buren's claim to the nomination by an antislavery party, and he hoped the candidate
would be Charles Francis Adams. What he saw and heard
at the Buffalo convention, however, did much to dispel
his doubts about Van Buren and to give him confidence
in the party. He was impressed by the speeches of such
men as Salmon P. Chase, Joshua R. Giddings, and Joshua
Leavitt, political antislavery leaders whom he met for
the first time. He was convinced now that the Free Soil
movement, "wholly unhampered by a southern wing,"
could not possibly compromise with the Slave Power. Nor
was there any longer reason to doubt Van Buren's faith-
fulness to the antislavery cause, for he had been driven to
retirement by Southerners with whom he could never
align himself again and had pledged himself to support
the strong antislavery platform of the new party.[40]

When Julian returned home he was appointed a Free
Soil elector, and undertook a vigorous campaign for the
party candidates—a campaign that turned out to be the
opening of a great crusade that would continue for twenty-
five years. However, for an understanding of Julian's development, at this time in his life, into a full-fledged reformer, it is necessary to go beyond his campaign speeches,
which consisted of attacks on the Whigs and a defense of
Van Buren as a true Free Soiler, and to consider his own
interpretation of his role in the campaign. Years later
Julian described the campaign with the same fervor that
he felt in 1848. Whig leaders tried to coerce him back
into their party, he wrote, but

[39] Richmond *Palladium,* August 2, 1848; Centreville *Free Territory
Sentinel,* August 16, 1848.

[40] Julian, *Political Recollections,* 59-60; Clarke, *Julian,* 78-79; Richmond *Palladium,* August 23, November 1, 1848.

I was obliged to offer them open defiance. . . . I was subjected to a torrent of billingsgate which rivalled the fish market. . . . I was an "amalgamationist" and a "woolly-head." I was branded as the "apostle of disunion" and "the orator of free dirt." It was a standing charge of the Whigs that I carried in my pocket a lock of the hair of Frederick Douglass, to regale my senses with its aroma when I grew faint.[41]

In the middle of the campaign Julian's brother Jacob requested that their law partnership be dissolved, and George found himself not only an outcast from his old political party but, as he said, "thrown on my own resources" professionally. ". . . men who *know* that I am honest in my convictions and that I could have no sinister motives," he lamented, would "prostrate me. . . . And now even a brother, chiming in with the popular clamor, sees proper to join in the general cry of 'mad dog.' "[42] Although the attack on Julian was harsh enough to provoke an emotional reaction, it is evident that he viewed himself as a martyr to his cause. This sense of martyrdom is further borne out in Julian's own explanation of how he handled the bad treatment accorded him:

[41] Julian, *Political Recollections,* 65.

[42] Julian's Journal, quoted in Clarke, *Julian,* 80-81. Jacob Julian had good reason for dissolving his partnership with his brother. He had been elected as a Whig to the Indiana House of Representatives from Wayne County in 1846 and re-elected in 1848. He was also seeking appointment to the post of United States District Attorney for Indiana and needed the help of Caleb B. Smith, Whig Congressman from his district. In a correspondence with Smith, Jacob informed him about the activities of the local Free Soilers and the possible effects on Whig fortunes. Caleb B. Smith Papers, Manuscripts Division, Library of Congress. Jacob did not receive the appointment as district attorney.

George's lament that he was thrown on his own professionally is illuminating in respect to his insecurity in the legal profession at this time and his feeling of martyrdom. In 1848 he was a man thirty-one years old who had been practicing law for eight years.

I was so perfectly swallowed up in my work and dominated by the singleness of my purpose, that I took no thought of anything else. . . . With the truth on my side, I was delighted to find myself perfectly able, single-handed, to fight my battle against the advantages of superior talent and the trained leadership of men of established reputation on the stump.[43]

In the summer of 1848 Julian appealed not only to the Whigs of Wayne County and the Fourth Congressional District of Indiana to reject the candidacy of Zachary Taylor, but also to a wider audience through the columns of the Washington *National Era.* His letters to the editor of that journal, under the pseudonym "A Northern Whig," rebuked northern Whigs who would vote for Taylor and contained castigations of the Whig candidate that were as malevolent as the charges of local Whigs against Julian. Taylor, he said, was a "mere military chieftain . . . exclusively in the hands of the South, and the undoubted exponent of Southern . . . policy and interest." The time had come for northern men to take their stand "in behalf of Northern rights . . . regardless of any supposed consequences of their separate and independent political action." The man chosen by the Whig party as its standard-bearer had waged an unconstitutional war at the bidding of a "Presidential usurper"; he had

waded up to his eyes in the blood of a people with whom we were at peace. . . . He stands before the country as the chief of our national cut-throats; and while his hands are yet reeking with the blood of his victims, and the gore is still dripping from his garments, he asks the American people, *in return for* his sweet services in the merciless work of death, to elect him President of the United States![44]

43 Julian, *Political Recollections,* 67.
44 Washington (D. C.) *National Era,* August 31, 1848.

VI

By 1848 Julian had been drawn into the current of reform whose effects were so vital in America during the three decades before the Civil War. His commitment to the Free Soil party, while its importance should not be underestimated, was merely the most obvious manifestation of a deeper and more complicated commitment. The decisions he made at this juncture, the direction in which he headed, are consequential enough to warrant a somewhat more searching analysis, one embracing the social and personal forces that combined to make Julian a reformer.

Julian's concentration on slavery during the campaign of 1848 does not accurately reflect the scope of his reform interests. He shared with other Free Soilers a concern for land reform that would soon make him a leader in the homestead movement, and he had been converted to woman's rights. Antislavery was merely the most urgent reform, and it is unlikely that Julian and other antislavery men were fully aware of the extent to which, and for how long, it would preclude other reform activities.

In a letter to Joshua R. Giddings soon after the election of 1848, Julian gives us a clue to the nature of his conversion to the antislavery movement. "I owe to you, to John Quincy Adams and to Dr. Channing," he said, "my emancipation from the thraldom of the truckling and time-serving policy which has so long characterized alike the politicians and the people of the Northern states."[45] Where Channing helped Julian to find through antislavery an emancipation from religious and emotional restraints, Giddings and Adams suggested a specific program of action. Logically, too, Adams' and Giddings'

---

[45] Julian to Giddings, December 5, 1845, quoted in Clarke, *Julian*, 82.

argument that slavery jeopardized civil liberties appealed to a son of the Valley of Democracy in the Jacksonian era.

We have noted how one of the effects of Channing on Julian was the adoption of a doctrine of good works as an antidote for the troublesome mysteries of religious doctrine. Even more comforting to Julian, whose intellect was making him more skeptical (and undoubtedly more guilt-ridden) about the Quaker faith, must have been Channing's criticism of Friends for their overemphasis on the depravity of man and for their tendency to worship too much with the emotions and too little with the mind.[46] Even so, in Channing Julian did not find a complete denial of Calvinist beliefs. Channing gave him Calvinism tempered with Christian rationalism, of a sort that would appeal to one who thought of himself as semi-orthodox. Channing did not reject the idea of human depravity; man was sinful, but he could act in such a way as to atone for his sins. Although imperfect, man through his own efforts was perfectible and capable of Godlike qualities.[47] The idea of progress was implicit in Channing's thinking about religion, as it was to be in Julian's about politics and reform.

[46] It is possible the connection between Julian's antislavery stand and his rejection of the Quaker faith for Unitarianism was more complicated than he himself was aware. In joining the antislavery movement he was adopting a cause in which Quakers had been active for a century. Conceivably his qualms resulting from deserting the faith in which he had been reared might therefore have been eased. Many years later when Julian was rereading Channing he noted in his journal that Channing "does not charm me as he did when I first met with his writings. He was far more of a prophet and a saint than a philosopher." Julian's Journal, March 30, 1873, Indiana Division, Indiana State Library.

[47] Arthur W. Brown, *Always Young for Liberty. A Biography of William Ellery Channing* (Syracuse, N. Y., 1956), 72-74, 86, 136, 172. For Channing's views on religion and slavery the author has found this short biography very useful. The one-volume edition of *The Works of William E. Channing* (Boston, 1881) has also been helpful.

While the effect of Channing's works on Julian was far-reaching, there were tenets of the Unitarian's thought that Julian had to reject in determining his particular course of action. Channing was critical of political abolitionists in general and of James G. Birney and the Liberty party in particular. Antislavery would triumph, he felt, "not by force or appeals to interest, but by becoming a living part of the public conscience and religion. Just in proportion as it is complicated with political questions and feelings it is shorn of its strength." And with some prescience Channing feared "a class of politicians who will use Abolition to rise by, but will disgrace it by want of principle."[48]

Channing was also concerned that antislavery men "in forming a just moral judgment of slavery" might pass moral sentence on slaveholders, two subjects that were distinct, since "men were not always to be interpreted by their acts or institutions." Slavery was the South's calamity rather than its crime, and the proper role for Northerners was to share this burden with the South by helping them to end it.[49] Malevolence toward the South would be only an obstacle to the realization of this goal. Such an approach toward slavery was a far cry from that of Julian and other antislavery leaders who were influenced by Channing but whose antislavery creed included an abiding hatred of the South.[50]

48 Brown, *Always Young for Liberty*, 233.

49 *Ibid.*, 229.

50 Charles Sumner, in his initial antislavery speech in 1845, paraphrased some of Channing's views. It is clear, however, that at this early date Sumner was incapable of accepting Channing's benevolent attitude toward the white South and that he was not going to share the South's guilt. "God forbid that the lash of the slave-dealer should descend by any sanction from New England! God forbid that the blood which spurts from the lacerated, quivering flesh of the slave should soil the hem of

It is evident that religion was a major factor in Julian's conversion to the antislavery cause, but not in any direct or simple sense, not in the way that antislavery evangelists such as Charles G. Finney or Theodore Dwight Weld appealed for converts to the crusade. Rather, Julian's turning to a more thoughtful religion in an effort to solve personal problems led him into the antislavery movement. Moreover, his frustrating experience as an aspiring young Whig politician and his less than conspicuous success as a lawyer provided a conditioning that was favorable for the development of a "True Believer." If, as Eric Hoffer suggests, action is often a cure for frustration,[51] Julian could not have found an opportunity better suited to his needs than the antislavery movement.

The formation of the Free Soil party was indeed fortunate for Julian. It was an instrument for the combined utilization of his crusading zeal and the realization, in some measure, of his political ambition. Without it he could have had no political career; as a leader in it he would soon take his place on the national scene.

the white garment of Massachusetts." This speech is quoted and discussed in David Donald, *Charles Sumner and the Coming of the Civil War* (New York, 1960), 140.

[51] Eric Hoffer, *The True Believer* (Mentor Edition, New York, 1958), 112.

THE FREE
SOIL YEARS

⊲⊳⊷⊶⊲⊳⊷⊶⊲⊳⊷⊶⊲⊳⊷⊶⊲⊳⊷⊶⊲⊳

AN important political consequence of the antislavery movement in the Old Northwest after 1848 was its effect on the Democratic party. Although the "doughface" Lewis Cass carried every northwestern state in 1848, antislavery sentiment within the Democracy was growing by leaps and bounds. The attitude of certain party leaders in the Old Northwest, such as Cass and Stephen A. Douglas, indicated to some that the Democracy was unified and ready to acquiesce in the southern leadership. But a more penetrating look disclosed that within the party there were men dedicated to the antislavery crusade who hoped to succeed under the banners of the Democracy. People who looked to Congress could find further evidence to support this view. After Taylor's election in 1848, a resolution in the House to appoint a special committee to report a bill to abolish the slave trade in the District of Columbia received the votes of twenty-two of the twenty-seven Democratic members from the states of the Northwest. And, increasingly, Democratic contestants for Congressional seats were forced to avow their support of the Wilmot Proviso. Ties with the Democracy of the South were further weakened when Taylor, as Whig candidate, carried seven southern states. Why should the Northwest be compelled to remain loyal to a section rapidly going into the Whig camp, Democratic leaders were asking, especially when there seemed to be fundamental differences over the issue of slavery?[1]

One effect of Democratic antislavery sentiment was the weakening of the Free Soil organization. Because both major parties now contained antislavery factions, many antislavery men believed it more expedient to try to capture a major party than to divert their energies in the cause of a third party. Even so, a nucleus which no longer had faith in the old parties as instruments of antislavery policy remained to insure the existence of the Free Soil party. Early in 1849 even the weak Free Soil organization in Indiana began looking toward the August elections, and before the end of January Hoosier Free Soilers had a state ticket in the field headed by James H. Cravens, the candidate for governor.[2]

Both the existence of a Free Soil organization and the antislavery feeling among the Democrats had an immeasurable influence on Julian's political fortunes. His Congressional district, composed of the counties of Wayne, Henry, Union, and Fayette, was the most ardently antislavery one in Indiana; and, equally important, the Democracy there, too weak to have the remotest hope of defeating the Whigs, might be persuaded to adopt the Free Soil candidate. The situation seemed propitious for the cause of a Free Soil aspirant to Congress.

As 1848 drew to a close the Free Soilers in Wayne County increased their activity. On December 30, they held a meeting in the Centreville Courthouse where they nominated delegates to the forthcoming Indianapolis convention, recommended candidates for governor and lieu-

---

1 Theodore C. Smith, *Liberty and Free-Soil Parties*, 154-55; William O. Lynch, "Antislavery Tendencies of the Democratic Party in the Northwest, 1848-50," in *Mississippi Valley Historical Review*, 11 (1924-25):322-25.

2 Smith, *Liberty and Free-Soil Parties*, 187-93.

tenant governor, and nominated Julian for Congressman from the fourth district. Before adjourning, the convention resolved that the Free Soilers could support "no man for any Legislative or Executive office, the *Presidency included,* who [was] not distinctly opposed to the extension of slavery and in favor of its abolition wherever Congress has power over the subject."[3] Soon afterward Henry and Union counties also announced in favor of Julian, and the *Free Territory Sentinel* began to carry his name as the Free Soil candidate.[4]

By the time the Whigs of the fourth district made their nomination, in June, the campaign was well under way. Their candidate was Samuel W. Parker of Fayette County, brother-in-law of the incumbent, Caleb B. Smith.[5]

Except for slavery the campaign was singularly free of discussion of issues, but an important feature was the effort of the Whigs, not without some success, to attract the Free Soil vote. Even some Free Soilers thought it expedient to support the state ticket of the Whigs, and one of them presented a resolution to this effect at the Free Soil convention in Indianapolis. His argument was that the Whigs had nominated men of Free Soil principles, and that it would be foolish to divert antislavery strength into a third party. Although the Free Soilers overwhelmingly rejected the resolution, the Whigs repeatedly used the incident to their own advantage.[6] The *Indiana State Journal* pleaded for free-soil Whigs to beware of the third party, which, it claimed, was more a tool of the Democrats than a true antislavery organization. In 1848, said the *Journal,* the Free Soilers had been mere stalking-horses for Cass, and many had voted for him with

3 Centreville *Free Territory Sentinel,* January 3, 1849.
4 *Ibid.,* February 7, 1849.
5 Richmond *Palladium,* June 20, 1849.
6 Indianapolis *Indiana State Journal* (weekly), January 27, 1849.

the result that Ohio and Indiana had been handed over to the Democrats. Now the Free Soilers were using the same tactics in an effort to elect Joseph A. Wright, the Democratic candidate for governor. The *Journal* also appealed to Free Soilers not to waste their votes on candidates who had no chance of being elected.[7]

In Julian's district the *Palladium* joined in the chorus. It took issue with a list of questions published by the Free Soilers which candidates would have to answer in the affirmative to demonstrate the soundness of their antislavery doctrine; no candidate who refused to do so could expect to receive any Free Soil votes. Whig candidates, said the *Palladium,* had been answering such questions affirmatively long before the existence of the Free Democracy.[8] For Democrats who would vote for Julian the *Palladium* had a caveat: they could "lose their identity as a great political party, and be completely swallowed up in the vortex of Old Abolitionism, a 'consummation devoutly' to be deplored by every lover of his race." Nor should Democrats be fooled by the argument that Julian was an "independent" candidate, which he was not in any sense of the word.[9]

Even before Parker's nomination the Free Soilers had begun their campaign with an attack on Caleb B. Smith, the Whig incumbent. They made the charge that he had been absent from the House of Representatives when antislavery resolutions were voted on and that he had tried to weaken the Gott resolution, to abolish slavery in the District of Columbia, by amending it so as to compensate slaveowners for the loss of their property. Such an apostate, they said, could not truly represent the anti-

[7] Indianapolis *Indiana State Journal* (weekly), May 28, 1849.
[8] Richmond *Palladium,* June 13, 1849.
[9] *Ibid.,* June 27, 1849.

slavery fourth district; in fact, his very presence in Congress was proof of the emptiness of Whig antislavery pledges. Parker, they said, was a mere replica of Smith and a man "ardently attached to the President" who so thoroughly detested Free Soilers.[10]

By the end of June, it was apparent that no Democratic candidate would enter the Congressional contest in the "Burnt District" and that Julian stood a chance of being elected in this Whig stronghold. One correspondent wrote to the local Democratic organ, the *Jeffersonian,* that Julian held Democratic views on internal improvements, the bank, and the tariff and that Democrats could vote for him in good conscience.[11] Another Democrat, rejecting the *Palladium's* warning, said in the *Free Territory Sentinel* that Julian, more an independent than a party candidate, deserved Democratic support. The rejoinder of the Whigs was that a corrupt bargain had been arranged between Democrats and Free Soilers.[12]

The personal abuse which characterized the campaign precluded any significant discussion of issues. On one occasion, however, Julian spoke in favor of a policy of free trade. Not missing the opportunity for a gibe, the *Palladium* retorted, "Geo. W. Julian and John C. Calhoun—side by side! Delightful position for a Free Soiler!"[13] Julian's opponents also charged him with being a turncoat and a sorehead who had gone over to the Free Soilers only after the Whigs had turned him out of their party. Julian's friends answered that the Whigs—and especially David P. Holloway—were disgruntled because Julian had risen above mere party politics in supporting

[10] Centreville *Free Territory Sentinel,* January 31, June 6, 27, 1849.
[11] Richmond *Palladium,* June 13, 1849.
[12] Centreville *Free Territory Sentinel,* July 18, 1849.
[13] Richmond *Palladium,* July 11, 1849.

the Butler bill. Moreover, said Julian, it was impossible to talk about issues with the Whigs, since they refused to join in any discussion of national policy.[14]

Ultimately Julian did receive enough Democratic support to win the election by a small majority. His victory was part of a sweeping Democratic triumph throughout the state in which they elected their candidate for governor as well as all the Congressmen except two. Julian was the only Free Soiler elected.[15] Among election postmortems were the laments of the *Indiana State Journal,* the most important Whig organ in Indiana. Having all but ignored Julian throughout the campaign, the *State Journal* now deprecated the defeat of Parker, a distinguished man who had faithfully fought Locofocoism in all its "deformed shapes" for more than twenty years. His defeat, the editors said, had been brought about by a "Union of Locofocoism, Free Soilism, and some Whig renegadism," as well as by the cholera.[16] The campaign of 1849 remained vivid in Julian's memory as a victory brought about by a combination of Free Soilers, Democrats, and Independent Whigs, and "bitter beyond all precedent."[17]

II

During the campaign Julian experienced his first serious illness—a lung infection accompanied by severe hemorrhages. Forced to cancel several speeches, he returned to the hustings late in the canvass, but after it was over he suffered a relapse that theatened his political career, and possibly his life.

14 Centreville *Free Territory Sentinel,* July 25, August 1, 1849.
15 Riker and Thornbrough (comps.), *Indiana Election Returns, 1816-1851,* 119; Esarey, *History of Indiana,* 1:547-49; Lynch, "Antislavery Tendencies," in *Mississippi Valley Historical Review,* 11:327.
16 Indianapolis *Indiana State Journal* (weekly), August 13, 1849.
17 *Political Recollections,* 72.

GEORGE W. JULIAN, LEGISLATOR

Julian's election in 1849 and his illness bring into focus again some of his family relations and some changes in the family situation. By this time his mother and his favorite brother, Isaac, had moved from Centreville to Linn County, Iowa. In a melancholy tone, Isaac wrote to George of his fear that George might never recover, "that, in the prime of life, in the dawn of fame & fortune fairly won, you may be cut down . . . in a land of strangers, deprived of" loved ones. Only George, among all Isaac's acquaintances and relatives, he said, "had sufficient breadth of judgment & generosity of spirit to make allowance for my past errors, & to hold fast some faith in my capacity for better things." Only to George had he been able to turn for "intelligent sympathy."[18] Repeatedly Isaac would rely on George for emotional and material support, and his message is probably a clearer indication of Isaac's state of mind than of George's physical condition.

Isaac's letters are in sharp contrast to those of Jacob Julian, George's older brother and former law partner, who was still soliciting the support of his Whig Congressman for an appointment to public office. Jacob, writing during and at the end of the campaign, made predictions about what George and other Free Soilers would do in the approaching session of Congress, but there was no reference to George's illness and no indication that he would not be able to take his seat in the Thirty-first Congress.[19]

On December 10, before he was fully recovered from his illness, George and Anne set out for Washington. The

[18] Isaac Julian to George W. Julian, January 2, February 1, 1850, Giddings-Julian Papers, Manuscript Division, Library of Congress.

[19] Jacob B. Julian to Caleb B. Smith, April 8, September 13, November 4, 1849, Caleb B. Smith Papers.

nine-day journey was divided into three parts, the first
by coach to Cincinnati, the second by steamboat up the
Ohio to Pittsburgh, and the third by coach over the mountains to Washington. In the national capital the stimu-
lation of active political life, the solicitude of a circle
of new-found friends, and the care of his wife combined
to effect a gradual recovery in Julian's health.[20]

Upon his arrival in Washington, Julian went to the
House of Representatives where he sought and found
Joshua R. Giddings. This was Julian's first personal contact with his political mentor and future father-in-law.
Giddings received him cordially and immediately sent for
the other Free Soil members, a group that came to be
known as the "immortal nine." In addition to Giddings
and Julian there were David Wilmot of Pennsylvania,
author of the "Proviso," Preston King of New York,
Joseph M. Root of Ohio, Charles Allen of Massachusetts,
Charles Durkee of Wisconsin, Amos Tuck of New Hampshire, and John W. Howe of Pennsylvania. The coterie
also included Gamaliel Bailey, editor of the *National Era*.
In this company George and Anne found an immediate
and warm acceptance. Anne, a girl of twenty-two, soon
became a favorite.

The United States Hotel was the Julians' first lodging
in the national capital, but soon Giddings found room
for them at Mrs. Spriggs's boarding house, sometimes
called Abolition House, which was located on the north
side of the public grounds facing the Capitol, and a well-
known dwelling place of antislavery men including Giddings and Theodore Dwight Weld.[21]

20 Clarke, *Julian*, 85-87.

21 Grace Julian Clarke (ed.), "Home Letters of George W. Julian,
1850-1851," in *Indiana Magazine of History*, 29 (1933):130-35; Julian, *Political Recollections*, 73-74; Barnes, *Antislavery Impulse*, 182.

Julian assumed his Congressional duties as the prolonged and bitter speakership contest was drawing to a close. The chief contestants were the Whig, Robert C. Winthrop, of Massachusetts, and the Democrat, Howell Cobb, of Georgia. The House, nearly evenly divided between Whigs and Democrats, was also deadlocked between pro-Wilmot Proviso men of the North and anti-Proviso men of the South. With most Northerners supporting Winthrop and most Southerners supporting Cobb, neither candidate had been able to muster a majority during nearly three weeks of balloting. The Free Soilers, holding the balance of power, could on several occasions have elected either man if they had voted for him en masse. Their opposition to Cobb was to be expected, but they might have given their votes to Winthrop, a northern Whig. But Winthrop, who opposed the Wilmot Proviso and was now the opponent of Charles Sumner in Massachusetts, was too conservative for them. Thus as the Free Soilers alternated their votes among themselves the fruitless balloting continued. Even before his arrival a few such votes were cast for Julian on several ballots.

On the twenty-fifth ballot one vote was cast for William J. Brown, a Democratic representative from the Indiana fifth district. On the thirtieth ballot he received twenty-one votes and continued to rise until on the fortieth ballot, taken on December 12, he received 112 votes, only two short of election. Then an exchange of letters between Free Soiler David Wilmot and Brown came to light, wherein Brown in return for enough Free Soil votes to elect him agreed to make certain committee appointments which would be satisfactory to Free Soilers. After this disclosure Brown withdrew his name from the contest.

Julian was not in the House during the excitement that prevailed following this disclosure of the letters; he cast his first vote for speaker on the fifty-sixth ballot—the lone vote for David Wilmot—on December 19. However, he regarded Brown as a Hoosier of pro-southern leanings, and after he reached Washington he made known to his Free Soil colleagues that he regarded Brown's offers to them as completely specious. Thereafter Julian could no longer count on the Democratic votes that had made his election possible. Howell Cobb was elected speaker on the sixty-third ballot on December 22, but only after a change in House rules had been adopted which permitted election by a plurality instead of the usual majority vote. Julian continued to vote for Wilmot.[22]

Cobb's election enraged the northern Whigs, who accused the Free Soilers of combining with the pro-slavery Whigs to defeat Winthrop. Horace Greeley, in the New York *Tribune,* called it an act of gross ingratitude as well as a stupid betrayal of the Free Soil cause. Winthrop, he said, had demonstrated his sympathy with Free Soilers by his opposition to the resolution to censure Joshua R. Giddings in an earlier session. Greeley was willing to excuse a man like Julian, who had been elected with Locofoco votes, but for most of the Free Soilers he felt only contempt.[23]

The *National Era,* in reply to Greeley, attempted to show that the Free Soilers could not have elected Winthrop and that if Congressmen had voted in accordance with a straight party alignment Cobb would have been

22 Julian, *Political Recollections,* 74-76; Allan Nevins, *Ordeal of the Union* (2 vols. New York, 1947), 1:251-52; James Ford Rhodes, *History of the United States from the Compromise of 1850* (7 vols. New York, 1893-1910), 1:118-19; Henry Wilson, *History of the Rise and Fall of the Slave Power in America* (3 vols. Boston, 1872-77), 2:212-16; *Congressional Globe,* 31 Congress, 1 session, 19-20, 20-22, 24, 25, 30, 66; New York *Tribune* (daily), December 11, 14, 15, 1849.

23 New York *Tribune* (daily), December 25, 1849.

elected on the first ballot. The Whigs themselves, it concluded, had finally thrown the election to Cobb by agreeing to the plurality rule which they knew would elect him. By supporting Winthrop the Free Soilers would have undermined the very existence of their party, a sacrifice they could not be expected to make.[24] Whatever the merits of these opposing arguments, Winthrop's defeat aggravated the growing animosity between Free Soilers and northern Whigs, and Horace Greeley had begun a campaign against Free Soilers that would end only with the demise of the movement itself.

III

The Washington which Julian discovered in 1849 was by no means an impressive national capital. Rather, as one observer put it, the city was one of "impure water, muddy roads, [and] squalor which sat in poverty." Yet Julian agreed with this same observer that it was also a place of natural beauty and that there was much of interest to see.[25] He and Anne set about seeing the many interesting places and making the acquaintance of some of the celebrities. Instead of being overawed in the presence of the "great men" of Washington, as he expected, Julian found that meeting them was not such a "wonderful privilege." They looked and acted, he discovered, very much as other people. After meeting President Taylor, George wrote to his brother:

I can't see now how it was that I was so anxious to see Old Zach, . . . an old outrageously ugly, uncultivated, uninformed man; & sure enough a *mere* military chieftain. He can't converse in decent language, mispronouncing words, stuttering,

[24] Washington (D.C.) *National Era*, January 3, 1850.
[25] Josiah B. Grinnell, *Men and Events of Forty Years* . . . (Boston, 1891), 51-52.

stammering, & frequently making a break-down in the middle
of a sentence. Certainly, he could not write a decent letter or
make a decent speech on any subject. Ignorant of politics or
any thing like statesmanship, he *cannot* be otherwise than a
perfect *tool*. . . . I was thunderstruck when I saw him, &
whilst I felt ashamed for my country, I felt secretly thankful
that *my* vote had not contributed to her dishonor, by helping
such an old ninny into the chair once filled by Washington.[26]

Henry Clay, he discovered, still commanded more attention than any other man in Washington, and Julian was
delighted with the opportunity to call on him in the
company of Giddings and others. Long attracted by
Clay's magnetism, Julian found him "perfectly eloquent
in conversation." Even though he no longer believed
Clay to be a "great statesman & pure patriot," he found
still a "peculiar power in his presence . . . which makes
you admire & love him," a nebulous quality that Julian
found it difficult to explain.[27]

Early in January, 1850, Anne went to Boston, where
she remained for several weeks. Julian wanted her to see
the historical places nearby and wrote her to be sure to
visit Quincy and Plymouth. Moreover, she was not to
worry about his health, for an old Wayne County friend,
Mrs. Underwood, had promised to care for him if he
should become sick.[28] But his social life did not end with
her departure. Soon he was writing to her of a presidential
levee which he had attended, where he had seen many

26 George Julian to Isaac Julian, January 25, 1850, Giddings-Julian
Papers. Later Julian revised his opinion of Taylor. In his *Political Recollections* he wrote of the old man's kindly, honest, farmerlike face, his
"old-fashioned simplicity of dress," and admitted that in saying some of
the things about Taylor which he had said in 1848 he had "unintention-
ally" done him an injustice. Pages 82-83.

27 George Julian to Isaac Julian, January 25, 1850, Giddings-Julian
Papers.

28 Clarke (ed.), "Home Letters," in *Indiana Magazine of History*,
29:132.

finely dressed women, but few handsome ones. He was confident that she would outshine them all when she returned.[29] As the days passed and as Julian heard of the gay time Anne was having in New England, he missed her more and more and was peeved that her visit had become so extended. He admitted that he was jealous and that her enjoyment of Boston had awakened the "green-eyed monster" in him. He feared that it was quite possible for her to fall in love with somebody with a more "jovial disposition [and] prepossessing manners" than he had. And, he complained, "You don't write such letters as you did when I was at Indianapolis before Channing was born."[30]

However, his longing for Anne undoubtedly was lessened by the growing companionship with men in the Free Soil circle, especially Giddings and Judge Charles Allen of Massachusetts. There was pleasant conversation at the table, and every day the three walked together or pitched horseshoes. Julian's room was close enough to Giddings' that he could hear the older man's "kind and mellow voice every day in answer to a knock at the door."[31] Julian had also become the Washington correspondent for the Centreville *True Democrat*,[32] a task which took much of his time. His frequent columns give an excellent running account, from the Free Soil point of view, of the activities in Congress and in the capital.

IV

Most engrossing of all to Julian must have been his observance of the Thirty-first Congress in action, bringing

29 *Ibid.*, 29:133-34.
30 *Ibid.*, 29:134-35.
31 *Ibid.*, 29:132-33.
32 Formerly the *Free Territory Sentinel.*

together as it did what may have been the most remarkable array of talent ever assembled on Capitol Hill. In the Senate was the great triumverate of an ebbing generation—Clay, Webster, and Calhoun—none of whom was to belong to another Congress. All had served, off and on, since the years of intense nationalism during and immediately following the War of 1812. They had seen parties rise and fall and had experienced the great depression of the 1830's. They had witnessed and been affected by the rise of Jacksonian democracy. They had seen the Union threatened, and on two memorable occasions had been involved in working out settlements to preserve it. Under the same roof were men of a new political generation, such as William H. Seward, former governor of New York; Salmon P. Chase, the Ohio Democratic and Free Soil antislavery leader; John P. Hale, New Hampshire Free Soiler; and Stephen A. Douglas, the rising young leader of the Democratic party. Not so well schooled in the mechanics of compromise as their political forebears, these men were probably more truly aware of the realities of the day.

The acquisition of new territory from Mexico as a result of the Mexican War had given the already difficult slavery question a new emphasis. Now it was up to Congress to make some provision regarding the status of slavery in the new states and territories. Since 1846, antislavery men had tried without success to adopt the Wilmot Proviso, which would have excluded slavery from territories acquired as a result of the Mexican War. Now, with California asking to be admitted as a free state, action could be delayed no longer. The California question was a vexatious one, because her admission would break the precarious balance between the free and slave states. Most Northerners were ready to admit California as a free state, but Southerners were determined to prevent it. Tension was heightened still further by the concern that a southern convention to be held soon in Nashville would organize a movement to take the South out of the Union if the California question, among others, was not settled to her satisfaction.

It was in this atmosphere that Henry Clay introduced, on January 29, his eight compromise resolutions, designed to settle for all time the issue of slavery in the United States. Clay's resolutions called for the admission of California as a free state, the organization of two additional territorial governments without any provision about slavery, the settlement of a Texas-New Mexico boundary dispute in favor of New Mexico, the assumption by the Federal government of the Texas debt, the abolition of the slave trade—but not slavery—in the District of Columbia, and a new and more stringent fugitive slave law. These resolutions were referred to a joint committee formed for the specific purpose of framing an acceptable measure, from which they finally emerged in the form of an Omnibus Bill. President Taylor, to the surprise of many, became a staunch ally of the anticompromise forces. His plan was for California to come in as a free state without passing through the territorial stage, and it was his belief that the territories of Utah and New Mexico would follow suit so that there would be no need for a compromise.

The Omnibus Bill was a conundrum for Congress, primarily because it contained provisions that were unacceptable to southern proslavery and northern antislavery men. Moreover, "Old Zach's" opposition to the Compromise had not been expected.[33] Eventually his death and

[33] Brainerd Dyer, *Zachary Taylor* (Baton Rouge, 1946), 368-92; Holman Hamilton, *Zachary Taylor, Soldier in the White House* (Indianapolis, 1951), 254-339.

a new political strategy led to the adoption of the Compromise measures, but not before Congress had engaged in a bitter and frustrating contest of eight months' duration.

Among Julian's earliest impressions of the Thirty-first Congress was the sensitivity of southern members on the subject of slavery. He could well believe the opinion expressed by a Congressional observer who, during a period of nearly thirty years, had "never before seen half the intensity of feeling and rashness of purpose that the Southern members now manifest." If there was a "one idea" party, Julian wrote, it was the slavery party, composed of both Whigs and Democrats of the slave-holding states. Southern Senators, he reported, were "aroused almost beyond measure" by some very mild remarks of Senator Chase by which he meant no malice toward the South. Julian felt that they were "morbidly sensitive" on the subject of the "peculiar institution."[34]

He registered an even greater disgust with northern Whigs and Democrats who habitually aided in the tabling of resolutions designed to effect the principles set forth in the Wilmot Proviso. On one occasion he found that fourteen northern Whigs and eighteen northern Democrats had voted to table such a resolution. The reason, he thought, was simply that "doughfaces" had been frightened by such cries as "The Union is in danger," "The South will not submit to the Wilmot Proviso," "We must compromise," "Beware of geographical parties." Hoosiers, too, he wrote to his newspaper, had in this way come to the aid of the South, in spite of the resolutions adopted by the Indiana legislature favoring the Proviso.[35] Throughout the crisis of 1850 Julian remained

34 Centreville *True Democrat,* January 30, 1850.
35 *Ibid.,* February 13, 1850.

convinced that there was no real danger of southern secession. Even if such a danger were imminent, he was convinced that it would not be ended by surrendering to southern demands.

But while Julian was complaining to his constituents of the apostasy of northern Whigs and Democrats, an incident occurred which was exceedingly embarrassing to him. On February 5 the vote was taken on tabling a resolution of Joseph M. Root of Ohio to prohibit slavery in all newly acquired territory. The result was 105 yeas to 79 nays, but there were over twenty-five absentees from the free states, including Julian. The *Palladium,* always on the alert, published a lengthy account referring to the incident as the "Julian Dodge," and demanded an explanation. From then on the "Julian Dodge" became a slogan for anti-Julian men in the fourth district, and it was years before Julian heard the last of it. Some of Julian's friends pleaded that he had just entered the hall when the vote was being taken and that he did not understand the question. The *Palladium* refused, of course, to accept this or any other explanation, and only reiterated that Julian was guilty of neglect of duty that could not be tolerated on the part of the Representative of the district. Julian's own explanation was that he knew the Root resolution was to come up for a vote that day and that he had planned to be present for the express purpose of voting for it; but he had remained too long in his room, where he had been writing, and had entered the hall too late to have his vote recorded. His friends tried to prove, by pointing to his whole voting record, that he intended no treachery. They also sought to exonerate him by pointing out that over twenty-five northern Whigs and Democrats did not vote on the resolution. but that their efforts were without effect on local Whigs. Never again was Julian so careless as to miss a vote on any antislavery question.[36]

During the early days of March, Julian went often to the Senate where he listened to the famous speeches on the Compromise. Webster, he wrote, had outdone every other northern man in the suddenness and completeness of his "remarkable . . . surrender to the slave-holders." This man, who Julian thought was the most intellectual-looking person he had ever seen, "had shown himself to be not only a doughface but a 'doughsoul,'" certain to receive the "scorn and contempt of his countrymen." Apparently failing to grasp the full implication of Seward's "higher law" doctrine, Julian reported merely that the New Yorker had made an able speech, but that there was still some fear that he had not cut himself off from the administration. Nor had Seward's words been effective, he continued, for *"compromise, compromise* is the incessant cry." Small "wonder that slavery should triumph when freedom had so many betrayers."[37]

As he listened Julian must have wondered what the effect of his own oratory would be when his turn came to speak in the House. So far he had participated in no debate and had arisen only to present a few petitions from his constituents. But he was preparing a speech in which he would answer southern arguments on the subject of slavery. His "darling purpose," he said, was to answer them as effectively as possible. And although "very curious to know how it would sound and what would be thought of it," Julian wrote later, "my consti-

---

[36] Wilson, *Slave Power,* 2:221-22; Richmond *Palladium,* February 20, 27, March 6, 1850.

[37] Russel B. Nye, *Fettered Freedom; Civil Liberties and the Slavery Controversy, 1830-1860* (Michigan State College Press, 1947), 193; Rhodes, *History of the United States,* 1:163-64; Centreville *True Democrat,* March 20, 1850.

tutional self-distrust made me dread the experiment unspeakably. My scuffle for the floor was a sore trial of patience."[38] He finally got the floor on the fourteenth of May.

In his maiden speech Julian set out to prove two major points: first, that the institution of slavery and the southern defense of it constituted a grave threat to freedom of speech, and second, that there had been no northern aggression against the South. "In this boasted land of free speech," he said, "we may talk of Northern labor and Northern pauperism," even of things as sacred as the Supreme Being. "But *American slavery* is an institution so precious, so beneficent, so exalted among the ordinances of God, so 'sanctioned and *sanctified* by the legislation of two hundred years,' that Northern men are not permitted to breathe an honest whisper against it." Indeed, had not a southern member just admonished Northerners to think what they liked about slavery but to keep their thoughts to themselves![39]

In attacking slavery as a restraint to civil liberties Julian was striking the institution, and the South, at one of its most vulnerable points. Northerners who had no sympathy with abolitionists or Free Soilers could combine with them in opposing this related evil. Slavery as a threat to civil liberties became an important corollary to the growing belief in a Slave Power conspiracy to control the Federal government and force the "peculiar institution" on the whole country.[40] Therefore, men who spoke as Julian did had an immeasurable influence in preparing

---

38 Julian, *Political Recollections*, 88-89.

39 *Congressional Globe*, 31 Congress, 1 session, 988, Appendix, 573-79; George W. Julian, *Speeches on Political Questions* (New York, 1872), 1-33.

40 Nye, *Fettered Freedom*, 217-50.

the people of the North to make the decision to resort to force ten years later.

Since both the North and the South had accused one another of aggression, he continued, it was this whole question that he proposed to make the main topic of his speech. He admitted that some northern criticism of the South may have been exaggerated but denied unequivocally that there had been aggression against the South. "The truth rather seems to be," he said, "that under the lead of Southern counsels, both sections of the Union have united in enlarging and aggrandizing the slave power." Free Soilers, he claimed, agreed with northern Whigs and Democrats that the institution of slavery was dependent upon state sovereignty and that Congress had no constitutional right to touch it where it already existed. But the institution could be attacked by moral forces; this was the way in which men worked for reform of any kind; this was not aggression, and there was no legal way to block it. The continuing effect of Channing on Julian's thinking is evidenced in his remark that "opinion is stronger than kings, mobs, lynch-laws, or any other laws for the suppression of thought and speech."[41]

Reaction to the speech was varied. The New York *Tribune* stated laconically that Julian had made a "calm and decidedly Anti Slavery speech." The *Palladium,* while expressing agreement with Julian's ideas, went on to say that the speech had evoked almost no enthusiasm and would have no effect in furthering the Free Soil cause, especially if Mr. Julian persisted in remaining in bed when votes were being taken on important questions. Another sort of reaction was expressed by an antislavery Southerner who congratulated Indiana for having sent at least "one representative [to] Congress, who is worthy

41 *Congressional Globe,* 31 Congress, 1 session, 988, Appendix 573-79.

to be her exponent on the great question of 'Freedom or Slavery?' " Only one element was lacking, he believed, to make it *"the* Freesoil speech of the session," and that was "oratorical energy in delivery . . . necessary to bring out the thoughts in distinctness and force."[42] From Charles Sumner in Boston came the most gratifying acclaim: "You have gone over the whole field of the slavery question & have presented, in a most interesting manner, the true conclusions. Few have treated it in the same exhaustive manner. Your speech . . . cannot fail to influence all who read it." "I did not dream," Julian replied, "that my . . . speech . . . would call forth such commendation, especially from one so far above me in every respect, and whose judgment in my favor is so peculiarly welcome & gratifying to me."[43]

Julian's maiden speech was no mean achievement for a thirty-three-year-old Congressman who less than ten years earlier had been unable to deliver a public address even in his native village. His very want of confidence probably accounted for his manner of speaking. Never adept at extemporaneous debate, he thoroughly prepared himself before attempting to appear before an audience. He would spend weeks, sometimes months, in preparation for these occasions. His style was restrained and conversational rather than histrionic. His good looks, his recent illness, and the sincerity of his devotion to the antislavery cause evoked sympathy for him and interest in his career. The older men in the Free Soil circle were beginning to see in him the potential for leadership in the antislavery movement. Shortly after his speech a social magazine for

42 New York *Tribune* (daily), May 15, 1850; Centreville *True Democrat,* May 22, 1850; Richmond *Palladium,* June 5, 1850.

43 Julian to Sumner, June 11, 1850, Charles Sumner Papers, Harvard University Library; Sumner to Julian, June 6, 1850, Giddings-Julian Papers.

women published a description of Julian that was reprinted, probably facetiously, by the *Palladium*. In spite of its maudlin tone, it conveys at least one view of his appearance and demeanor:

> His lofty form, his noble air, modest mien, and blue and unflinching eye, give him an appearance of native grandeur not often met with. He would make a splendid military officer. His face is oval, fair and becomingly full, with soft carnation bloom, his forehead is deep, square and smooth as polished marble, and denotes capacity and a discriminating mind in which independence and the endearing affections are blended. His brow is handsomely arched, and serene and tranquil and bespeaks great equinimity of temper and a visible self-possession common to well-informed men. His full blue eye is cool, keen and penetrating, while his glance is elastic. His fine classic countenance is dignified and intelligent: thus learned, gentle and manly. There is nothing to hinder him from attaining to the first post of honor in the gift of his country.[44]

As spring passed into summer Julian became less hopeful than ever that the Thirty-first Congress would adopt any Free Soil measures. While the House talked the California bill to death, the Senate was busy attempting to amend the Compromise so as to please as many special interests as possible. The enervating heat and humidity of the Washington summer did not make life any easier.[45]

Then, early in July, the President died, and it seemed for a time that the Omnibus Bill would pass after all. But by the first of August the Senate was deadlocked again, and it seemed to Julian and others that to remain in Washington was the height of futility. Some members drifted back home or took self-appointed vacations at

---

[44] Richmond *Palladium*, June 26, 1850, quoted from *The Huntress*, edited by Mrs. Ann Royal.

[45] Centreville *True Democrat*, June 26, 1850.

that time. Although Julian felt some sympathy for old Henry Clay, he was contemptuous of the efforts of the compromisers. Their labor had been worse than wasted, he concluded, for not only had they prevented the Senate from accomplishing anything but they had also obstructed the House. The result of their herculean efforts to restore harmony to their country—efforts worthy of a better cause—was only more confusion than ever.[46] But just as Congress was about to give up and go home, the Senate began to pass the various parts of the Compromise as separate measures, a process which continued until September 12, when it was completed with the passage of the Fugitive Slave bill.

To Julian the "broken doses" were worse than the "whole pill." Although the Fugitive Slave law was most odious to antislavery men, he felt that the Texas boundary bill was an even more pusillanimous surrender to the Slave Power. It had turned over to the South forty thousand square miles more than the Compromise had provided for, to say nothing of the ten-million-dollar gift to Texas. Julian's friend Giddings attributed this graft to speculators in Texas bonds, and especially to Webster— now Secretary of State in President Fillmore's cabinet— who had "stamped his image" upon the policy of the administration.[47] The Fugitive Slave Act, Julian observed, could have been defeated by those Congressmen from the free states who had absented themselves or refused to vote. But whereas the Fugitive Slave Act could be repealed, the act for handing out land to the South seemed irrevocable.[48] To him the adoption of the Com-

---

[46] *Ibid.*, August 7, 1850.

[47] *Ibid.*, August 21, 1850; Wilson, *Slave Power*, 2:280; Holman Hamilton, *Prologue to Conflict. The Crisis and Compromise of 1850* (University of Kentucky Press, 1964), 118-32.

[48] Centreville *True Democrat*, September 27, 1850.

promise was a great southern triumph which had left the impression in Washington that "the Free Soilers and their principles are dead and buried and that no more 'agitation' will ever be heard of." But, he added, "We shall see."[49]

V

Early in June, Anne Julian, having returned to Washington from New England, departed for Centreville. After she left, George sank into a spell of despondency from which he found little relief in the depressing summer of 1850. The absence of his scintillating young wife now left a gap in his life which was almost intolerable. After an absence of six months, he was also eager to see his little son again. His letters expressed not only a longing for them but also "strange forebodings" about them. In June, and again in July, he suffered from spells of sickness with which he was now intermittently afflicted. One of these illnesses prevented him from attending the funeral of "Old Zach," for whom Julian had found new respect since his stand on the California issue. Even the novel pleasure of hearing praise for his speech was wearing off. And only in the event of the cholera spreading to Washington, it seemed, would there be an adjournment. When Anne pleaded with him to buy some new clothes—she was especially anxious to have him fitted out with a white vest—and to mingle more in society, George could only reply:

It would probably be good for me, but I have spent too much of my life, my "glorious youthful prime," in the solitude to which I was driven by my timid nature, my cowardly fear of men and women. I have done much to conquer nature and to neutralize the effects of an education which made no

49 Clarke (ed.), "Home Letters," in *Indiana Magazine of History*, 29:147.

effort to save me from my besetting sin; but I can never hope
to be the man I might have been with proper early education.

One thing Julian could do. He could spare his child
such a fate. With proper care and education, he wrote to
Anne, little Channing could be saved "from a world of
suffering and self-conflict," and could attain "the full
stature of manhood."

Anne had to bear most of the brunt of the irascibility
that accompanied Julian's depressed state. He complained
that her letters were unsatisfying to him and that, after
urging him to come to Washington, she had left him
when he needed her most. She should "think of this,
and how I must feel to be so far and so long away from
you and our boy. Give me good letters and I will *try* to
reciprocate." At least, she ought to give him "something
better than 'scraps' to live on." Could she not find time
to write a few lines every few days, for Congress was a
bore and life a "drag," and he really needed to hear often
from her and Channing "as a solace."[50] George's letters
to Anne in the summer of 1850 manifest the ambivalence
of his relationship with her; sometimes he was the father
scolding or cajoling his daughter; at other times he was
the husband and lover who needed her affection and support. And through them all is the consistent theme of
self-pity.

Toward the end of August he was ill again, but as he
recovered, his despondency also lifted. Perhaps it was
because the session was drawing to a close, or it could
have been that he was preparing another speech.[51] In
any event, his spirit became more buoyant again. Although fearful that he would be unable to get the floor
during the last days of the session, he finally managed it

50 *Ibid.*, 29:136-45.
51 *Ibid.*, 29:148.

on September 25. Congressmen were so eager to adjourn that Julian was fearful of "outraging the[ir] feelings" by using up precious time. Nevertheless, he made a speech in which he denounced Congress for its surrender to the Slave Power in adopting the Texas boundary bill and castigated Northerners for their abandonment of the Wilmot Proviso. He concluded with a few words on the Fugitive Slave law which, he said, would jeopardize the freedom of every Negro in the North, while "converting every man in the free States into a constable and jail-keeper for slaveholders." He ended with the prediction that, rather than bringing peace, the Compromise measures would bring more chaos.[52]

By the end of the session Julian was more thoroughly committed than ever to the antislavery crusade. He had the prescience to see that the question "would [not] be settled to-day, or to-morrow, or next year," and that after its settlement there would be no reorganization of political parties on the basis of old issues. Yet he was determined to fight the battle through to the bitter end.[53]

VI

By the time Congress adjourned late in September many of the members had already gone home. Julian stayed until the end, but left immediately afterward. Instead of returning at once to Anne and Channing, he went first to visit friends and to make new acquaintances in New England. After a brief visit with Lucretia Mott in Philadelphia, he went on to Boston. There he saw his old friend Judge Charles Allen, met Charles Sumner, dined with Charles Francis Adams at Quincy, and de-

[52] *Congressional Globe,* 31 Congress, 1 session, 1965; Julian, *Speeches on Political Questions,* 34-49.
[53] New York *Tribune* (daily), July 8, 17, 1850.

livered two speeches—one on the same program with Wendell Phillips. Before a week had passed he was nearly worn out with excitement; too much had happened to put into a letter, he wrote Anne. One of his exciting experiences in Boston was hearing Jenny Lind sing; Julian was one of thousands of Americans who were captivated by the Swedish nightingale.

We have noted that the route Julian followed into the antislavery movement was the one frequently followed by New Englanders along the lines suggested by William Ellery Channing rather than the western route laid out by Theodore Dwight Weld. Julian always enjoyed the company of northeastern antislavery leaders and rarely missed an opportunity to participate in their activities. The theme of the speeches Julian made during this New England sojourn was essentially the same as that of his last speech in the House, but there was one new note, the higher law doctrine that Senator William Seward had introduced into the Compromise debates, which now became Julian's rationale for defiance of the Fugitive Slave law. He admitted that there was an "allegiance . . . owed to the laws of the land," but there was a "higher and paramount allegiance by which all men are bound." This higher allegiance, he said, made it impossible for him to obey the Fugitive Slave law.[54]

There is no doubt that Julian made a favorable impression on his New England comrades of the antislavery movement. One of his new acquaintances probably expressed the common view when he described Julian as a "noble fellow" and warned his district not to "change him off for some doughface" at the next election.[55]

---

[54] Julian, *Political Recollections*, 99-101; Clarke (ed.), "Home Letters," in *Indiana Magazine of History*, 29:148-49; Grace Julian Clarke Scrapbooks, 1:[4], clipping from Boston *Commonwealth*, October 10, 1850.

[55] Clarke Scrapbooks, 1:[4], clipping from Burlington (Vt.) *Courier*.

Between Julian's arrival in Centreville, in mid-October,
and the reconvening of Congress for the next session there
was not a great deal of time for him to enjoy the family
life for which he was so desperate during the last weeks
of the previous session.[56] By the end of November he was
back in Washington for the opening of the second session, "bruised and fatigued beyond all former experience" from the journey by coach across the mountains,
but in high spirits and eager to resume his Congressional
duties. Quite in contrast to the previous session, Julian
now entered upon one of the happiest three months of
his life. The beauty of the capital city and the life of a
Congressman there made Centreville seem "more insig-
nificant than ever." It was now Anne's turn to complain
that she had to endure the drabness of an Indiana village
while he enjoyed the social season in Washington. Julian's
response was that he could do nothing about it and that
it was not customary to bring wives to the capital for the
short session. With more confidence in himself and better
health than he had enjoyed in a year, Julian strengthened
the friendships made during the first session and maintained an active social life.[57]

Among the Free Soilers who shared the boarding house
where he lived, Charles Allen soon became his closest
friend. It was with Allen, now affectionately called "The
Judge," that Julian often went to social gatherings, to the
Unitarian church, and on long daily walks. In December
Jenny Lind appeared in Congress; Giddings and Durkee
were "enchanted" by her, as Julian had been in Boston.
On New Year's Eve Julian attended a presidential levee

[56] Clarke (ed.), "Home Letters," in *Indiana Magazine of History,*
29:149; Grinnell, *Men and Events,* 60.

[57] Clarke (ed.), "Home Letters," in *Indiana Magazine of History,*
29:150.

which was followed by a visit to the house of Senator Benton and later by an evening gathering at Dr. Bailey's, where Julian also enjoyed a standing invitation for Saturday nights. His correspondence reveals that he partook of mild alcoholic beverages, such as apple toddy or eggnog, even though back home he had given some support to the temperance movement.

More than ever before, Julian seems to have taken pride in his acceptance into Washington society. He liked to write of the important persons with whom he came in contact, to describe their manners and appearance, even though he may not have held them in high esteem as public men. We have noted the spell that Henry Clay cast over him. Gen. Winfield Scott also held a kind of fascination for Julian—his majestic appearance, his great size, and the way in which he seemed to draw attention in any group where he was present. To Anne, Julian boasted that these numerous invitations had come to him even though he had not in any way solicited them.

In Julian's circle of acquaintances there were a few women with whom he developed warm, although apparently completely platonic, relations. Through the Baileys he came to know Grace Greenwood, the novelist, and Mrs. Emma Southworth, another novelist and spirited conversationalist, who was a favorite of the Free Soilers. A female correspondent from Boston, Miss Curtis, who had a room at the boardinghouse where the Free Soilers lived, overcame her initial antipathy for them and became one of their circle of friends.

While Julian was enjoying the life of a Congressman in the national capital, he was confronted more and more with the problem of his wife's growing restiveness back in Centreville. To assuage her feelings, he wrote that he would not be content until he had retired from the "strife

of politics" and was free to return home again,[58] a statement whose falsity is demonstrated by his personality and
his career from beginning to end. In his reaction to his
wife's situation, which was similar to his own a few
months earlier, in his insensitivity to her feelings, he was
displaying that characteristic of some reformers, an inability to succeed in direct and intimate human relations
while pursuing their humanitarian goals. In Julian's case
the incongruity is heightened by the fact that he was
involved not only in the antislavery movement but in the
woman's rights movement as well.

As a Congressman during the second session, Julian
was a new man. Undaunted by the constant cries raised
against the Free Soilers that they were engaging in "agitation," he branded those who made the charges as
inhibitors of freedom of speech. Such charges led to an
acceleration, rather than a diminution, of his antislavery
efforts. During the first session he had occasionally presented antislavery petitions from his constituents; now
many came to him from Massachusetts and occasionally
from other states.[59] More frequently than before, he
entered briefly into the give-and-take of debate. Soon
after New Year's day, 1851, he presented a petition from
the Yearly Meeting of Antislavery Friends in Indiana requesting the repeal of the Fugitive Slave law. Despite the
cry of "agitation" and over strong opposition, he succeeded in having it read and the yeas and nays taken.
The vote went against him, but the following day he was
on his feet again to complain that his remarks had not
been correctly entered in the Journal and to demand

[58] Clarke (ed.), "Home Letters," in *Indiana Magazine of History,*
29:151-61.
[59] *Congressional Globe,* 31 Congress, 1 session, 261, 701, 719, 778, 843,
863; 31 Congress, 2 session, 436, 449-50, 459, 490, 503, 521.

that it be amended.[60] In this he also failed, but he was effectively using the tactics of the Free Soilers to keep the question of slavery open for debate.

Some weeks later, while the House was debating a bill for the establishment of a board of accounts to assist in the adjudication of claims against the government, Julian introduced into the discussion an entirely new note in proposing an amendment that "nothing herein contained shall authorize said board to hear or decide any claim for the loss or service of any slave." After opponents had tried unsuccessfully to have him ruled out of order, Julian went on to elaborate on his amendment. It had been the accepted practice of the House since the beginning of the government, he said, to refuse compensation for loss of slaves, for slaves had not been regarded as property but as persons. The amendment was defeated by an overwhelming majority,[61] but again he had taken part in the sort of debate which helped prevent the Compromise from being accepted as the final settlement of the slavery question.

Not content with merely striking at the Compromise itself, Julian joined the antislavery attack on one of its most venerable proponents, Daniel Webster, and presented a resolution to appoint a committee to investigate the charge that Webster had asked for and received between $40,000 and $50,000 from merchants of Boston and New York to accept the office of Secretary of State. Here was an example, Julian said, of the way in which the "money power" and the "slave power" had united to get up "Safety Committees and call forth so much patriotic devotion to the Union, particularly among Wall Street bro-

60 *Ibid.*, 31 Congress, 2 session, 177, 180-82; Clarke (ed.), "Home Letters" in *Indiana Magazine of History,* 29:154-55.

61 *Congressional Globe,* 31 Congress, 2 session, 486-87.

kers." Again his resolution met defeat, and one member, probably correctly, accused Julian of knowing all along that there would be no such investigation.[62]

Meanwhile, during the debate on Andrew Johnson's homestead bill, Julian made one of the most important speeches of his political career, one that clearly marked him as a land reformer, a role in which he would later gain a national reputation.

The land reform movement had its roots in the agrarian fundamentalism of Jeffersonian America and was further stimulated by the economic and social dislocations of the depression of the 1830's and 1840's. Beginning primarily as a plan to ameliorate labor conditions, its spokesmen were George Henry Evans and John Cummerford. Horace Greeley also joined the movement and publicized its program in his New York *Tribune*. Inevitably the idea found its way into Congress, and it was not long before Andrew Johnson of Tennessee became its champion. The program of the reformers called for the disposal of the public lands by granting them, in plots of one hundred and sixty acres, to anybody willing to cultivate them. They also sought to make land secure against creditors and against alienation and to prevent land monopoly by prohibiting large grants to speculators.[63]

People in Julian's district had long been familiar with the subject of land reform. The *True Democrat* had carried frequent articles favorable to the movement and

62 *Congressional Globe*, 31 Congress, 2 session, 752, 755; Centreville *True Democrat*, February 27, 1851. Julian's attack on Webster seems to be in accord with David Donald's view that many antislavery men were, without necessarily being aware of it, attacking the newly rising industrial system, of which Webster was the most outstanding political spokesman. See *Lincoln Reconsidered* (New York, 1956), 19-36.

63 Roy M. Robbins, *Our Landed Heritage* (New York, 1950), 97-104, 113-16.

to the adoption of a homestead measure. Hence Julian naturally gravitated to Johnson and the other Congressional advocates of the homestead law. His eclectic speech was especially significant, however, because it indicated the mode of Julian's thinking on several related issues. At the outset he made it clear that his advocacy of the homestead bill did not imply socialistic ideas. He claimed no right for the government to interfere with the laws of property or the vested rights of citizens, but he believed it wrong for governments to "make merchandise of the earth." In arguing that God had intended the soil to be cultivated and that man had a right, perhaps even a duty, to put land to use, he was going back to good Puritan doctrine, and was, unwittingly, accepting one of the premises of "manifest destiny." Calling on the ideas of Locke, he argued that there was a natural law which prohibited monopoly of the soil. Here, too, he was echoing the mid-nineteenth-century concept of progress begun by Saint-Simon. According to this doctrine there was a law of nature under which political, moral, social, and now material progress were inseparable. As Julian stated it, "The sentiment is becoming rooted in the great heart of Humanity, that the right to a *home* attaches of necessity to the right to live, inasmuch as the physical, moral, and intellectual well-being of each individual cannot be secured without it." And Jeffersonian agrarianism was invoked in the statement: "It may be taken for granted as a general truth, that the nation will be powerful, prosperous and happy in proportion to the number of independent cultivators of its soil." Then he went on to a peroration on the virtues of rural life. Julian touched on slavery, as a related issue, by drawing a comparison between Virginia, which was dying under the curse of the "peculiar institution," and her neighbor, Ohio, whose people enjoyed great abundance. Finally, he argued, although politicians might denounce land reform as "agrarianism" or "demagogism," they would never be able to prevent its final triumph, for it was an "important part of the great reform movement of the age—a link in the chain of the world's progress in harmony with the 'power that moves the stars and heaves the pulses of the deep.' "[64]

Unlike George Henry Evans, who regarded Negro slavery as an evil secondary to wage slavery, Julian viewed the land reform movement ancillary to, but significantly connected with, the antislavery movement. Yet Julian's ideas, as presented in the land reform speech, suggest that if there had been no antislavery movement its leaders would not have been without a cause.[65]

VII

Julian liked the taste of politics which life as a Congressman gave him, and health permitting, he probably had every intention of running again in 1851. Even so, he went through the frequent rationalization of politicians that only an irresistible call to duty could induce him again to undergo the rigors of electioneering and serving. Throughout the first session of the Thirty-first Congress he had mentioned, from time to time, the prospect of entering the next election. Although he had never

[64] *Congressional Globe*, 31 Congress, 2 session, Appendix, 135-38; Julian, *Speeches on Political Questions*, 50-66.

[65] For a somewhat different interpretation of Julian's homestead speech, one that emphasizes the agrarian utopian myth in nineteenth-century America, see Henry Nash Smith, *Virgin Land. The American West as Symbol and Myth* (Cambridge, Mass., 1950), 170-73. Although Julian was a strong advocate of land reform, his crusade in 1850 was antislavery, with the homestead bill as one means to the accomplishment of that end. Toward the end of the Civil War, and during Reconstruction, Julian would make his great contribution to the land reform movement, per se.

denied that he would be a candidate, the tenor of his remarks was that he probably would not run in 1851. By the end of 1850 his statements were becoming more equivocal, and in November he told some of Anne's relatives that in the spring he would be "traversing the district" again.[66] With the arrival of 1851, he still had not publicly announced his plans, but he wrote to Anne, "If I can succeed at all next summer, it will be by firmness, unanimity and *faith* on the part of the Free Soilers. . . . If they give up in despair of course they can't influence the action of the old parties." Soon, under the urging of family and friends, he disclosed his intentions when he said that not to try for the office again would be a "cowardly surrender to the Whig hunkers."[67]

If there really was any doubt in Julian's mind about running, developments in the "Burnt District" before he returned home from Washington helped to remove them, for the Whigs had launched a vigorous campaign in favor of Samuel W. Parker, Julian's opponent of 1849. One Whig newspaper, while setting forth the well-founded claims of Parker for the office, lamented that the fourth district was "misrepresented" by the "caricature of a man, George W. Julian," and that it was a "humiliating" fact that the "gorgeous Whig banner of that noble district" had given way to the "disunion flag of ABOLITIONISM." The *True Democrat* answered by saying that Parker had "spued out all his freesoilism" and by accepting the Compromise had renounced his claim to being an antislavery man.[68] Eventually, after a display of im-

[66] Clarke (ed.), "Home Letters," in *Indiana Magazine of History*, 29:145; Lou Finch to Hampden Finch, November 30, 1850, Hampden G. Finch Collection, Indiana State Library.

[67] Clarke (ed.), "Home Letters," in *Indiana Magazine of History*, 29:158, 161.

[68] Centreville *True Democrat*, February 13, 1851.

patience by Julian's friends, the *True Democrat* announced that he was the Free Soil candidate. From then on Julian was in the race, as there was no formal nomination by a Free Soil convention.[69]

During the canvass there were three serious charges made against Julian. The first was that he was not intelligent enough to represent the district; the second, that he had absented himself often from Congress and had not done justice to the job—a gross distortion of fact; and the third, that he was an agitator who had advocated mob action against the Fugitive Slave law, also a misrepresentation of fact. Further, his enemies circulated a story that Andrew Johnson had cursed Julian after his homestead speech and had blamed the Hoosier's abolitionism for the failure of the bill to pass. Under the caption, "The Artful Dodger," the *Palladium* published another exaggerated version of the incident of the Root resolution in which the question was asked how long it would take a dodger such as Julian to dodge the Free Soil party and butt his head against the Democratic party.[70]

Another feature of the campaign was the repeated charge by each contestant that his opponent refused to debate the issues. In spite of the frequent exchange of invitations to share the platform the two met only twice during the campaign, and one of these encounters was accidental. It is unlikely that either really wanted to meet the other face to face on the hustings; yet the continual accusations of cowardice and the efforts to prove them occupied no small part of the candidates' time and much space in the local newspapers.[71]

[69] Centreville *True Democrat,* March 13, 20, 1851.
[70] *Ibid.,* March 13, 27, July 3, 1851; Richmond *Palladium,* June 11, 1851.
[71] Centreville *True Democrat,* June 26, July 3, 10, 1851.

The apathy following the Compromise of 1850 had its effect, too, especially on the statements concerning the Fugitive Slave law. Julian found it discreet not to take the same vigorous stand against the law which he had taken in Congress. He proposed, he said, to say very little about it and to speak more of other things, but finally he did state that he favored a modification of the law. He placed more emphasis on land reform, and both candidates advocated cheap postage and economy in government. Although neither candidate had much to say about the tariff, their parties did take definite positions, the Free Soilers in favor of a tariff for revenue only and the Whigs for a protective tariff.[72]

Julian found it much more difficult to muster Democratic support in 1851 than in 1849. One reason, undoubtedly, was the Compromise and its enervating effects on antislavery Democrats; another was the opposition of influential Democrats both in and outside the "Burnt District." William J. Brown, who had lost his bid for speaker of the House in 1850, became a powerful antagonist. As editor of the influential Indianapolis *Sentinel,* Indiana's leading Democratic newspaper, he maintained a constant barrage against the Free Soil candidate. As the campaign progressed Parker began to claim the support of such well-known Democrats as Brown, Jesse D. Bright, Judge Test, and Oliver P. Morton. Julian's friends answered that they were not surprised that the perfidious Brown or the slaveholder Bright were opposed to Julian, but they refused to believe it of Morton and Test.[73] As it turned out, the Julian adherents were mis-

72 *Ibid.,* June 12, July 10, 17, 24, 1851; Indianapolis *Daily Indiana State Journal,* July 15, 1851.
73 Centreville *True Democrat,* July 3, 1851; Indianapolis *Daily Indiana State Journal,* May 3, 16, 27, 1851.

taken, for it was an element of the Democratic party under Morton's leadership which threw the election to Parker. Originally Morton's aim was to have the Democrats nominate a candidate of their own, but when that tactic failed he went over to Parker and took enough Democratic votes with him to decide the election.[74]

Oliver Perry Morton, six years younger than Julian, was also a native of Wayne County and, by 1850, one of its leading lawyers. An anti-Wilmot Proviso Democrat, he would leave the Democratic party during the furor over the Kansas-Nebraska Act, join the People's party in Indiana and, in 1856, become its candidate for governor. Later he would serve as Republican Civil War governor and use the office to make himself the most powerful leader in Indiana history. An opportunist of rare political acumen, he became a postwar Senator and national Republican leader.[75]

Before 1851 personal animosities existed between Morton and Julian; now the two men became unremitting political foes. Never again would Julian be free of the strictures of Morton, growing ever more powerful in Indiana politics.

After the election Julian made his usual announcement that he was through with politics and intended to devote his full time to the practice of law. Probably Julian really intended not to run again for office, but he must have realized that he would not withdraw from active participation in politics. His actual beliefs and intentions are probably more accurately stated in his diary: "There is likely to be need for a Free Soil party for some time to

---

[74] Smith, *The Liberty and Free-Soil Parties*, 233-34; Foulke, *Morton*, 1:32-33.

[75] See John D. Hicks's account of Morton's life in the *Dictionary of American Biography*, 13:262-64; also Foulke's *Morton, passim*, and Stampp, *Indiana Politics during the Civil War*.

come, and it may be that in 1852 I shall be again on the stump, battling for John P. Hale, Joshua R. Giddings, or some other true man. Certain I am that I shall never desert the cause I have espoused."[76]

VIII

The Compromise of 1850 transformed the mood of the American people from anxiety to relief, convinced as they were that it had settled the conflict that threatened to destroy the Union; but within four years after the handiwork of the compromisers had been completed men would look back with remorse and shock at their credulity in accepting it as a final settlement. While its spell lasted, however, the Compromise had some profound political effects, one of which was to destroy—or at least to atrophy—the third-party movements that had been stimulated by the antislavery impulse. Never again could the Free Soilers expect such support as they had received from the Conscience Whigs or the Barnburners of the Democratic party. While the Thirty-first Congress was still in session forty-three members from the two old parties—thirty-three from the South and ten from the free states—had pledged themselves to support no man for the Presidency or any other public office who was not known to favor the Compromise,[77] and in 1852 both major parties supported it. In Indiana the Democrats returned to the Senate the slaveholder Jesse D. Bright.[78] At the same time, the *Indiana State Journal*, representing the Whigs, contended that only "certain reckless politi-

---

[76] Julian's Journal, August 21, 1851, quoted in Clarke, *Julian*, 122n.

[77] Wilson, *Slave Power*, 2:360-61; Centreville *True Democrat*, February 6, 1851.

[78] Nevins, *Ordeal of the Union*, 2:5; Charles B. Murphy, *The Political Career of Jesse D. Bright* (Indiana Historical Society *Publications*, vol. 10, no. 3, Indianapolis, 1931).

cians" kept the slavery issue alive. Another evidence was
the decline of the Free Soil press in the Northwest. Of
forty Free Soil newspapers in Ohio in 1848, only seven
remained by the end of 1851. In Indiana only the Centreville *True Democrat* remained, none was left in Michigan, one of ten in Illinois, and three of the original eight
in Wisconsin.[79]

Yet a small group of antislavery leaders who could not
accept the Compromise as a final settlement remained
active and managed to maintain a political organization.
Among these men were Giddings, John P. Hale of New
Hampshire, Henry Wilson of Massachusetts, Samuel Lewis
of Ohio, and Julian. In September, 1851, they met at
Cleveland with what remained of the Free Soil organization and made plans to continue their efforts into the
campaign of 1852. At this convention Julian was selected
as one of the vice-presidents and a member of the committee on resolutions.[80] In 1852 he was active again among
the Wayne County Free Soilers and as a member of the
Indiana state central committee. In April he spoke at
an antislavery convention in Cincinnati where he pointed
out that although slaveholders composed only one fortieth
of the population they were in control of the Federal government, a situation from which there was little likelihood
of relief because neither of the old parties could succeed
in any election without the vote of the slave states. Nor
could he see any valid reason for the existence of the old
parties, since the issues to which they were committed and
which had given them birth were all obsolete. In conclusion he reiterated his belief that slavery was bound to
disappear because it was an affront to the moral sensibili-

---

[79] Smith, *The Liberty and Free-Soil Parties*, 230-46; Indianapolis
Daily Indiana State Journal, March 13, 1852.

[80] Centreville *True Democrat*, October 2, 9, 1851.

ties, antithetical to the social and political interests of thirty-nine fortieths of the population, and in contradiction to the "mighty engine of progress." When offered the presidency of this convention, Julian declined in favor of John G. Fee, the abolitionist preacher from Kentucky. In June the Indiana Free Soilers nominated Julian, along with Stephen C. Stevens, for Congressman at large,[81] but other events intervened to prevent him from running for that office.

As Free Soilers awaited the convening of their national convention, to meet in Pittsburgh in August, John P. Hale emerged as the strongest candidate for the Presidency, and by the time the convention met his nomination was assured. Although there was less unanimity about his running mate, Samuel Lewis of Ohio, a respected antislavery leader of long standing, appeared to be the favorite. Cassius M. Clay of Kentucky also had some support for the second place on the ticket. There is no evidence to indicate that Julian had any expectation of becoming the vice-presidential nominee. Even his uncle, Henry Hoover, who undoubtedly would have been pleased to see him receive the nomination, did not mention his name when he wrote to the *National Era* expressing his preference for Hale and Clay. Yet at the convention, after Hale's nomination on the first ballot, Julian was almost unanimously selected for the vice-presidential place on the second. Somewhat embarrassed, Julian wrote to Lewis to express his regrets that he had not received the nomination; generously Lewis replied that he was more than satisfied with the ticket.[82]

81 *Ibid.*, May 27, June 10, 1852.
82 Nevins, *Ordeal of the Union,* 2:33-34; Wilson, *Slave Power,* 2:373-75; Julian, *Political Recollections,* 123-28; Pittsburgh *Visitor,* 1852, in Grace Julian Clarke Scrapbooks; Centreville *True Democrat,* August 19, 1852; Washington (D.C.) *National Era,* January 22, 1852.

The nomination of a thirty-five-year-old man who was a recently defeated candidate for Congress after only one term must have come as a surprise to many Free Soilers, but an examination of the developments in the Free Soil convention shows that the decision was no mere aberration. The elimination of Samuel Lewis, it appears, resulted from the enmity of Salmon P. Chase, who was powerful enough to block his nomination. Since Hale was a New Englander, political expediency demanded that the vice-presidential candidate represent the Northwest, and the selection of a Hoosier might attract some votes from a relatively weak Free Soil state. Another factor that must have worked in Julian's favor was the role of the land reformers at the Pittsburgh convention, who sought the nomination of George Henry Evans. When it became evident that Evans could not secure the nomination, his delegates would logically turn to Julian, a devoted advocate of the homestead bill in Congress. In other ways, too, Julian was a strong candidate. He had a good Free Soil record in Congress as well as the appeal of handsomeness and youth. In 1852 the Free Soilers were struggling more for their continued existence as a political organization than for victory in the presidential election, which they knew was unattainable. As a candidate, Julian might not only attract young people to the movement, but if the slavery contest were to continue for another decade or so, such a man would grow up with the party and bring it experienced leadership at a time when it would be most needed. Indeed, one of the fundamental demands of such a politico-reform organization was that its adherents be satisfied to look to the future for their rewards rather than to expect them in the present.

Julian's extensive canvass for the Free Democracy (the party name now adopted by Free Soilers) in 1852 carried him into Kentucky as well as into the six states of the old Northwest. It is unlikely that Julian expected to attract many votes in Kentucky to the cause of the Free Democracy, and his decision to venture into that slave state manifests a desire to give moral support to a small band of courageous antislavery men there, led by Cassius M. Clay and John G. Fee. Speaking in an area where the people were aroused by the recent escape of thirty slaves, Julian found Clay's presence by his side, "with his right hand in the neighborhood of his revolver and ready for any emergency," to be a great comfort, and admitted that he would not have undertaken such a venture alone. No emergency developed, however, and the small audiences which turned out apparently gave close attention to Julian's antislavery speeches.[83]

Another potentially dangerous situation faced Julian in Terre Haute, Indiana, where, a short time before his appearance, the Free Democracy's candidate for governor, Andrew L. Robinson, had been mobbed. Julian went there in spite of warnings of several friends. Upon his arrival at the county courthouse, where he was to speak, he found a restless crowd and a "gang of ruffians armed with brickbats." Julian pointed out that one of his chief reasons for coming to Terre Haute was that a friend of his had been mobbed there and that he wished to "vindicate free speech and the honor of the town against the rule of ruffians and cut-throats." Again he escaped injury. A Democratic newspaper of the town expressed its thanks to Julian for coming. The editor held nothing in common with him politically and assured his readers that he would not be driven from his political position "even by the keen, bright Damascus

---

[83] Clarke, *Julian,* 133, quote from Julian's Journal with no date given; Centreville *True Democrat,* October 21, 1852.

blade of a Julian," but that freedom of speech was as important to him as the political debate of the campaign.[84]

Although treated with kindness in most places and generally pleased with the reaction to his speeches, occasionally Julian felt that he had failed miserably. In Logansport, Indiana, for example, he was "chilled by the coldness of the atmosphere on the subject of freedom," and his two-hour address apparently made no impression on the "miserable Hunkerish crowd in the Court House." He was more than ready to take the first stage for Indianapolis after that speech.[85]

The stunning Democratic victory in 1852 left not only a mortally wounded Whig party but a Free Soil movement that seemed doomed by the overwhelming approval which the people had given the Compromise. Yet Julian did not view the situation with despair. Convinced that the Compromise was more of an ephemeral illusion than a reality, it now behooved Free Soilers, he thought, "to go to work and organize as an independent and permanent party, establish presses, employ speakers, circulate facts, make no compromises, and stand unswervingly by their colors." In this way, he believed, they could within eight years take possession of the government.[86] The history of the decade would prove his prediction more nearly true than the majority of the people could have believed in 1852.

By 1852 Julian had been involved in the antislavery movement for six years, four of which had been devoted to the cause of the Free Soil party. We have noted the religious and subjective aspects of Julian's conversion to the antislavery movement, as well as his speeches attacking southern aggression and advocating the application

84 Centreville *True Democrat*, November 11, 1852.
85 Clarke, *Julian*, 135-37.
86 Julian's Journal, December 5, 1852, quoted in *ibid.*, 137.

of the higher law doctrine to justify his refusal to obey the Fugitive Slave Act. He had also spoken of the backward economic condition of the slave states in contrast to the economic health and social progress of the free states. But nowhere, except possibly in his rejection of the Fugitive Slave law, do we find his attention centered on the lot of the Negro in America, slave or free. Although it is hardly likely that he had no direct contact with Negroes, it does appear that in 1852, for the first time, he associated with Negroes on a basis of social equality. Julian's reaction to this experience—on two occasions—might lend some credence to those interpretations of the antislavery movement which suggest that men were not always rationally conscious of the true source of their commitment to the cause.

The first occasion was the Cincinnati convention which met in April, 1852. Here Julian met Frederick Douglass for the first time. He was charmed by Douglass' personality and moved by his oratory, and was especially grateful for this opportunity of seeing and hearing him because it helped Julian to overcome the "ridiculous and wicked prejudice against color which even most anti-slavery men [found] it difficult to conquer."[87] The second, and the more revealing, occasion was the one when Julian spoke

[87] Julian's Journal, May 5, 1852, quoted in *ibid.*, 123; Centreville *True Democrat,* May 27, 1852. We ought to remember, of course, that not many men of the 1850's were free of racial prejudice and that the belief in the inherent inferiority of the Negro was widespread. Note the use of this prejudice for political purposes by the *Indiana State Journal,* soon to be the state's leading Republican paper, in referring to the Cincinnati convention: "A number of the abolitionists of Cincinnati have engaged an artist to paint a portrait of FRED DOUGLASS, the negro orator, as they call him. The [Cincinnati] Commercial is of the opinion that the artist will not be troubled much in the mixture of the colors for his paint, as a little oil and lampblack is all that will be required." *Daily Indiana State Journal,* May 4, 1852.

in Detroit to a Negro audience. In recreating this experience in his diary, Julian's emphasis is on the fact that the speech on the subject of the wrongs of slavery was some sort of personal victory for *him*. Although admittedly still trying to overcome his racial prejudice, Julian conjures up a mental picture of the shocked expression of his "doughface" Hoosier enemies if they could see him in that setting. "I . . . was never more favored with the gift of effective utterance," he wrote. "Large numbers wept like children when I portrayed the wrongs of slavery, and I could see that what I said was appreciated as it could be by no white audience."[88]

Again Julian announced that he was through with politics and that it was his intention to attend industriously to his profession. This time the claim was more valid, for he did not hold political office again until 1861. Even so, he was never far from the political scene, and indeed, played a vital role in the political history of Indiana during the eight years preceding the Civil War.

Julian's conversion to the Free Soil movement in 1848 and his activities in the movement during the next four years remained, in his own mind, the most significant experience of his life. Here, he believed, he had fought the hardest in what he saw as a continuing battle for human rights; here he had made the greatest sacrifices; it was to the rigors of these years that he attributed the illnesses which burdened him throughout his remaining years. And in the succeeding decades, when he was particularly anxious to justify or vindicate his beliefs or actions, he would often look for an analogy between new situations and his role as a Free Soiler.

[88] Julian's Journal, October 12, 1852, quoted in Clarke, *Julian,* 134.

HOOSIER REFORMER
AS POLITICIAN

◆◇◆◇◆◇◆◇◆◇◆◇◆◇◆◇

THE relief from tension and crisis following the Compromise of 1850, which had helped to elect the "doughface" Franklin Pierce and had made moribund Hale's and Julian's Free Democracy, could not prevail for very long in the atmosphere of mid-nineteenth-century America. Romantic reform—especially antislavery—had affected the nation more deeply than it knew. Personal liberty laws and the continuing operation of the underground railroad in the North soon demonstrated that the Fugitive Slave law of 1850 was unenforceable. And in the year of Pierce's election Harriet Beecher Stowe expressed for the North its moral indignation on the subject of slavery in the publication of *Uncle Tom's Cabin.*

In politics the slavery question was reopened in 1854 with the passage by Congress of Douglas' Kansas-Nebraska bill. With this measure Douglas not only made his bid to establish himself as the undisputed leader of a Democratic party that would not be sundered by dissension between North and South over slavery, but also sought to clear away political obstacles to a transcontinental railroad along a central route. When in August,

1854, Douglas departed for Illinois after the adjournment of Congress, he expected his journey to be triumphal, with the people of the North recognizing his great service to the nation in guiding the Kansas-Nebraska bill through to adoption. Instead, it was a sad journey punctuated with jeers and insults.[1]

The Kansas-Nebraska Act provided for the organization of the two territories and repealed the Missouri Compromise, which had excluded slavery from the northern portion of the Louisiana Purchase. It was the removal of the restriction against slavery that was to cause Douglas the most trouble. In championing this measure the Illinois Senator had made an egregious miscalculation. His own approach to slavery was amoral; he did not care, he said, whether slavery was voted up or down. If the people of the North had reasoned similarly, popular sovereignty might have been a workable plan for solving the problem of slavery in the territories. But what Douglas failed to grasp was that people in the northwestern states did not agree with him. Men who were not themselves abolitionists had been moved by the moral fervor of the abolitionist attack on slavery, and those who were not so moved did not relish the prospect of sharing western lands with slaveholders. In short, Douglas had grossly underrated the attachment of the people of the North to the Missouri Compromise. Douglas was to find also, to his sorrow, that the South was not easily beguiled by popular sovereignty and that the southern interpretation of it was not the same as his. The Kansas-Nebraska Act destroyed the delicate balance which the Compromise of 1850 had made; the slavery question was in the open again, to be settled in a more decisive and tragic way. Douglas was

[1] George Fort Milton, *The Eve of Conflict: Stephen A. Douglas and the Needless War* (Boston and New York, 1934), 175-76.

in a political dilemma from which he was never able to extricate himself. It was a political dilemma entangled with a moral dilemma which Douglas never clearly understood, for in the 1850's one could not escape moral involvement by proclaiming that he did not care whether slavery was voted up or down. Successful politicians were apt to be those who, although projecting themselves as practical men who abhorred abolitionism, did not do violence to the axiom that slavery was antithetical to American democracy. Thus Abraham Lincoln, who was willing to make all sorts of concessions to the South and repeatedly rejected abolitionism, would not be forced out of the position that the essential difference between him and Senator Douglas was that he and his party believed slavery to be wrong whereas Douglas and his party did not believe it to be wrong.[2]

The most immediate effect of the Kansas-Nebraska Act was to accelerate political realignments. It gave hope to various political groups which, in opposing the Democrats in 1852, had met with disastrous defeat. With the North almost solidly opposed to the measure, skillful political manipulation might well unite Whigs, Free Soilers, Know Nothings, temperance advocates, and even some northern Democrats in a new party. If leaders were careful not to antagonize these elements on points of disagreement, while emphasizing their common opposition to the extension of slavery into the territories, the end of the dominance of the Democratic party might not be far away.

As early as May, 1854, a number of Congressmen, fully aware of the possibilities, met in a Washington boarding-house to discuss the formation of a new party and recommend that it adopt the name Republican. Within two

2 Roy P. Basler, *et al.* (eds.), *The Collected Works of Abraham Lincoln* (9 vols. Rutgers University Press, 1953-55), 3:245-83.

months similar activities resulted in fusion organizations in at least six states. Of particular significance were the meetings at Jackson, Michigan, and Ripon, Wisconsin.[3]

In Indiana the movement developed through a series of county conventions where Whigs, anti-Nebraska Democrats, and temperance men joined together in a fusion organization soon to be known as the People's party. As an anonymous Hoosier, using the sobriquet "Old Jackson Man," viewed the situation, "Parties are pretty low in the heel just now. . . . The party kettle wants cleaning out, and the best way to do it, I guess, will be turn it bottom upwards, even if you do spill out some of the old Hunkers with it."[4] It was evident from the beginning that the Whigs would be the dominant force in the new party, and through their organ, the Indianapolis *Journal,* they called for a mass meeting of all who were opposed to the Democracy. According to the *Journal,* the Democratic party was committed to the dominance of the Slave Power and had already begun to organize for the extension of slavery; hence it was high time for the opposition forces to begin to work together. It was logical that the Democrats would counter by pinning to the People's party the abolitionist label. The Indianapolis *Sentinel* warned its readers that the leaders of this "Peoples' Mass Convention" were certain to be Free Soilers and abolitionists bent on forcing upon the convention the "doctrines of Sumner, Giddings, Theodore Parker, Julian & Co."; men

3 Nevins, *Ordeal of the Union,* 2:322, 333-37; Theodore C. Smith, *The Liberty and Free-Soil Parties,* 292-96. The subsequent dispute as to which of these meetings constituted the formation of the Republican party has never been settled.

4 Indianapolis *Morning Journal,* April 17, June 13, 1854. See also Charles Zimmerman, "The Origin and Rise of the Republican Party in Indiana," in *Indiana Magazine of History,* 13 (1917):233-37.

should beware of this so-called "army of freedom" whose banner was really the "black flag of disunion." The *Journal*, to reassure doubtful followers, avowed that the abolitionists would not be there.[5] The Whigs, however, could not be rid of the abolition menace so easily, for it would have been difficult, if not impossible, to hammer into shape a political coalition on the anvil of Free Soil doctrine and at the same time exclude the Free Soilers. In spite of Whig promises, the Free Soilers were there, and Julian was their leader.

II

As leader of the antislavery contingent of the People's party of Indiana in the 1850's, Julian reached the apogee of his career as a reformer-politician. Although the possibility of returning some day to a political office could hardly have been absent from his mind, Julian refused to make the compromises and to indulge in the equivocations that would have placed political office within his grasp. Imbued with the millenialism of the true reformer, he was willing to wait for the ultimate victory, not only of party but of principles. On both the slavery issue and the nativist issue he made himself the conscience of his party. While Garrison and Wendell Phillips, with their lack of faith in institutions to accomplish reform, appealed to the moral sensibilities of the North to cleanse itself of the sin of slavery, if necessary by lopping off those segments of the nation infected with it, Julian and his fellow political abolitionists appealed to their *party* on moral grounds to become the agency for eradicating slavery under the Constitution. The political and the apolitical abolitionists shared the conviction that democ-

5 Indianapolis *Daily Journal*, June 20, July 10, 1854; Indianapolis *Daily Sentinel*, July 11, 1854.

racy could not exist along with slavery; both resorted to the natural rights philosophy as expressed in the Declaration of Independence, and both appealed to the Christian ethic. The only major difference between them was in the means of realizing their goals.

At this period of Julian's life his own statements about his beliefs and actions have a veracity and an accuracy that they do not have earlier or later. If there are rationalizations, they are not so obvious, and are closer to reality. Even more than before, the religious theme was brought into his discussion of political matters, especially in relation to the Free Soil party, now becoming sacrosanct as it faded out as a political organization. In April, 1853, in expressing his regrets that he could not accept an invitation to speak in Boston at a dinner in honor of John P. Hale, he wrote, "The great central truth of Christianity is the great central truth of our movement as a party. The platform on which we stand embodies in it the unfashionable political virtue of recognizing the distinction between right and wrong, and the government of the world by a providence."[6]

Following his defeat for Congress in 1851, Julian found it necessary to devote more of his energies to the rebuilding of his law practice, but there was still time for local politics. He made many speeches in the Whitewater Valley, and became corresponding secretary of the Wayne County Free Democracy.[7] To the fainthearted his message was for them not to forsake their labors. The anti-

[6] Julian to Committee of Invitation, April 29, 1853, Giddings-Julian Papers.

[7] Smith, *The Liberty and Free-Soil Parties,* 263-64; Indianapolis *Indiana Free Democrat,* January 20, March 3, April 7, 1853; Washington (D.C.) *National Era,* March 17, 1853. Rawson Vaile discontinued publication of the Centreville *True Democrat* with the issue of December 23, 1852, and announced that he was moving to Indianapolis to start a similar paper to be known as the *Indiana Free Democrat.*

slavery cause was not lost. "The Democracy is awfully swollen, whilst all Whiggery capable of salvation is preparing to come into our embrace. There is a good time coming."[8] A true antislavery man, he pleaded in addressing the Free Soil State Convention, May 25, 1853, at Indianapolis, no more doubts the progress and triumphs of his cause

than he doubts his own existence, or that of his Maker. He has faith in rectitude, and in the government of the world by a Providence. . . . He is not blinded or disheartened by the irregular ebbing and flowing of political currents. . . . Abolitionists have often been branded as infidels; but I am acquainted with no body of men since the introduction of Christianity . . . who have evinced so strong, so steadfast, and so vital a faith in the Fatherhood of God and the brotherhood of man.

In spite of the poor showing of the Free Democrats in 1852, he said, it was not their party but the Whigs who had been destroyed by that election, and the issues that had given the Whig party a reason for being—internal improvements, protective tariffs, and a national bank— were obsolete. Now the grand issue, indeed the only issue, was slavery. The destruction of the Democratic party would inevitably follow, for the only reason for its existence was opposition to Whiggism. And with the demise of the two old parties the field was now cleared for the battle over slavery. Although it would be bitterly contested, there was no doubt in Julian's mind about the ultimate result. Divine guidance and the omnipotent law of progress would assure victory to the forces of freedom.[9]

8 Julian's Journal quoted in Smith, *The Liberty and Free-Soil Parties,* 264.
9 Julian, *Speeches on Political Questions,* 83-88; Indianapolis *Indiana Free Democrat,* June 2, 9, 16, 1853.

This analysis of the political situation in the early 1850's demonstrated both the perceptiveness and the blindness that are apt to be combined in the mind of the reformer. The Free Soil ideology was not dead, and slavery was to be the major, although not the only, issue. But the Free Democratic party was finished as an independent political movement. The economic program of the Whigs was anything but obsolete. So alive was it, in fact, that already railroad legislation and tariffs were intricately enmeshed in the political antislavery movement. Much of the battle that Julian predicted for the Free Soilers was to be fought within a larger party of of which they were only a minority faction.

July 13, 1854, was the day appointed for the state People's convention, and as it approached Hoosier Free Soilers formulated and published the conditions under which they would co-operate. Their position, as set forth by the *Free Democrat* early in June, shows that they were not yet viewing realistically the political situation in Indiana. They were still unaware that they were bargaining for a place in the new party from a position of weakness rather than strength. Both of the old parties, said the *Free Democrat*, were "hopelessly corrupt and utterly unworthy of [their] confidence," and Free Soilers would not abandon their separate organization to go along with a party whose platform merely advocated the repeal of the Kansas-Nebraska Act. Suppose the fusionists did succeed in repealing the Kansas-Nebraska Act, then what would be the party's stand on the slavery question? The Free Soil answer was that it would then be committed to the Compromise of 1850, including the Fugitive Slave law, and "pledged to discountenance all attempts, whether in or out of Congress, to renew the slavery agitation." What Free Soilers demanded was a People's platform calling for "the complete severing of the Federal Government from all responsibility for the institution of slavery by its prohibition and abolition wherever the Federal Government has jurisdiction, and the repeal of all national laws recognizing and sustaining it."[10] Julian, as he readied himself to be the Free Soil spokesman at the convention, publicly stated this doctrine to be his own.[11]

The People's convention drew a crowd of ten thousand to Indianapolis. Although the Whigs were in the majority, the power of the Know Nothings, who had met secretly two days earlier to draw up a state ticket, was soon in evidence. The Know Nothing or American party was the outgrowth of various secret anti-Catholic, anti-foreign groups. Among the leading Indiana Know Nothings were Schuyler Colfax, a promising young politician and a future Vice-President who it was believed would strengthen the new party in the northern part of the state, and Stephen S. Harding, a former Free Soiler. But it was to Henry S. Lane, the old Whig, that the convention looked for leadership. Nobody in the state and few in the country could match his oratorical eloquence. A fellow Hoosier described him as a "master of the stops of eloquence — argument, sarcasm, ridicule, anecdote, pathos—he knew how to attach the willing to a cause, to shame the hesitant, to raise the laugh when it served, and set men to swearing when that was best. . . ."[12] One future Republican leader was not there. Oliver P. Morton, who habitually hesitated to join any movement until

10 Indianapolis *Indiana Free Democrat,* June 2, 1853; Indianapolis *Daily Sentinel,* June 7, 1854.
11 Indianapolis *Daily Sentinel,* July 7, 1854.
12 *Lew Wallace. An Autobiography* (2 vols. New York, 1906), 1:231-32. Wallace did not include Julian among the leaders of the convention, saying that like Garrison and Phillips he was more an enemy of slavery than a Republican.

the signs of its success were unmistakable, came in later—in time to enjoy the victory.

The platform adopted by the convention showed conclusively that the Free Soilers were not a power in the new party to be taken seriously, at least not at this early stage of its existence. The slavery plank expressed opposition to the extension of slavery and called for the restoration of the Missouri Compromise. Thus, in its predictions about the role of the antislavery men in the party the *Journal* had been essentially right and the *Sentinel* essentially wrong. Although Julian was there, this was not an antislavery convention. For the Maine law advocates, there was an evasive recommendation favoring prohibition.

Julian was going to be heard from, however. He would not submit, without some show of defiance, to a diluted platform, which did not mention the power or duty of Congress to prohibit slavery in the territories and said nothing about the denationalization of the "peculiar institution." His counterproposals, introduced to the convention as a minority report, included a resolution demanding the denationalization of slavery to the fullest extent permissible under the Constitution. Another resolution called for an effective prohibition law to forbid the manufacture and sale of intoxicating beverages. Both resolutions were defeated by a large majority.[13]

The rejection of Julian and his program by the People's party was not simply the result of a struggle for control of the party, in which Julian was the loser. In view of Hoosier attitudes about antislavery and the

---

[13] Zimmerman, "Origin and Rise of the Republican Party," in *Indiana Magazine of History*, 13:215-16, 226-47; Carl F. Brand, "The History of the Know Nothing Party in Indiana," in *Indiana Magazine of History*, 18 (1922):65-69.

Negro, Julian's presence in the party was, in fact, a considerable liability. These attitudes toward the Negro ranged from indifference to outright hostility. As in other states of the Old Northwest, the way of meeting the race question was to exclude Negroes and mulattoes, and in 1851 Indiana voters had approved an exclusion clause in the new state constitution by a slightly larger vote than that for ratification of the constitution. The clause also voided contracts with Negroes or mulattoes, and imposed heavy fines on persons encouraging them to remain.[14] Little wonder, then, that men trying to build a political organization strong enough to defeat the entrenched Democratic party should be reluctant to embrace an avowed antislavery man like Julian.

Throughout the following campaign the Democrats pictured the People's party as a multifarious combination of malcontents dominated by abolitionists and Know Nothings, with Julian held up as one of the outstanding leaders. The Indianapolis *Daily Sentinel* played up the Julian resolution as representative of the true spirit of the movement. The resolution, it asserted, had really passed in the convention, but had been suppressed by Whig and Know Nothing leaders; it also accused the *Journal,* falsely, of refusing to print the resolution. Nor was it only Julian's antislavery that played into the hands of the Democrats. There was also his earlier affinity for the Democrats and the fact that it was not slavery alone that caused him to leave the Whig party. The argument had some merit, for if there had been no slavery issue, Julian probably would have been a Democrat by 1854. Moreover, while the Democrats used Julian to smear the People's party with abolitionism, they agreed with him that the

---

14 Riker and Thornbrough (comps.), *Indiana Election Returns, 1816-1851,* 388-90; Smith, *The Liberty and Free-Soil Parties,* 336.

Know Nothings were odious and that the party was funda-
mentally weak.

What to do about Julian became an even more knotty
problem to the fusion leaders as the campaign progressed.
If they disavowed him completely, they might lose badly
needed Free Soil votes; but if they accepted him too
warmly, there was danger of antagonizing the anti-Nebraska Democrats, whom they were anxious to keep
within the fold. The People's party was embarrassed by
its effort to be all things to all men, and Julian made that
problem all the more obvious. There was only one way to
handle him in this situation—to ignore him—and this
was the tactic employed. He was left out of the party
councils, his speeches were not reported in the newspapers, he was neither praised nor condemned. When
it did become necessary to discuss Julian's role in the
party, the technique was to stress his personal peculiarities,
or to pass him off as a disorganizer who did not support
the party. In this way the party leaders might discipline
him while avoiding an open discussion of the issues. After
the election the charge was made against him that he did
not vote for the People's ticket—a charge that he, of
course, denied, pointing out that not only had he voted
for it but he had "publicly advocated it in more than a
dozen speeches."[15]

The election of 1854 resulted in a notable victory for
the inchoate People's party. While losing the upper house
of the state legislature to the Democrats, the fusionists
won a substantial majority in the lower house and an
over-all majority of twelve. Even more significant were
the Congressional elections in which People's candidates

[15] Indianapolis *Daily Journal*, July 18, 24, November 13, 14, 1854;
Indianapolis *Daily Sentinel*, July 13, 14, 19, 1854.

were successful in nine of the eleven districts.[16] In Julian's district David P. Holloway, his perennial antagonist, was the successful candidate.[17]

On November 1, Indianapolis was the scene of a mass meeting to celebrate the victory. Resolutions were adopted to the effect that the Declaration of Independence, the Constitution, and the Ordinance of 1787 composed a program broad enough for the whole American people to stand on. Among the exultant leaders who spoke on this occasion were Henry S. Lane and Samuel W. Parker, both former Whigs, and the Know Nothing Godlove S. Orth. Morton, the Democrat who had joined the People's party a month before the October election, was also there.[18] But Julian did not participate in the victory celebration.

III

As Julian looked back on political developments in Indiana in 1854 and on the People's party after its first campaign he concluded that the reason for the party's feebleness on the slavery issue was the effect of the Know Nothings within its ranks. "I predicted it," he wrote to Giddings in Washington, "and hoped for nothing better from the accursed heresy of Nativism which skulked into our camp to divide our friends and break the force of our movement."[19] Julian had not changed his mind when he wrote some years later that it was an intentionally planned and

---

16 Zimmerman, "Origin and Rise of the Republican Party," in *Indiana Magazine of History*, 13:244-45.

17 *Ibid.*, 13:241-42.

18 *Ibid.*, 13:247; Indianapolis *Daily Journal*, September 19, 1854; Roger H. Van Bolt, "The Rise of the Republican Party, 1855-1856," in *Indiana Magazine of History*, 51 (1955):185-86.

19 Julian to Giddings, January 12, 1855, Giddings-Julian Papers.

well-timed scheme to divide the people of the Free States upon trifles and side issues, while the South remained a unit in defense of its great interest, . . . a cunning attempt to balk and divert the indignation aroused by the repeal of the Missouri restriction, which else would spend its force upon the aggressions of slavery.[20]

It followed that if the People's party was to be saved and made to fulfill its rightful purpose, the canker of Know Nothingism must be removed, and Julian took upon himself the task of surgeon in performing the operation.

His first public broadside against the Know Nothings came on June 27, 1855, at an antislavery convention in Indianapolis where he delivered the main address. He began the speech with a plea to his antislavery friends to remember that they were engaged in a Christian crusade. "Let us say to the world," he exorted them,

that we wage war against slavery *because we are Christians,* and that to us rightfully belongs the prerogative of sitting in judgment upon the popular religion of the country, and pronouncing upon it according to its fidelity or infidelity to the great doctrine of human brotherhood.

He regretted that there was so little awareness of the magnitude of the slavery question, for if people had really understood it this great question of human rights would not be "dragged down to the level of our current politics, and confounded with the strife of parties and the schemes of place-hunters." There was too little genuine hatred of slavery and too much anti-Nebraska sentiment, "the product of political rather than moral causes, of transient influences rather than deep-rooted convictions."

20 Julian, *Political Recollections,* 141; Julian, *Speeches on Political Questions,* 122-23.

Now Julian was ready to deal with the Know Nothings. He admitted that there was some danger of an undue growth of Romanism in America, but he was certain that the methods of the Know Nothings would aggravate rather than diminish the evil: "Secrecy, indeed! Our Model Republic loving darkness better than light! American Democracy carrying concealed weapons! American Protestantism stealing the livery of the Jesuit, and at the same time raising the war-cry against Rome." If this was Protestantism, he could not be a Protestant. Indeed, the Protestant churches had become the great bulwarks of slavery and the Slave Power and without them the "peculiar institution" could not exist. The accident of birth, he continued, did not make native Americans better citizens than foreigners. In concluding he called on all true antislavery men to denounce Know Nothingism and not to lose sight of the real issue, and he wanted it distinctly understood that "an anti-slavery man is, of necessity, the enemy of caste, bigotry, and proscription."[21]

The Know Nothing party that Julian so vigorously attacked was no mere phantom in the mid-1850's. Stemming from the secret society organized in New York in 1849, the Order of the Star-Spangled Banner, it was essentially an anti-Catholic organization whose original purpose was to work within the two major parties to elect nativists and anti-Catholics. The victory of Franklin Pierce in 1852, which nativists and Whigs had attributed to the foreign-born vote, gave the order a great boost, and by 1854 it had emerged as a separate party and won political control of a number of eastern and border states. The movement nourished itself on the chaos of the 1850's—slavery, the industrial revolution, immigration,

21 Julian, *Speeches on Political Questions,* 102-25.

and the disruption of the political parties. This was neither the first nor the last time that Americans would turn to foreign scapegoats when faced with internal problems that seemed to be insoluble, and the Know Nothings' boast that they would elect a President in 1856 could not be taken lightly.[22] After 1856 the movement rapidly declined; but this was not the prospect in 1855, and to expose it as Julian did was an act of real courage.

Even though the nativists were not so formidable in the Northwest as in the East, they were numerous enough in Indiana that Julian was certain to antagonize some of his antislavery friends. In his audience at the antislavery convention were men who, although Know Nothings, regarded themselves as good antislavery men who would not allow Julian's charges to go unchallenged. In replying to him Stephen S. Harding, an old and honored antislavery fighter who foresaw the demise of the movement, said that Know Nothingism was a "dead lion" and that Julian was wasting his efforts in fighting it. But he defended the Know Nothings against the charge that they were proslavery and challenged Julian to cite one election where Know Nothing votes had been detrimental to the antislavery cause.

Rawson Vaile, former editor of the Free Soil organ, the *Free Democrat,* and an ardent Julian champion in his Congressional campaigns and in the presidential election of 1852, followed Harding and denounced Julian more bitterly. He pointed out that all over the North Know Nothings had helped to elect antislavery men to Congress, among them Charles Durkee of Wisconsin, Henry Wilson of Massachusetts, William H. Seward of New York, and John P. Hale in New Hampshire. Vaile, now a

22 Ray Allen Billington, *The Protestant Crusade, 1800 to 1860* . . . (New York, 1938), 380-437.

loyal People's party man and one of the editors of the Indianapolis *Journal,* asserted that Julian's sentiments were not those of the majority of Free Democrats, who were co-operating in a "common endeavor to rescue [the] country from the Slave Power." He also predicted that at its next convention the People's party would adopt a platform satisfactory to all antislavery men. Before adjournment the convention decisively rejected Julian's anti-Know Nothing resolution and adopted one committing the convention to support the People's party.[23]

From that day the friendship between Julian and Vaile rapidly deteriorated. Soon Julian wrote to the *National Era* that Vaile had deserted the antislavery movement and that his editorship of the *Journal* was a Know Nothing "job office." Vaile denied the accusation, and answered that Julian had turned against him before he had left the *Free Democrat* because, in the absence of a Free Soil candidate, he would not oppose the election of David P. Holloway to Congress from the fifth district.[24]

It soon became evident that Know Nothingism was not a "dead lion" but still a force to be reckoned with in the People's party. The party convention which met in Indianapolis in July, 1855, chose as its president the Know Nothing, Charles Test, and three of the eleven vice-presidents were Know Nothings. Henry Wilson, the Massachusetts antislavery and Know Nothing leader, delivered the main address. The party platform was hardly

---

23 Brand, "Know Nothing Party in Indiana," in *Indiana Magazine of History,* 18:196; Indianapolis *Daily Journal,* June 29, 30, July 2, 1855; Van Bolt, "The Rise of the Republican Party," in *Indiana Magazine of History,* 51:195.

24 Indianapolis *Daily Journal,* August 8, 1855. Wayne County was now part of the Fifth Congressional District along with Union, Fayette, Randolph, Delaware, and Henry counties.

more antislavery than it had been in 1854, but the hand of the Know Nothings could be seen in the additional plank which demanded that the franchise be limited to native or naturalized American citizens. Among the prominent leaders in the convention were Morton, Lane, and Colfax. Julian, if he was present, was not heard from.[25]

As the summer of that year drew to a close Julian grew more despondent about the future of the Republican party. He wrote to a friend predicting that 1856 would bring a series of defeats, not only in Indiana but in other states as well. He was especially concerned about the gubernatorial race of Salmon P. Chase in Ohio and feared that the Know Nothings would "secretly and systematically cut his throat and throw back the antislavery men of the North upon their radical doctrines to fight their battle single handed . . . under all the distractions and divisions that will have overtaken us." But he admitted that his association with the Hoosier brand of Republicanism may have made him too pessimistic.[26]

Throughout most of the 1850's Julian was so deeply involved in antislavery reform and so fully committed to shaping the emerging Republican party to that specific end that the political impulse and the ambition that remained alive in him is apt to be lost sight of. But as he watched more equivocal men and more adroit politicians such as Colfax and Morton take charge of the party, he experienced acute personal suffering. Then he could write ruefully to a friend,

[25] Zimmerman, "Origin and Rise of the Republican Party," in *Indiana Magazine of History*, 13:248-49; Brand, "Know Nothing Party in Indiana," in *Indiana Magazine of History*, 18:200-1; Indianapolis *Daily Journal*, July 14, 1855; Richmond *Palladium*, July 19, 1855.
[26] Julian to E. A. Stansbury, September 14, 1855, Miscellaneous Manuscripts, Manuscript Division, Library of Congress.

I have held on to my integrity most inflexibly as an anti-slavery man, without any variables or shadow of turning, and yet the Republican politicians in this state fear and hate me more than any man in it. My straight onward course . . . from the very start, has laid me prostrate, and precipitated me out of politics as completely as I could have desired, though not exactly in the way most flattering to my popularity. *That* is all gone, and I have nothing left but character, which nobody but a "fanatic" thinks worth [having].[27]

IV

While Julian was engaged in the unrewarding work of the political abolitionist in Indiana, he could look beyond the borders of his native state and see developments that were propitious for the formation of a national Republican party more in accord with his ideas. To participate actively in the formation of such a party would provide him with some constructive work to do quite in contrast with his political efforts at home. Thus the forthcoming convention in Pittsburgh, scheduled for February, 1856, for the purpose of organizing a national Republican party was fortunate for Julian from both a personal and a career standpoint.

Just on the eve of the convention Anne presented him with another child, a son named Louis Henry, and he was reluctant to leave her. But her insistence that he should go overcame any hesitancy that he might have felt, and he had the exhilarating experience of stepping out of Indiana's tepid antislavery air into the rarified atmosphere provided by such reformers as Giddings and Owen Lovejoy. Indeed, the Pittsburgh convention was a turning point in Julian's life. Not that the old battles were over—they never were to be for him. But thereafter Hoosier politicians could not ignore him so ignomini-

27 *Ibid.*

ously as in the past, and a few years brought such changes that his seeking political office could no longer be thought absurd.

The assemblage of Republicans in Pittsburgh was really a mass meeting rather than a political convention in the usual sense. Men came voluntarily and not as delegates from the states. As Julian pointed out, "No candidates were to be nominated and no offices were to be divided." Although most of the members had had little political experience, the leadership fell to those who had already "arrived" politically or were on the rise in state and national politics.

At least three of the leaders—Giddings, Preston King, and David Wilmot—had been Free Soil associates of Julian's in Congress. Zachariah Chandler of Michigan, a former Whig who had rejected Free Soilism but was now a staunch antislavery Republican, was also there. Morton was present, but at this convention in which "the element of uncalculating radicalism . . . baffled the policy of timidity and hesitation and saved the cause," he could not harass Julian as he could at home. Francis Preston Blair, Sr., the former Jacksonian who had followed Van Buren and the Free Soilers in 1848, was elected permanent chairman of the convention. Blair's antislavery ideal, according to Julian, was the Compromise of 1850, and he "strangely misconceived the spirit and purpose of the convention."

There were many speeches, mostly of a strong antislavery flavor. Horace Greeley stopped off in Pittsburgh on his way home from Washington and was called on for a speech, but his message was disappointing to much of his audience. Fearful of antagonizing the Know Nothings, Greeley brought a warning from the national capital that the convention should proceed with caution.

Giddings answered him with a speech that scoffed at such advice and suggested that Washington was the least likely place to look for wisdom on the formation of a new party. The speech that most impressed Julian was the one delivered by Charles Reemelin, a German immigrant from Cincinnati, whose "arraignment of Know-Nothingism as a scheme of bigotry and intolerance, and a mischievous side-issue, was vigorous and unsparing."

Julian was also one of the speakers, but his important work in the convention was done as a member of the Committee on National Organization. As chairman of this committee, which was composed of one person from each state and included among its members such anti-slavery leaders as Owen Lovejoy, Chandler, and Charles Durkee, Julian reported the committee's plan for interlocking party organizations in states, districts, counties, and towns, all under a national executive committee to consist of a member from each state. The committee report also called for a national Republican convention to meet in Philadelphia on June 17 to nominate candidates for President and Vice-President.[28]

When he returned home from Pittsburgh, Julian soon found himself again caught up in the maelstrom of Indiana politics. In the Wayne County People's convention he won acceptance of a recommendation that temperance be abandoned as a party objective, and the convention approved the anti-Know Nothing resolution that he introduced. The *Sentinel,* speaking for the Democratic party, exaggerated the import of these actions, implying that they meant an "abolitionist" victory in "Old Wayne." "Morton's denunciations of Julian,"

28 George W. Julian, "The First Republican National Convention," in *American Historical Review,* 4 (1898-99):313-22; Indianapolis *Daily Journal,* February 26, 1856.

it said, "were deep and bitter, but he was no match for Julian in tact or talents and Julian 'used him up.' " Actually, Julian still had Morton and his coterie and their local organ, the *Palladium,* to contend with. Although the *Palladium* eased up on Julian somewhat after the Pittsburgh convention, it did not abandon its condescending and sarcastic tone. It was not yet sure of Julian's loyalty to the party and would readmit him only when he ceased his attacks on Morton and other loyal men. And it doubted the sincerity of Julian's opposition to "fusionism," to which he had voiced no objections a few years ago when he had "courted the Democracy as a candidate for Congress."[29]

In Wayne County there may have been some basis for Julian's boast that he would compel the Indiana fusionists to "walk up on to a clean Republican platform on the single issue of slavery," but outside the "Burnt District" he found the task an impossible one. The Indiana People's convention of May 1, 1856, was still permeated with fusionism; some of the delegates advised against joining the national Republican movement, and only with considerable reluctance did the convention decide to send delegates to Philadelphia. The platform expressed opposition to the extension of slavery, advocated the admission of Kansas as a free state, and included a Know Nothing plank for withholding suffrage from foreigners until after naturalization. And Oliver P. Morton was the party's nominee for governor.[30]

[29] Julian's Journal, March 5, 1856, quoted in Clarke, *Julian,* 171-72; Richmond *Palladium,* April 17, 24, 1856; Indianapolis *Daily Sentinel,* March 17, 1856.

[30] Julian's Journal, March 5, 1856, quoted in Clarke, *Julian,* 171; Zimmerman, "Origin and Rise of the Republican Party," in *Indiana Magazine of History,* 13:256-60; Indianapolis *Daily Sentinel,* May 2, 3, 1856.

Soon after the convention Julian denounced the People's party even more harshly than he had in 1854, and this time he carried on the attack outside as well as inside the state. In a letter to the Washington *National Era* he charged that the People's convention had neatly evaded any positive stand on the two important issues, slavery extension and nativism. Again, there was no demand that Congress use its constitutional powers to prohibit the extension of slavery into the territories; there was nothing to indicate any opposition to the Know Nothing aim of extending the required period of residence to twenty-one years before a foreigner could become a citizen. Julian frankly stated what he believed to be the duty of men who could not support the People's ticket. They ought to "do everything in their power, by honorable means, to overwhelm it with an inglorious defeat." This castigation was too harsh even for the radical *National Era,* which cautioned men who thought as Julian did to "do nothing rashly," and while agreeing that there was reason for dissatisfaction, the newspaper advised against precipitating a crisis before the Philadelphia convention assembled in June.[31] But Julian refused to recant; instead, he wrote back to the *National Era* reaffirming his position. He asserted that not only was the platform a "sneaking dodge of the great issue before the country," but that the men nominated were not entitled to the support of antislavery men. He refused to support a man like Morton, who regarded the Fugitive Slave law as constitutional and wanted it enforced, and who had stated that he would vote for the admission of new slave states under "popular sovereignty."[32] These harsh words presented the *Palladium* with another open-

31 Washington (D.C.) *National Era,* May 22, 1856.
32 *Ibid.,* June 12, 1856.

ing for a gibe: "What a miserable feeling it must be to be covered up with such intense hatred—personal hatred—as George exhibits! May the Lord have mercy on his poor soul!"[33]

Julian's relationship to the People's party was developing into a regular pattern. In each of the election years— 1854, 1856, and 1858—he either asserted that he would not vote the People's ticket, or his opponents accused him of apostasy. Yet, despite his near contempt for the party's program and his continued efforts to shape it to his own ideas, he never carried through with his threats or gave others the satisfaction of truthfully branding him a self-made exile from the cause. In each case he eventually announced publicly that he supported the People's ticket. The reformer was still enough politician not to have himself thrown out of the only party that was available to him.

If Julian's indiscreet remarks following the state convention had temporarily separated him from the People's party in Indiana, the national Republican convention in Philadelphia eased his move back into it. The presidential nominee, John C. Frémont, although a man of little political experience, was acceptable to the antislavery element of the party, and the platform embraced much of the old Free Soil program. It called for the preservation of republican institutions guaranteed by the Constitution and the Declaration of Independence and demanded that Congress exert its constitutional right and "imperative duty" to prohibit slavery in the territories.[34] When the Indiana fusionists endorsed this platform, Julian could argue cogently that they had repudiated their earlier position. Not only could he now join

[33] Richmond *Palladium,* June 5, 1856.
[34] *Proceedings of the First Three Republican National Conventions of 1856, 1860 and 1864* . . . (Minneapolis, 1893), 43.

the movement in good faith, he was also duty bound to hold the party to its pledge.

Hence, after midsummer Julian appeared from time to time as a speaker on the same platform with such party leaders as Godlove S. Orth, Morton, and Samuel W. Parker. Julian glowingly remembered the campaign of 1856 as "pre-eminently a conflict of principles" where the vital issues could hardly have been better defined, "a struggle between two civilizations, between reason and brute force, between the principles of Democracy and the creed of Absolutism." The memory of it was a delight and his role "a real jubilee of the heart":

I was welcomed by the Republican masses everywhere, and the fact was as gratifying to me as it proved mortifying to the party chiefs who, a little before had found such comfort in the assurance that henceforeward they were rid of me. With many wry faces they submitted, after all sorts of manœuvers early in the canvass to keep me in the background, varied by occasional threats to drive me out of the party.

According to Julian's account of the Indiana election of 1856, victory was in the grasp of the People's party until it was thrown away. The nomination of Morton and the party's refusal to engage in a vigorous campaign so as not to offend old Whigs and Know Nothings, he asserted, had prostituted a great cause. Instead of making war against slavery, lamented Julian, the People's party was more intent on proving itself a white man's party. Anti-slavery speakers from outside were prevented from coming into the state, and the well-known proslavery attitude of southern Indiana frightened the party leaders away from that area, where the campaign should have been carried on with the greatest vigor.[35]

35 Julian, *Political Recollections*, 151-57; Clarke, *Julian*, 174-75; Zimmerman, "Origin and Rise of the Republican Party," in *Indiana Magazine of History*, 13:267; Indianapolis *Daily Sentinel*, August 8, 1856.

Although Julian's explanation tends toward the specious—he omitted any consideration of the long-established power of the Hoosier Democracy—his evaluation of the People's party weaknesses has some validity. Its defensive position was manifested in its repeated efforts to disprove the charge that it was abolitionist in sentiment. Late in the campaign a friend wrote Julian from Jeffersonville in southern Indiana that his name had been mentioned in the vicinity more than fifty times as "an ultra Abolitionist in favor of everything offensive to these proslavery parties, and the prejudice of the uninformed." The writer wanted Julian to come immediately to deliver a speech which would "show slavery no quarter . . . [but] convince the laboring class that it is at war with the genius of our Republican institutions and opposed to their rights and interests."[36] Even the ardent fusionist Indianapolis *Journal* attributed the Democratic victory to betrayal by Know Nothings, and offered as proof that every strong Fillmore county had gone against Morton.[37] Julian stated it more succinctly: "Fusionism has debauched and defeated us."[38]

V

During the 1850's Julian was not engaged exclusively in fighting the antislavery battle in the People's con-

[36] N. Field to Julian, September 19, 1856, Giddings-Julian Papers; Ruhl J. Bartlett, *John Frémont and the Republican Party* (The Ohio State University Studies, *Contributions in History and Political Science*, No. 13, Columbus, 1930), 45-46.

[37] Indianapolis *Daily Journal*, October 18, 1856.

[38] Julian's Journal, December 5, 1856, quoted in Clarke, *Julian*, 181; Zimmerman, "Origin and Rise of the Republican Party," in *Indiana Magazine of History*, 13:267. In the election of 1856 Morton lost the contest for governor by 5,842 votes. The General Assembly was split, with the Democrats having a majority in the House and the Republicans in the Senate. The Democrats had a substantial over-all majority. The Republicans elected five of the eleven Congressmen.

ventions or on the hustings. Having returned to the practice of law, he made a living from the profession, although it was not remunerative enough to provide any substantial savings. There were times when he seriously considered moving from Centreville to Indianapolis, where his wife would have been happier and where he would have found a more lucrative law practice. But he was not to be lured away at this time from the pastoral region of his birth, for which he always maintained a strong sentimental attachment. A factor in his decision not to move was the new railroad from Centreville to Indianapolis, which was completed in 1853 and made the state capital more accessible.[39]

But the most persuasive reason for staying in Centreville was probably his knowledge that only from the "Burnt District" could he again return to Congress.

Sometimes there were opportunities outside politics for him to carry on the antislavery crusade. Two brothers, Andrew and Solomon Bidwell, of Indianapolis, in an effort to establish in Indiana "a higher standard of public opinion, particularly on the question of American slavery," undertook publication of a weekly newspaper entitled *The Western Presage*. It was to be an experiment; if it did not attract subscribers or if compromises had to be made between truth and policy to keep it going, it was to be abandoned. The Bidwells contracted with Julian to write five articles. The venture, however, turned out to be a failure and Julian had written only three articles when the paper expired.[40]

After 1850 a lawyer in any of the states lying on the north shore of the Ohio River could, if he were so in-

[39] Clarke, *Julian*, 143-45.

[40] Grace Julian Clarke (ed.), "A Letter from Daniel Worth to George W. Julian and Other Documents," in *Indiana Magazine of History*, 26 (1930):152-57.

clined, devote some of his practice to fugitive slave cases. Julian, inescapably, became involved in several of these cases. In one of them he was defense attorney for Benjamin Waterhouse, who was shown to be guilty of aiding in the escape of fugitive slaves. Julian succeeded in getting Waterhouse off with a fifty-dollar fine and one hour in jail, despite legal opposition from the able Richard W. Thompson, the Hoosier Know Nothing leader.[41]

By far the most important fugitive slave case of Julian's legal career, and the one which he remembered with the greatest pride, was the West case. In November, 1857, Austin W. Vallandigham, a Kentucky slaveholder, sent his agent into Illinois where he captured a Negro known as West, or Weston, whom Vallandigham claimed as his slave. As West and the agent passed through Indianapolis en route to Kentucky, proceedings were instituted in the city courts against Vallandigham for kidnaping a free Negro, on an affidavit filed by a local Negro. The argument centered on the legality of a Negro filing an affidavit against a white man. The court discharged West and immediately the deputy United States marshal arrested him and took him before the commissioner, John H. Rea, on the charge that he was a fugitive slave. Here the first of two trials occurred. Julian and his colleagues requested three weeks' time to bring witnesses to the trial. When the request was denied and when Vallandigham was able to call in an array of witnesses for his side, the decision became a mere formality. But as soon as the commissioner had issued the necessary certificate to Vallandigham permitting him to take West to Kentucky,

41 Charles H. Money, "The Fugitive Slave Law of 1850 in Indiana," in *Indiana Magazine of History*, 17 (1921):275; Indianapolis *Daily Journal*, November 26—December 10, 1857.

Julian and his colleagues took the case to the court of common pleas where they tried a second time to secure West's freedom on a writ of habeas corpus. Hence there ensued a second trial—in the hall of the House of Representatives this time—which attracted widespread attention. In the course of the proceedings Julian branded the commissioner a usurper of human rights bent on sending a legally free Negro to the slave pens of Louisville. The Fugitive Slave Act he denounced as a "Godless law, . . . an unutterably infernal law" designed to "drag God Almighty from his throne, and inaugurate the reign of the devil upon the earth." The decision of the judge returned West to slavery. One of Julian's purposes had been to arouse public opinion in favor of West and possibly resistance to the authorities, which might assure his freedom. During the trial Julian had stated that, in the event of a miscarriage of justice in the courts, more direct action ought to be taken—action in which Julian would be happy to be a participant. Anticipating trouble, the commissioner arranged for a posse of forty men to prevent West's escape. Despite these precautions, a group of antislavery men working with Julian aided West in escaping from the jail where he was being held. Apparently he failed to get away only because he made the mistake of mounting a slow horse instead of the fast one which was awaiting him.[42]

Thus ended the West case. Even though Julian and his friends did not succeed in freeing the Negro, they were undoubtedly furthering their aim of making slave hunting in Indiana as expensive and as difficult as possible. And Julian had demonstrated that he would "agi-

[42] Money, "The Fugitive Slave Law in Indiana," in *Indiana Magazine of History*, 17:257-68; Indianapolis *Daily Journal*, November 26—December 10, 1857.

tate" for the antislavery cause not only on the floor of Congress and in political conventions but within courts as well.

VI

By 1858 the People's party had officially adopted the name Republican. Meanwhile, the Hoosier Know Nothing movement was rapidly declining, so that by 1858 all that was left of it was a splinter group led by the recalcitrant Richard W. Thompson, who refused to co-operate with either of the major parties. For all practical purposes, Know Nothingism had merged with Republicanism.[43]

The result was not, as might have been expected, an end of internecine strife within the Republican party. Other developments were keeping the situation complicated. The Kansas War and the efforts of the Buchanan administration to bring the territory into the Union under the proslavery Lecompton Constitution had led to a rupture in the Democratic party with Buchanan and the administration in one faction and Stephen A. Douglas and his followers in the other. Increasingly, fusion-minded Republicans were flirting with anti-Lecompton Douglas Democrats, for if this numerous group could be brought within the Republican fold, victory in 1860 seemed all but certain.[44]

Thus Republicans who assembled for the state convention in Indianapolis on March 4, 1858, were faced with the old problem of molding together potentially antagonistic elements. All were now opposed to the extension of slavery, but the method to be used to achieve

[43] Brand, "The Know Nothing Party in Indiana," in *Indiana Magazine of History*, 18:292-97.

[44] For a thorough coverage of the Democratic split see Roy F. Nichols, *The Disruption of American Democracy* (New York, 1948), *passim.*

it was still a delicate subject. On the evening of March 3, Republicans gathered for a political rally. The leaders were all there. Henry S. Lane, with his customary eloquence, scored the Dred Scott decision, the Lecompton Constitution, and the generally bankrupt condition of the Democracy. Morton pleaded that a cold prevented him from making a speech, but he related some "historical reminiscences" showing the "past false professions of the leaders of the democratic party." After an array of lesser lights had their say, Julian was called on for a speech. He responded by reminding his listeners that the issues of 1856 were still very much alive and that it was necessary for Republicans to adhere to their principles of that year.[45] It was apparent that Julian was going to fight for a positive reaffirmation of the Philadelphia platform. It must have been equally clear that there was going to be trouble.

The next day Morton, as chairman of the convention, pointed out that it would be impossible to please everybody and urged all to work for party harmony. Under his guiding hand a platform was drawn up which denied the validity of the Dred Scott decision and asserted the constitutional power of Congress to prohibit slavery in the territories. But instead of demanding that Congress use its power, it merely advocated that slavery extension be prohibited by "proper constitutional means," a proposal vague enough to appeal to the whole Republican spectrum from Free Soilers to Douglas' popular sovereignty Democrats. Julian branded the platform as a "milk and water affair," the work of party managers and not representative of the views of the party. He demanded a reaffirmation of the Philadelphia platform. Morton, not to be outdone, called one of the vice-

45 Indianapolis *Daily Journal,* March 4, 1858.

presidents of the convention to the chair and took the floor to combat Julian. The platform, he argued, was *essentially* the same as the Philadelphia platform. There was nothing sacred about that platform which made its adoption mandatory on every occasion. In drafting their platforms, said Morton, political parties were compelled to consider the circumstances of time and place, a rule which the convention had wisely followed. With consummate skill, Morton made Julian the butt of a joke and expertly disposed of him.[46]

Even though Julian failed in his efforts to have the convention accept his views, his very presence was significant. Not since 1854 had he figured prominently in one of these meetings. Perhaps his role at Pittsburgh and his concise estimate of the party's weaknesses in Indiana were having an effect. Now that there was a nationally organized Republican party there was something to be said for his argument that Hoosier Republicans were damaging their own cause by refusing to accept its platform. Although Julian was never successful in converting many Hoosiers to his radical views, he had become the recognized leader of the radical faction of the party in Indiana. And despite continued opposition from Morton and his henchmen the time was approaching when Julian might again successfully appeal to the voters of the antislavery fifth district comprised of Wayne, Union, Fayette, Randolph, Delaware, and Henry counties.

In June, 1858, the Free Soil newspaper, now named the *True Republican,* began publication at Centreville, again under the editorship of Will C. Moreau, a radical who had joined Julian in his contest with Morton at the

46 Mildred C. Stoler, "The Democratic Element in the New Republican Party in Indiana," in *Indiana Magazine of History*, 36 (1940):193-94; Zimmerman, "Origin and Rise of the Republican Party," in *Indiana Magazine of History*, 13:363-64; Foulke, *Morton*, 1:61-64.

Indianapolis convention. Despite Moreau's claim that the paper was committed to no candidate, it was in fact a Julian organ, and in September Julian's brother Isaac became its editor.[47] The *True Republican* was the foremost radical newspaper in eastern Indiana, if not in the whole state. Its existence was a kind of indicator of Julian's political fortunes, and he never won a nomination except when it was being published. It was to serve him well throughout his ten years in Congress.

Early in July the *True Republican* placed Julian's name among those seeking the Republican congressional nomination in the fifth district. Reviewing his record, the newspaper reminded its readers that throughout his political life Julian had been advocating the true program of the Republican party and that he was one of the founders of the party. Who could be a more logical party candidate? To Julian's critics, who again claimed that he was an abolitionist, the *True Republican* replied that if this were true all men who adhered to the Philadelphia platform of 1856 were abolitionists. And to those who were fearful of having Julian's name on the state ticket, or felt his nomination would weaken the party in the "Pocket" of southern Indiana, radicals answered that it was not the business of one region of the state to dictate to another region. But if people must resort to such reasoning, the *True Republican* reminded them not to overlook the damage that might result in eastern Indiana if Julian were not nominated. But Julian had proved his disloyalty to the party, said his enemies, by opposing the platform at the Indianapolis convention, and if he did not win the nomination he would bolt the party. In answering this charge the *True Republican* pointed out that party managers were now disclaiming

47 Centreville *Indiana True Republican,* July 8, September 9, 1858.

any difference between the Philadelphia platform of 1856 and the Hoosier platform of 1858; hence there was no cause for worry about Julian on that score. Those who were still in doubt about him were reassured—Julian would support the state ticket and the Republican nominee for Congress from the fifth district, whoever he might be.[48]

The contest for the Republican Congressional nomination in Julian's district was important enough to the leaders in the state organization that they were to be seen politicking there for several weeks before the August 19 nominating convention, and the most active among them was Morton himself. Different versions appeared as to what he was doing. The Indianapolis *Journal* said he was there to fight for the Republican cause and was sacrificing himself as he had done in 1856.[49] The *Sentinel* thought he was advocating the Philadelphia platform, a reversal from his earlier position favoring popular sovereignty.[50] Julian men, and some others, believed that Morton was himself a candidate for the Congressional nomination, along with the four avowed candidates: the incumbent David Kilgore, Holloway, William Grose, and Julian. A plan had been made, said the *True Republican,* whereby Holloway and Grose were to withdraw in favor of Morton, whose primary concern was to defeat Julian.[51]

Perhaps at one time there had been such a plan, but Morton's name was not mentioned as a candidate at the Cambridge City convention. From the beginning it was apparent that the contest was between Kilgore and

48 Centreville *Indiana True Republican,* July 22, 1858.
49 Indianapolis *Daily Journal,* July 29, 1858.
50 Indianapolis *Daily Sentinel,* July 16, 1858.
51 Centreville *Indiana True Republican,* July 15, August 5, 12, 1858.

Julian. On the first ballot Kilgore had forty-eight votes to Julian's forty-one, with Holloway and Grose far behind. Kilgore gained and Julian lost as the voting progressed, but not until the seventh ballot did Kilgore get a majority. Julian gracefully accepted the result and pledged his support to the Republican candidate. Many of Julian's followers were of the opinion that in defeat he had won a notable victory. His conduct during the campaign and his conciliatory tone at the convention had disproved the charges against him; the reception given him at the convention was enthusiastic. The *True Republican* predicted that his nomination two years hence was a certainty. For the "Burnt District" had given its wholehearted support to the Philadelphia platform, and the radical spirit there was increasing.[52]

When the Republicans failed in 1858 to elect their state ticket, the *True Republican* and Julian again attributed the defeat to the failure of the Republican party to stand on sound antislavery principles. Whereas the Know Nothings had forsaken the party in 1856, he said, the Douglas Democrats had failed to support it in 1858. And again the conservative Indianapolis *Journal* agreed that Democrats, while helping in the election of Congressmen, had not come to the support of the state ticket. Indeed, Julian was much concerned over the growing power of Douglas, not only in Indiana but in the nation. The "Little Giant," not Buchanan, Julian believed, was the real leader of the Democracy, and his victory over Lincoln in Illinois Julian viewed with some alarm. Republicans had helped to elect him there, and Republicans were hurting their party by flirting with him. "No man in the Union," Julian charged, "hates

52 *Ibid.*, August 26, September 2, 1858; Indianapolis *Daily Journal*, August 20, 1858.

the Negro with a more withering and malignant hatred than he; nor is there a dough-face in all the land more uncircumcised in heart."[53]

The election of 1858 and Julian's strengthened political position in his home community did not immediately alter his role in the Republican party. More than ever Republicans sought to prove that their organization was a white man's party.[54] The best that Julian could hope for was that continued "agitation" would gradually inculcate the Republican party with his own conviction that slavery was an evil with which there was no possible compromise.

Throughout his crusade of the 1850's Julian adhered to orthodox Free Soil doctrine. He held that slavery was incompatible with the nature of American institutions and in order to make them function as the "founding fathers" had intended, it eventually would have to become extinct. In this doctrine there was no hint of disunionism; instead, it was in tune with the intense nationalism of the era. When a friend wrote Julian suggesting that he take part in a movement to separate the free from the slave states, Julian replied with a resounding rejection of such a policy:

Like yourself I have hitherto acted with the Republican party. My hope is still with that party. I am in favor of its early and thorough reorganization, on the basis of the Philadelphia platform, believing that basis to be sufficient, as an enunciation of essential anti-slavery truth. Fairly interpreted by its obvious letter and spirit it asserts the principle of congressional prohibition of slavery in all our territories; the non-admission of any more slave states to be formed out of

53 Julian's Journal, December 5, 1858, quoted in Clarke, *Julian*, 195; Centreville *Indiana True Republican*, November 8, 25, December 2, 1858.

54 Centreville *Indiana True Republican*, June 2, 1859; Indianapolis *Daily Journal*, September 17, 1859.

them; the abolition of slavery in the District of Columbia, and in all places under the exclusive jurisdiction of the Federal Government; the repeal of all Federal enactments in favor of slavery. . . . It goes still further, by referring authoritatively, and by way of example, to the policy of our "Republican fathers" on the subject of slavery; for that policy, by abolishing it in all Federal territory and in seven of the old states; by cutting off the Foreign supply, which all parties understood to be the life-blood of the system, . . . clearly contemplated the *extinction* of slavery in all the states. It was through the firm belief of our fathers that the evil was only to have a transient suffrance, a brief hospitality, and then quietly disappear from the country, that they were induced to assent to those clauses of the Constitution which compromised, to some extent, the freedom of the colored race. . . . Limitation is recognized as an essential part of the whole process of cure, just as the first dose of medicine given to a sick man forms a part of the general treatment for his recovery. . . . I am for the Union, simply as the servant of liberty, and I shall go for its dissolution the moment I become convinced that it can be preserved only through the perpetual enslavement of four millions of people and their descendants.[55]

[55] Julian to T. W. Higginson, October 24, 1857, Giddings-Julian Papers.

SECESSION

◇◈◇◈◇◈◇◈◇◈◇◈◇◈◇◈◇◈

JULIAN's *Political Recollections,* published in 1884, shows very clearly that the election of 1860, which brought Abraham Lincoln to the Presidency, the Republican party to power, and the return of Julian to Congress, was one of the milestones of his life.[1] If he viewed the election more glowingly, from the antislavery point of view, than the facts warranted, we can account for it as an understandable bit of wishful thinking following his decade-long struggle in Indiana to commit the Republican party to the antislavery cause.

There were other events on the eve of the election, too, that might help to explain Julian's somewhat distorted account. Two personal friends who were active in the antislavery movement became victims of the South's proslavery policy. One was the Reverend John G. Fee who was expelled from the state of Kentucky for his continued antislavery activity.[2] The second was Daniel Worth, a North Carolina Quaker and antislavery advocate who was imprisoned for violation of a state law that forbade the circulation of incendiary literature. The book that Worth was accused of circulating was Hinton R. Helper's *Impending Crisis,* which had become a *cause célèbre* throughout the nation and had precipitated one

[1] Julian, *Political Recollections,* 174-80.
[2] Clarke, *Julian,* 198.

of those caustic arguments in Congress so characteristic of that body in the immediate prewar years.

In reply to a letter from Julian, Worth wrote from his Greensboro prison:

At sixty-five a prison is but a dreary abode, travelling the down hill of life with accompanying physical infirmities. Yet I have my consolations. Though prosecuted as a criminal, faithful conscience witnesses that I have intended wrong to none; neither has any injury accrued to any, to master or slave, as far as I know, in consequence of my labors in Carolina.

If convicted of the crimes with which he was charged the punishment might be whipping, imprisonment, or even death.[3]

In Julian's version of the election the Republican party had become a powerful antislavery organization whose strength rested on the growing belief in the North in the inherent evil of the "Peculiar Institution." The principles set down in the Republican platform of 1856, he asserted, were "broadly stated and fully reaffirmed," and the canvass, like that of 1856, was one in which true antislavery men could proudly participate. If there was any note of expediency, it was to be found in the nomination of Lincoln instead of Seward or Chase.

Julian's account is valid in stating that the Republican victory was a big step toward ultimate emancipation, but it becomes questionable when Julian attributes to it the qualities of a crusade, for not many voters in 1860 were aware of the historical meaning of the election. The

---

3 The letter, dated February 6, 1860, is in the Giddings-Julian Papers. Worth was found guilty and sentenced to one year in jail. He lost his appeal to the North Carolina Supreme Court and rather than go to jail forfeited his $3,000 bond and fled to the North. He wrote to Julian again in May from Brooklyn, New York, asking financial help.

typical Republican voter of 1860 did not take seriously southern threats of secession in the event of a Republican victory and did not foresee a civil war which would bring an end to the institution of slavery. Hence Julian's overemphasis of the antislavery aspects of the election reminds us that he was writing *recollections* and not history.

Actually, the national Republican organization in 1860 was similar in many respects to the fusion party in Indiana with which Julian had contested so vigorously throughout the 1850's. The platform was a masterpiece of expediency designed to draw the votes of as many northern groups as possible while offending none. The effect of the guiding hand of professional politicians was unmistakable. To attract the antislavery men there was a tribute to the spirit of the Declaration of Independence, insisted on by Giddings in the Chicago convention, and a denial of the power of Congress or of territorial legislatures to legalize slavery in the territories. For those opposed to the extension of slavery but fearful of abolitionism there was the assertion that the states had the right to control their own domestic institutions. There were planks favoring a protective tariff and a transcontinental railroad, both designed to attract eastern business and industrial interests. Republican leaders of 1860 remembered that Pennsylvania, with its powerful iron interests, had been lost four years earlier. The homestead plank would lessen the objections of western Free Soilers to those concessions to the East. This platform and the nomination of Abraham Lincoln—an "available" candidate from a pivotal western state—made it apparent that a Republican victory in 1860 would be a fusion victory.

Governor Salmon P. Chase of Ohio was Julian's first choice for the Republican presidential nomination. Julian had become acquainted with Chase at the time of the formation of the Free Soil party, and in succeeding years the acquaintance had ripened into friendship. Seward, the leading contender for the nomination, was Julian's second choice. Julian did not attend the convention, which nominated Lincoln on the third ballot, but he was intensely interested in it and had questions about it that he wanted answered. For information he went to Joshua R. Giddings. How did it happen, Julian asked, that Chase made so poor a showing? And why did the Chase men oppose Seward? Julian had become "excited over the matter" because of a rumor that "doughface" Republicans of Indiana and Pennsylvania had combined to defeat Chase:

Did Lane of this State threaten to decline the race for Governor and give up the contest as hopeless, if Seward should be nominated? The anti-slavery men of this state want to know how this is; for though they will cordially support Lincoln, & have perhaps as much faith in him as in Seward, they will *not* relish the idea of supporting a candidate for Governor who only labors for the spoils.[4]

Giddings answered that Chase's poor showing was the result of the inroads Ben Wade had made in the Ohio delegation and that Seward's cause was weakened by the constant assertions of his friends "that they had the money to secure his election, that they could buy up the doubtful states, etc. etc." Lane's argument was that it would be difficult, if not impossible, to carry Indiana for Seward, but that he could assure it for Lincoln. "Indeed," said Giddings, "Lincoln was selected on account of his *location,* not from objections to Seward or to Chase. . . . It is also true that some of the Doughfaces seemed to think him more popular because his anti-slavery senti-

4 Julian to Giddings, May 21, 1860, Giddings-Julian Papers.

ments had been less prominent." Lincoln would be just as trustworthy on the subject of slavery as Seward or Chase. "I have been well acquainted with him and I think I understand his whole character. I know him to be *honest* and faithful."[5]

Julian expressed his gratitude to Giddings for his threat to leave the convention if the "self-evident truths" of the Declaration of Independence were not included in the platform, as they had been in 1856. Julian was convinced that the "conservatives . . . meant to cheat us," but Giddings had foiled them and had succeeded in getting the plank included in the platform.[6]

The Hoosier campaign was a near facsimile of the national party strategy. The convention of February 23 had nominated the former Whig, Henry S. Lane, for governor and the former Democrat, Oliver P. Morton, for lieutenant governor. The platform, a forecast of the Chicago document, merely denounced the doctrine that the Constitution by itself carried slavery into the territories and promised in a general way to oppose its extension by all constitutional means. The Republican victory in the state, the first Democratic defeat in a national election since 1840, was the result of a combination of forces as far apart as German immigrants and Know Nothings.[7] The effort of Julian and his followers to purify the party was even more blatantly rejected than in 1858.

Julian's interpretation of the election as an antislavery victory is more valid when applied to his own campaign in Indiana's fifth district. Here there was a genuine dis-

5 Giddings to Julian, May 25, 1860, Giddings-Julian Papers.

6 Julian to Giddings, May 21, 1860, Giddings-Julian Papers.

7 Foulke, *Morton*, 1:66-67, 73-84; Stampp, *Indiana Politics during the Civil War*, 34-48; Centreville *Indiana True Republican*, March 1, 1860; Indianapolis *Daily Journal*, February 23, 1860.

play of antislavery ardor, and Julian could profitably act on the advice of Giddings to "assume the whole movement to be anti-slavery, and *on that account* call on all men to support it."[8] In fact, in no other way can Julian's election be explained. The state Republican organization did not favor his nomination; Lane was fearful that Julian's candidacy would injure the party's chances of success, and the most influential Republican newspaper in the district vigorously opposed him. But the majority of the electorate of the fifth district now shared Julian's view that slavery was the only major issue and that the time had come to take a decisive stand. Julian's radical following was in agreement with conservatives on one point, that the South did not intend to carry through with its threats to secede in the event of a "Black Republican" victory, but with a difference. These radicals were ready to call the bluff of the secessionists and were tiring of the conservative representation they had been getting from such men as Parker, Smith, and Holloway. Their attitudes were reflected in the mass meetings they held throughout the district and in the antislavery resolutions they adopted. One typical meeting expressed sympathy for the imprisoned Daniel Worth and promised him a warm welcome in the Whitewater Valley if he should ever return there.[9]

The campaign in the fifth district was singularly free of the personal enmity that characterized both former and later elections in which Julian was a candidate. The immediate question causing the greatest controversy seemed to be the proper method of nominating the Republican Congressional candidate, still tantamount to

8 Giddings to Julian, May 25, 1860, Giddings-Julian Papers, quoted in Clarke, *Julian*, 206-7.
9 Indianapolis *Daily Journal*, February 10, July 20, 1860.

election in the district. Julian men held that the nomination ought to be by popular vote rather than in a district convention, and the *True Republican* advocated this method as the time-honored system of the district to avoid "wire-pulling and trickery" and gave warnings of the schemes of "a well known set of politicians . . . determined to put an end to the popular system." Despite the objections of the *Palladium,* the Wayne County Republican convention resolved in favor of the primary, and this was the method used.[10]

In the primary Julian won a decisive victory over his opponent, Nelson Trusler, of Fayette County. Still, the clamor for a nominating convention did not cease. Even though the Indianapolis *Journal* recognized Julian's candidacy, the *Palladium* refused for three months to carry his name among the list of candidates, and when he was finally accepted, it was only "to promote the harmony and success of the Republican party."[11] Thus ended open Republican factionalism for the remainder of the campaign. In October, although he ran slightly behind the Lane-Morton ticket, Julian won a substantial victory over William Bickel, his Democratic opponent.

II

During the summer and autumn of 1860 Julian labored through the campaign in the shadow of impending personal sorrow. Anne Julian was in the last stages of tuberculosis and died on the fifteenth of November at the age of thirty-four. Although they both knew that her

10 Centreville *Indiana True Republican,* January 26, February 2, 9, March 15, 29, 1860; Richmond *Palladium,* February 23, 1860; Indianapolis *Daily Journal,* February 8, 1860.

11 Indianapolis *Daily Journal,* April 9, 1860; Centreville *Indiana True Republican,* April 19, 26, May 3, 1860; Richmond *Palladium,* April 26, July 6, 1860.

death was near, George was not emotionally prepared for it, and he carried his grief with him to Washington. During the last months of her life Anne had found solace in Spiritualism and she had tried to interest George in it. Now he began "investigating it with all his might." Appealing to Giddings for help, Julian wrote pathetically, "Can you comfort me? She was a believer in 'spiritualism.' Her bright intuitive mind seems to have accepted the new philosophy before it was known among us, years ago. . . . I *want* to believe, & to be convinced. I would give the world if I could. I do not disbelieve, but I want to *believe* & to *know* for myself. I want to communicate with my dear lost one. Do you think that I can?"

Giddings, who was himself a believer in spiritualism, did not discourage Julian but advised him to become more placid in his mind before attempting to communicate with Anne through a medium. It is doubtful that Julian found any real comfort here, for he was a man who took pride in applying logical thought to human problems and used what he believed were intellectual processes in working through emotional problems. Before long he was dismissing spiritualism with a quotation from Emerson on the subject: "Shun them [spiritualists] as you would the secrets of the undertaker and the butcher. . . . The whole world is an omen and a sign. Why look so wistfully in a corner? Man is the image of God. Why run after a ghost or a dream?"[12]

III

Northerners who refused to take seriously southern talk of secession were shocked to discover soon after the

---

[12] Clarke, *Julian*, 202, 204, 207-8; Grace Julian Clarke, "George W. Julian: Some Impressions," in *Indiana Magazine of History*, 2 (1906):66-67; Julian to Giddings, December 11, 1860, Giddings-Julian Papers.

election that the threats from Dixie were not idle ones. To be sure, the majority in the slave states did not regard Lincoln's victory over Douglas, John Breckinridge, and John Bell sufficient reason for immediate secession, but the leaders of the immediate secession faction—men such as William Yancey of Alabama and Robert Barnwell Rhett of South Carolina—had done their work well. The mistakes of a decade earlier when the Nashville convention was captured by the moderate, antisecession forces taught them a lesson they were not to forget, and the secessionists of 1860 avoided such a danger by arranging for the states to secede one at a time. They refused to join with the co-operationists who would take the South out of the Union as a whole, or with those who preferred to await an overt act before seceding. South Carolina was the logical state to take the lead. She seceded on December 20, 1860, and was followed by the other states of the Lower South. By early February seven states, from South Carolina to Texas, had seceded and had met in Montgomery, Alabama, to establish a provisional Confederate government.

Four months before the bombardment of Fort Sumter, therefore, the nation entered that brief but tense period of its history dominated by the "secession crisis." And during nearly three months of that time the government was in the hands of the "lame-duck" Buchanan administration.

The difficult questions relating to the "secession crisis" have intrigued historians for nearly a century, with little indication that the last word has yet been said. Did the states of the Lower South secede because of a weak and vacillating Buchanan administration that was prosouthern in sympathy? Or did Buchanan act wisely in not making the crisis worse by "coercing" southern states?

What is the meaning and what the implication of the words "coercion" and "enforcement of the laws" as they were used by both the outgoing and the incoming presidents? Why did the compromise efforts fail? Did Lincoln reject compromise proposals to save his party without due regard for the nation? And what of Lincoln's "Sumter strategy"? Was it a device on the part of the President to precipitate the attack on the fort and thus start the war in a way that was psychologically favorable to the North? Or was it a manifestation of Lincoln's awareness of the inevitability of the conflict?

Although we must avoid entanglement in the historiography dealing with these questions, the biographer of a Radical Republican must concern himself with his subject's reaction to and understanding of them. Unfortunately, in Julian's case, the documentary evidence is fragmentary. Neither his *Political Recollections* nor the surviving manuscript material is rewarding; it is necessary to construct the story from a few letters and an occassional article written by Julian to his newspaper from Washington following Lincoln's inauguration.

On one point, however, we can be certain—Julian was opposed to the compromise proposals, both the Crittenden Compromise in the Senate and the proposals of the Washington Conference which met on the call of the Virginia legislature. His condemnation of Buchanan was not so severe as one might expect from a Radical— Buchanan was wrong in his prosouthern attitudes and was morally obtuse on the subject of slavery; but Julian gave him credit for his insistence that secession was unconstitutional and that the President had the right to enforce the laws in all the states. It follows that Julian still disagreed heartily with those abolitionists who would allow the southern states to depart from the Union in peace. After all, Julian was a western politician, a son of the Valley of Democracy, and it would have been strange indeed for him to embrace disunionism, to have acquiesced in foreign domination of the lower reaches of the Ohio-Mississippi river network. His statement of principles of 1858 on the abolition of slavery *with* the preservation of the Union still prevailed, and would not be subject to change.

Yet, despite Julian's repeated protests that the Republican party should act in accordance with the anti-slavery principles as stated in the 1856 platform, in 1860 and 1861 he was still so involved in local politics that his role in the secession crisis was somewhat parochial. Early in January, 1861, he visited Lincoln in Springfield. The purpose of the visit was twofold—to make the acquaintance of the President-elect and to discuss certain patronage matters. Indiana had given her electoral vote to Lincoln, and seemed to be entitled to representation in the Cabinet. Indeed, the matter had already been taken care of, but in a way not to Julian's liking. During the Chicago convention a deal had been made by some of the Lincoln delegates whereby Caleb B. Smith was to be given the Interior Department. Not only was Smith a member of the Morton faction, but Julian thought him totally incompetent, and he hoped to dissuade Lincoln from going through with the appointment. Lincoln rejected Julian's appeal on the ground that he could not violate his commitment, but after his return home Julian continued his campaign to keep Smith out of Washington. Soon he was writing to Lincoln that he had discovered that Smith would be willing to accept a foreign mission and recommended such an appointment as an alternative to a place in the Cabinet. "There is, I know," Julian wrote, "a very general and decided opposition to his appointment among the great body of the people of Indiana. No man's record as a businessman and financier for the past twenty years and more is so uniformly and consistently bad, and this is too well known to allow his appointment to the post in question to be regarded as even tolerable by this country." (Not long before this Julian's brother, Jacob, had written to Lincoln praising Smith as a man of outstanding ability whose appointment would be well received in Indiana. In a long and laudatory editorial about Smith the Indianapolis *Journal* took Jacob's side.)[13]

Smith was only the first of a trio of Hoosier Republicans whose appointments to office Julian tried without success to block. The second was his old nemesis, David P. Holloway, whom Lincoln appointed Commissioner of Patents. Shortly after the inauguration Julian went to the President to protest this appointment, for which he blamed Caleb B. Smith. According to Julian, Lincoln had already come to regret the appointment of this incompetent office seeker. From then on Julian dogged Holloway. Two years later the pressure was still on, and it was Julian who submitted a resolution which the House of Representatives adopted that called for a thorough investigation of the Patent Office.[14]

The third appointee whom Julian opposed was Col. Sol Meredith, another Morton follower from Julian's district, who was given command of an Indiana regiment.

13 George W. Julian to Lincoln, January 23, 1861, and Jacob B. Julian to Lincoln, January 1, 1861, Lincoln Papers, Manuscript Division, Library of Congress; Indianapolis *Daily Journal*, March 15, 1861; Winfred A. Harbison, "Lincoln and the Indiana Republicans, 1861-1862," in *Indiana Magazine of History*, 33 (1937):279.

14 Centreville *Indiana True Republican*, March 21, April 4, 1861; Indianapolis *Daily Journal*, March 18, 1861; *Congressional Globe*, 37 Congress, 3 session, 280.

Julian's effort to block Meredith started a feud that went
on for several years and culminated in Julian receivng a
severe physical beating from Meredith and some of his
friends. Again Julian's argument was that the President
had been duped by misinformation given him by the
Morton clique. During this episode both Julian and
Meredith, who later commanded the famous "Iron
Brigade," resorted to the most caustic language and conduct so undignified that it must have astonished a generation accustomed to hyperbole in public office.[15] It
is difficult to see how either man could have benefited
in any way from this encounter.

The matter of Julian versus Smith, Holloway, and
Meredith typifies a persistent Julian penchant for personal combativeness. It is difficult to find a period in his
life when he was not engaged in a controversy with
somebody, and Julian was often responsible for publiciz-
ing these quarrels. Just what he expected to gain for
himself or his cause from the Meredith affair is not
clear, but with Morton molding for himself a sort of
Hoosier dictatorship this foray and others like it did not
make Julian's political road any easier. It should be said
for Julian, however, that even a more phlegmatic person
might have been provoked by Oliver P. Morton. While
Julian was unable to check Morton's growing power in
the state, his leadership did constitute the most effective counterforce to an adroit and efficient political
machine. Perhaps only such a man as Julian could have
done this. His election to Congress for five successive
terms in the face of increasing opposition from the Morton camp attests his more than ordinary appeal to the
people of the "Burnt District."

15 Centreville *Indiana True Republican,* June 27, July 18, 1861;
Indianapolis *Daily Journal,* July 3, August 22, September 6, 1861.

IV

Late in February Julian went to Washington, where he remained until nearly the end of April. Thus he was in the national capital for the inauguration and during the last weeks of the secession crisis. Through his dispatches to his newspaper we get a glimpse of his attitudes about the new administration during the first six weeks of its existence, a precarious time when Fort Sumter was becoming a symbol and a test both of southern intransigence and the determination of the Federal government under Republican control to take a stand against secession.

Washington, Julian found, had changed little since his Congressional term ten years earlier, except that the emergency had made it a more exciting city. He attended Lincoln's first presidential levee at the White House, which he felt must have equaled Andrew Jackson's inauguration in its exuberance.

The most immediate problem for Julian and other members of Congress was what to do about the endless procession of office seekers who pressed for local or national positions as the Republican party assumed power for the first time. He could well sympathize with the President, too much of whose time and energy was expended in dealing with these rapacious followers. "Everybody has a 'Blue Book,' " Julian wrote, "searching for a fat place, looking at the pay of Consulships, Indian Offices, Surveyorships, Clerkships, &c., &c., and crowds and squads of men are to be seen at every turn, canvassing the prospects of different aspirants, entering into combinations, and looking as anxious, hungry, and fierce, as wolves." The national capital, Julian concluded, was not a place favorable to the development of virtue.

After the inauguration Julian's accounts began to show a greater concern about the issue of secession and war and to reflect his attitudes toward Lincoln and the other party leaders. Soon after the election William H. Seward had taken command of the Republican ranks, and his assumption that he would be the directing force in the new administration did not change even after the inauguration. Seward's program for dealing with the crisis was one of conciliation with the South, including the evacuation of Fort Sumter. His performance was a shock to the Radicals, some of whom had favored his nomination at Chicago. Julian felt that Seward had "fallen very far in the opinion of many of his best and truest friends. . . . They believe he has trifled with the *principles* of Republicanism, and they cannot forgive."

Even Charles Sumner, Julian charged, had succumbed to the spell of conciliation in urging the selection of John Crittenden of Kentucky, author of the compromise proposal, for the Supreme Court. "After this, who can be surprised at any thing?" Even so, "nobody . . . would pretend to doubt the fidelity of Charles Sumner."

The Sumter crisis was bringing with it confusion and chaos as well as a dangerous schism within the Republican party. Julian was fearful that Stephen A. Douglas, who was "shrewdly playing with existing circumstances," might be more troublesome in 1861 than in the last presidential race "should our organization go into fragments in consequence of the endeavors of its leaders to surrender its vital principles."[16]

In his attitudes toward Abraham Lincoln, Julian, like some of the other Radicals, was ambivalent. Despite his failure to have Lincoln reject Caleb B. Smith for a Cabinet post, Julian had left Springfield favorably impressed in some ways with the President-elect. There was an undeniable appeal in Lincoln's "plain western manners

16 Centreville *Indiana True Republican,* March 21, 28, 1861.

and old-fashioned appearance," and the "care-worn sad expression about his face" aroused Julian's sympathy.[17] Although there were times when Julian could be caustic in his criticism of the President, he never developed that personal aversion to Lincoln that usually accompanied disagreement with other men on public issues. Nor was Julian the only Radical who softened on coming into contact with Lincoln's homely magnetism and charm. As David Donald has shown, the relations between Lincoln and the Radicals were never so harsh and uncompromising as some historians, in search of anti-Lincoln villains, would have us believe.[18]

But there were times when the Radicals were frustrated and angered by the President, and one of these times was the early spring of 1861, when nobody seemed to know what Lincoln was going to do about Fort Sumter. Julian apparently concluded that Lincoln had decided to abandon the fort. The President looked to Julian "very much like a physically 'used up man.' He seems quite feeble, and shakes hands with his friends as if all his power of grasp has departed. Can anybody wonder that a man so jaded should be willing to give up Fort Sumter?"[19]

In this instance, Julian could hardly have been more wrong in his estimate of the President, for Lincoln had arrived at a decision about Sumter—a decision that has come to be known as the Fort Sumter strategy by which Lincoln shifted the burden of responsibility for a precipitant act from his shoulders to those of the southern leaders. His decision was to provision the fort without militarily reinforcing it, and to inform the South Caro-

17 Julian's Journal, quoted in Clarke, *Julian,* 210-11.
18 Donald, *Lincoln Reconsidered,* 103-27.
19 Centreville *Indiana True Republican,* April 4, 1861.

lina governor of his decision. From this point on, whether Sumter stood or fell, Lincoln could not be the loser. The decision, moreover, made Lincoln master in his own political house; no longer would there be a pretender to the position of party leadership.

Julian's miscalculation about Lincoln's plans for Fort Sumter might be accounted for by the President's taciturnity and his tendency to remain quiet on important policy matters until he had made up his mind. It was this habit which frequently led men to believe that he had no policy and that he allowed important matters to drift until they were beyond control. The impression created was often one of indecision or weakness, or even of vertigo. Even William Seward, occupying the first place in Lincoln's Cabinet, was not aware of the formulation of a policy a month after the inauguration.

But for a true understanding of the differences between Lincoln and the Radicals it is necessary to look beyond mere personal predilections in the conduct of public affairs to philosophical differences in the realm of government and politics. And it is well to be aware of the areas of agreement as well as the differences between the two factions. Except for an occasional aberration, the Radicals were in agreement with Lincoln in his insistence on the preservation of the Union as a major war aim. We have seen how Julian refused to be persuaded that antislavery and disunion could be linked together. They also shared a hatred for the institution of slavery. But what the Radicals could not fathom about Lincoln was his refusal to use the war to destroy slavery while preserving the Union. Perhaps the major difference between them was the fact that Lincoln was a pragmatist, par excellence, while the Radicals—especially those, like Julian, whose commitment to antislavery had preceded the launching of their political careers—were apt to be doctrinaire. To such men Lincoln's concern to distinguish between "coercion" and "enforcement of the laws" was abstraction carried to the point of absurdity. The determination of the President not to exacerbate the border states on the subject of slavery was proof enough for the Radicals that they had been sold out by their leader. They did not yet grasp that Lincoln's refusal to make slavery an issue in 1861 did not preclude emancipation at a later and more propitious time.

CONDUCT
OF THE WAR

6 ⬦⬦⬦⬦⬦⬦⬦⬦⬦⬦⬦⬦

IN the early morning hours of April 14, 1861, the Confederate guns in Charleston harbor surrounding Fort Sumter opened fire, and later that day Maj. Robert Anderson surrendered the garrison. This was the southern reply to Lincoln's announcement that he was sending provisions to the fort. The period of watchful waiting had ended; the war had begun.

The following day President Lincoln proclaimed the existence of insurrection in the seven states of the Lower South and called on the state militias for seventy-five thousand men to quell it. Four additional slave states— Virginia, Arkansas, Tennessee, and North Carolina—protested that the President had now entered upon a policy of coercing the seceded states with which they could never co-operate, seceded, and joined the Confederacy. Lincoln's border state policy, with some timely application of military force, prevented the secession of Missouri, Kentucky, Maryland, and Delaware, the remaining slave states.

Julian followed these events from his home in Indiana, then left for Washington to attend the special session of Congress which the President had called for July 4. Arriving several days early, he found only a few of his fellow members on hand. Despite the presence of a number of regiments from the northern states that were now encamped around the city, there was a welcome quietness. Washington was enjoying one of those rare respites from enervating summer heat and humidity; the days were clear, the evenings cool, and Julian's room, just south of the Capitol, was situated amidst "the most beautiful landscape . . . ever beheld." He occupied his time in visits to Georgetown, to the surrounding countryside, and to Arlington, the ancestral home of the Lees, whose "architectural plan . . . and delapidated condition," Julian felt, were fitting symbols of old Virginia.

With the assembling of Congress, however, Julian sensed "an intense and irritating restlessness," which would soon be transformed into a clamor for action—a clamor in which the northern press joined. After all, the military forces under Gen. Irvin McDowell were poised and ready to strike the Confederates under the command of Gen. P. G. T. Beauregard, located some twenty miles southwest of the capital. Ninety days was the time expected to be required to put down the southern rebellion, an estimate shared by the President himself. There were, in fact, some Radicals who even feared that an early defeat of the South might fail to bring the abolition of slavery and who were willing to take a few defeats and to prolong the war. But in July, 1861, Julian was not one of them; immediate action, he believed, was necessary to avoid demoralization.

Nor was Julian one of the Congressmen and government officials who ventured out to the hills around Centreville, Virginia, to witness the first Battle of Manassas. Hence he was spared the worst scenes in the rout of General McDowell's army. But he saw the aftermath in Washington, an army which had become an undisciplined and uncontrolled mob with men in uniform milling around disorderly and drunk. To Julian, as to others, the spectacle was so shocking that he could hardly find words to describe it. Either there was some terrible mystery about the debacle, he believed, or there had been a planned breakdown of leadership, both tactical and administrative. But before long Julian had discovered, at least to his own satisfaction, the cause of the humiliating defeat. There were simply too many avowed secessionists and Democrats in the military and other sensitive government posts.[1] It was the sort of reasoning that was to become the standard Radical explanation of northern defeats. There were times during the war when such assumptions were not altogether invalid, and as a factor in the over-all conduct of the war they must be given due consideration. But such an explanation of first Manassas indicates a stubborn refusal to face facts. The defeat of the northern army resulted from the inadequate training of its soldiers and the absence of a staff that could cope with the problems of moving and fighting an army, especially one opposed by such formidable adversaries as Stonewall Jackson and Joseph E. Johnston. The attitudes of northern generals about slavery had nothing to do with it.

Here was an opportunity, however, to demand a house cleaning and to show the determination of Congress to have a voice in running the war. Toward the close of the special session Julian introduced a resolution which the House adopted that the retention in or appointment to office in Washington or elsewhere "of men of well-known secession sympathies, merits the condemnation of all loyal citizens."[2]

1 Julian, *Political Recollections*, 195-96; *Congressional Globe*, 37 Congress, 1 session, 459; Centreville *Indiana True Republican*, June 27, July 11, August 1, 1861.

2 Centreville *Indiana True Republican*, July 4, 1861; *Congressional Globe*, 37 Congress, 1 session, 357, 366.

First Manassas turned out to be a Pyrrhic victory for the South. It ended much of the wishful thinking and the naive optimism in the North about the probable duration of the war. And for a time, at least, it brought a unity that could not otherwise have been achieved. It also brought the appointment of some new military commanders to high positions as well as a reorganization of the army along corps rather than divisional lines.

The battle also set men thinking about the nature of the war, in such a way as to bring a hiatus in the dispute between the Radicals and the moderates concerning war aims. In his message to Congress Lincoln had defined the war as an insurrection which must be suppressed as soon as possible in order to restore the Union. On the day following the battle the House of Representatives supported this view by adopting the Crittenden Resolution, which asserted that the war was not to be waged for the oppression or subjugation of the South but to "defend and maintain the *supremacy* of the Constitution." Julian, along with nearly all the Radicals, voted for the resolution. Only two Republicans voted against it, and two others absented themselves; in the Senate there was only one dissenting vote.

An explanation of this very unusual performance on the part of the Radicals can be found in the warning of Ben Wade not to weaken the popular support of the war at this critical moment. According to Professor T. Harry Williams, the Radicals "were willing, temporarily, to subordinate their own convictions in order that the conflict might be continued. For they knew that war meant the death of slavery, and they were confident that the exigencies of the struggle would enable them to circumvent the Crittenden resolution."[3] The session ended with

3 T. Harry Williams, *Lincoln and the Radicals* (University of Wisconsin Press, 1941), 33.

the passage of the first Confiscation Act, legalizing the seizure of rebel property actually used to aid the rebellion. Thus, as Congress adjourned, the administration's moderate concept of the war prevailed. But by authorizing the enlistment of 500,000 volunteers for three years Congress recognized the probability of a long struggle.

Julian's votes in favor of the Crittenden Resolution and the Confiscation Act were by no means an accurate indication of his feelings. He viewed the concept of a war merely to preserve the supremacy of the Constitution and the Union as a weak apology on the part of the North "and a most ill-timed revival of the policy of conciliation." The Confiscation Act he regarded as a way of notifying the rebels "that we are slightly inclined to take our part, but very anxious to do it in such a manner as shall occasion the least possible inconvenience."[4]

In addition to measures that related to the conduct of the war or the war aims of the administration, the tariff bill passed by the first Civil War session of Congress deserves mention. Although it is unlikely that this bill was designed as a protective measure, subsequent measures did have protection as an objective, in fulfillment of the commitment of the Republican platform in 1860 to protect manufacturers. Also, as one of the critical issues on which Radicals did not agree, it is significant because of its bearing on the potential factionalism within the Radical ranks.

Julian did not participate in the debate on this tariff, but he did vote for it as a revenue measure. It is clear from his correspondence to his newspaper that if he had considered it a protective measure he would have voted

---

4 Julian's Journal, September 5, 1861, quoted in Clarke, *Julian,* 215; Julian, *Political Recollections,* 197-98.

against it. His opinion about this bill was that there was no other important measure about which there was so much acknowledged ignorance. "Every thing was trusted to the wisdom of the leading tariff men, whilst the sufficiency of their wisdom . . . may well be questioned." In no sense could this bill be construed as having settled the tariff question in favor of protection, he wrote, for it was carried only "on the ground of its necessity as a war measure, having reference to revenue alone." Julian felt that opposition to the bill under the circumstances would be "awkward if not inexcusable," but he feared that "mischief, rather than good," would "be the fruit of it."[5]

In August Congress adjourned and Julian returned to Indiana where he immediately launched a campaign to aid the war effort. He hoped to educate Hoosiers to the true meaning of the conflict and to encourage men to enlist in the armed forces. The press reports on Julian's activities show that he spoke in nearly every town and village in his district. This local campaign to arouse the participation of his constituents soon became involved with a matter of national importance—the President's dismissal of Gen. John C. Frémont from his command in Missouri. It brought an immediate reaction in Indiana, as in other western states, and was soon a major point of contention between Lincoln and the Radicals.

The President's selection of Frémont to command the Western Department, with headquarters at St. Louis, was one of his most popular early appointments. Frémont, the western explorer, son-in-law of Senator Thomas Hart Benton, and the first Republican presidential nominee, was already a somewhat legendary and certainly a very romantic figure, and his views on slavery were in

5 Centreville *Indiana True Republican,* July 25, 1861.

accord with those of the Radicals. The assignment in Missouri, a slave state where there was fighting to be done as well as touchy political problems to handle, would have taxed a man of much greater capacity than Frémont. His method of handling the rebellion in Missouri was to issue a proclamation freeing all the slaves in his Department belonging to persons engaged in the rebellion. Lincoln could see only trouble from such a policy in a slave state that he was trying to hold in the Union. Moreover, Frémont's proclamation, going in the face of the expressed war aims of both the President and Congress, could have been a serious challenge to civilian authority. Lincoln asked Frémont to rescind the order, and when the General refused, Lincoln himself issued an order countermanding it. But Frémont's proclamation enhanced his popularity with the Germans in the Middle West, with the antislavery people, and with many rank-and-file Republicans. "As often as I would mention the name of 'Frémont,'" Julian wrote in his *Recollections,* "the prolonged hurrahs of the multitude followed, and the feeling seemed to be universal that 'a war on peace principles' was abandoned, and that slavery, the real cause of the war, was no longer to be the chief obstacle to its prosecution." Lincoln's revocation of the order, Julian believed, was the beginning of an unfortunate proslavery reaction which encouraged "timid and halting men to become cowards," "gave new life to slavery, and encouraged fiercer assaults upon 'abolitionism,'" and helped revive Democratic sympathy for treason and thereby prolonged the war. Although Julian's account is exaggerated and inaccurate, this is the more understandable if we keep in mind the extreme pro-Frémont atmosphere of the Hoosier state. Indeed, the Frémont episode provided one of those rare issues on which Julian and his conservative opponents in Indiana could agree. When Lincoln dismissed Frémont from his command, the Indianapolis *Journal* joined in condemnation of the act as a disastrous blunder which could only have resulted from the work of somebody in Washington who was jealous of the General.[6]

II

Upon his return to Washington in December, 1861, for the first regular session of the Thirty-seventh Congress, Julian found that his political training of the past twelve years was about to pay off more handsomely than ever before. Now his place in the Radical wing of the Republican party was far from inconspicuous. Although there were differences among the Radicals, there was enough agreement among them to formulate a recognizable Radical program. Rejecting Lincoln's concept of the war, the Radicals wanted to apply the military might of the nation to destroy the Slave Power and to remold the South in the image of the North. Slavery was, of course, to be abolished. Nor would the Radicals tolerate Lincoln's "Border State" policy. Tenderness to slaveholders in Maryland, Kentucky, or Missouri, would only subvert Radical aims, would be a source of weakness rather than strength, and would prolong the conflict. While bringing about the destruction of the South, many of the Radicals were ready to work with their more conservative Republican brothers to enact a protective tariff, a sound banking and currency system in the Hamiltonian tradition, a transcontinental railroad along a

[6] Clarke, *Julian*, 217-18; Julian, *Political Recollections*, 199-200; Harbison, "Lincoln and the Indiana Republicans," in *Indiana Magazine of History*, 33:288; Centreville *Indiana True Republican*, August 29, September 5, 12, 1861; Indianapolis *Indiana Daily Journal*, October 23, November 13, 19, 1861.

northern route, and the Homestead Act which the platform of 1860 had promised the western farmers. If Julian was not in complete agreement about the tariff, there was ample compensation in the Radical attitudes on slavery and the Homestead Act. Indeed, the very presence of this powerful group which now took Julian into its fold seemed to be a final reward for past virtue. No longer would he have to stand alone against fusionists; no longer would he be hooted down, as in the old Hoosier days, as a mere "abolitionist." True, there would be opposition, but behind him when he attacked the Slave Power or Northerners who catered to it would be a Thaddeus Stevens in the House, a Ben Wade in the Senate, and the powerful Joint Committee on the Conduct of the War.

Valid generalizations about the Radicals themselves—their origins, their personalities and ambitions, their political philosophies, and their motivations—are not so easily determined. In the Senate they ranged in background, personality, and education all the way from the erudite Charles Sumner, scion of Back Bay Boston, to Zachariah Chandler, the crude self-made millionaire of Michigan. In their ranks in the House were to be found the vindictive and brilliant Jacobin, Thaddeus Stevens, the iron master of Pennsylvania, side by side with an Illinois preacher, Owen Lovejoy, brother of the martyred Elijah.

The power of the Radicals stemmed not so much from their numbers—they were a minority in the Republican party—but from their program, their personalities, and the *milieu* in which they worked. In aggressiveness and talent they were favorably endowed in comparison with their conservative colleagues. What some lacked in polish, they amply compensated for in energy. Their concept of the war could be more cogently, more clearly stated and defined than the Lincoln policy of moderation. They were not caught in the dilemma of waging a war against the South while claiming not to be waging war, for as the conflict continued it became apparent that the nation was engaged in an all-out war. Whether the administration admitted it or not, the South was a nation to be conquered, not merely a collection of states in rebellion which must be shown the error of their ways. But to explain the Radicals' ultimate triumph over the moderates in terms of their determination or their vindictiveness, which many of them had in ample measure, is much too simple. The greatest source of their power lay in the very nature of total war.

Before the end of the year 1861 Julian's position as one of the Radical leaders was given recognition by his appointment to the Joint Committee on the Conduct of the War. As originally proposed, the committee was not to have a policy-making function, but was to investigate specific errors in the military or civil conduct of the war. But after a Congressional debate on the subject, it was given power to examine the whole conduct of the war and to make recommendations for its prosecution. From the beginning the committee became an instrument for forcing Radical policies on the administration. Throughout its existence the Radical Republican members dominated it, with little or no opposition from the Democratic members, who were carefully chosen so as not to obstruct or embarrass the Radicals. The most serious charge made against the committee, by both contemporaries and later historians, has been that it adopted a star-chamber procedure. Persons being investigated were not permitted to face their accusers and were not always informed of the source of accusations against them. Nor were persons brought before the committee permitted legal counsel.

The most important single objective of the committee was to bring about the dismissal of Gen. George B. McClellan from his command. The greatest miscarriage of justice was perhaps the dismissal and arrest of Gen. Charles P. Stone, whom the committee held responsible for the Union defeat in the Battle of Ball's Bluff, where Col. Edward Baker, a former Radical Senator, was killed. After six months' imprisonment and repeated requests for a military trial which were never granted, Stone eventually resigned his commission. For nearly two years he was unable to determine what were the specific charges against him. In this case it is evident that the committee, through its hearings and the influence it exerted in the War Department, ruined the career of an able officer.

The misuse of power by the committee was particularly unfortunate since it was the only civilian agency officially charged with any responsibility for the conduct of the war. With greater objectivity and fairness, it might have been a real force for efficiency in both civil and military matters.

Senator "Bluff Ben" Wade of Ohio was the committee chairman. He had won his seat in 1851 as a compromise candidate of the Whig party who had denounced slavery but had not deserted to the Free Soilers in 1848. As a good Whig during his early years in the Senate, he labored for protective tariffs and internal improvements for the northwestern states. With the demise of the Whig party he became a Republican, and after the enactment of the Kansas-Nebraska bill he gained a reputation as a vigorous opponent of the Slave Power. Possessed of uncommon physical courage and loving a fight, he was well suited for effectiveness in the truculent atmosphere of Congress in the 1850's. He became a hero of the anti-slavery men when he accepted—to the astonishment of his fellow Senators—the challenge of a Southerner to a duel, naming as weapons squirrel rifles at twenty paces, thereby inhibiting the resort of southern gentlemen to their code of honor in Congressional battles.[7]

Zachariah Chandler of Michigan, another former Whig and a close friend of Wade's, joined with the chairman to give the senatorial portion of the committee a predominately radical flavor. Chandler refused the chairmanship of the committee on the ground that he was not a lawyer, but the force of his personality and influence was ever present. Andrew Johnson, Tennessee Democrat, was the third member from the Senate. His strong opposition to secession and his intense dislike of McClellan made him a logical choice for Democratic representative. Committee members from the House of Representatives, in addition to Julian, were Daniel Gooch of Massachusetts, Moses F. Odell of New York, and John Covode of Pennsylvania.[8]

Although Julian was engaged to some extent in the work of the committee, his selection as a member of it is more significant than the actual work he did for it. Wade and Chandler were the dominant figures and were frequently the only members present at the committee's hearings. Daniel Gooch, exceptionally adept as legal adviser and cross-examiner, was the most active member from the House. But of all the seven members Julian was probably the most ardent and doctrinaire

[7] Columbus *Daily Ohio State Journal*, March 17, 19, 1851; Cleveland *Plain Dealer*, July 31, 1852; Benjamin F. Wade Papers, Manuscript Division, Library of Congress.

[8] Williams, *Lincoln and the Radicals*, 65-71.

antislavery man, and he was proud to be associated with the committee, whose existence he attributed to "the popular demand for a more vigorous prosecution of the war, and less tenderness toward slavery." The work was gratifying to him "because it afforded a very desirable opportunity to learn something of the movements of our armies and the secrets of our policy."[9]

III

When Julian returned to Washington in 1861 he was forty-four years old and at the height of his intellectual powers; he was ready to assume the duties and responsibilities of an influential Congressman. Although his health was far from perfect, it was better than it had been during his Congressional term a decade earlier, and his grief over Anne's death abated as he entered actively into a new stage of his career. Standing slightly over six feet, he was considerably taller than the average. He had grown a beard that in the fashion of the day was cropped short and bristled over his chin and the sides of his face. His eyes were still piercing under brows that were apt to be drawn into a frown, showing the intensity of the man. His straight and slender nose gave character to a face that, on the whole, showed determination. If any feature indicated a tenderer side of his nature, it was his sensitive mouth with a slightly protruding lower lip. Although Julian never completely overcame his inherent timidity, his confidence was now greater than it ever had been. He was never an outstanding extemporaneous debater, but he spoke more frequently now and with greater force.[10]

[9] Julian, *Political Recollections*, 201.
[10] There are a number of sources that seem to substantiate this description. See especially Clarke, "George W. Julian: Some Impressions," in *Indiana Magazine of History*, 2:62-63, 67-68.

Soon Julian was involved in the work of the Committee on the Conduct of the War, as it set out to achieve its most immediate and most pressing objective, the dismissal of Gen. George Brinton McClellan from his command.

After first Manassas Lincoln had called McClellan from western Virginia, where he had won victories in the battles of Philippi and Rich Mountain, to replace McDowell as commander of the Army of the Potomac. Before the end of 1861 McClellan had maneuvered the retirement of Gen. Winfield Scott and had, himself, become general in chief of all the United States armies. With the appointment of McClellan began Lincoln's long and painful search for a general who could coordinate the Union effort and win victories over the Confederates in the Virginia theater of war. The advent of McClellan brought renewed confidence in government circles and among the people that now the work of crushing the rebellion would proceed to a successful conclusion. Even some of the Radicals were, for a brief time, impressed; but it soon became evident that in McClellan were combined characteristics and ideas about the war that were intolerable to the Radicals. McClellan was a Democrat and a West Pointer who insisted that the abolition of slavery was not a valid war aim.

Before the end of 1861 McClellan had demonstrated his unusual ability as a parade ground soldier and organizer. The diverse collection of military units on the Potomac was being transformed into an army. And, most threatening of all from the Radical point of view, that almost mystical devotion which the soldiers of the army of the Potomac were to have for McClellan was becoming manifest. But as the months went by and 1861 gave way to 1862, more and more people began to wonder when this magnificent army was going to move, and by early January, 1862, the Committee on the Conduct of the War was determined to find out. During the first three months of the new year the committee met frequently with Lincoln and the Cabinet to try to determine what McClellan was going to do and when he was going to do it. While the General demanded more time to ready his army, the Radicals became more impatient and more hostile toward him. To Julian it seemed that the President did not know what McClellan's plans were or when he proposed to execute them. Lincoln at this stage of the war was taking pains not to interfere with the military, and refused to be pressured by the Radicals into forcing McClellan to reveal his plans. Soon Julian came to the dismal conclusion that "the fate of the nation was coiled up in the little brain of one man, called General-in-chief . . . who communicated his wisdom, if he had any, to no human being."[11] Julian suspected that McClellan was a traitor, and was convinced that he cared nothing about what happened to the country.

The pressure that the Radicals kept on the President was not without its effect, however, and in February Lincoln ordered McClellan to take the offensive. At this point began a protracted argument between the President and the General which culminated in the Peninsular Campaign. Out of it have arisen questions pondered by military historians and about which they have never arrived at a consensus. Was McClellan right in his insistence on a vast envelopment with a final advance toward Richmond up the peninsula between the James and the York rivers? Or was Lincoln right in opposing

11 Julian's Journal, February 5, 1862, quoted in Mabel M. Engstrom, *George Washington Julian* (M.A. thesis, University of Chicago, 1928. Typewritten copy in Indiana Division, Indiana State Library), 25.

it? Did McClellan's plan leave Washington unprotected, or was Lincoln to blame for the ultimate failure of the campaign by withholding a corps from McClellan's enveloping force? Or was the failure the result of McClellan's overcaution and faulty tactics on the peninsula?

The Radicals did not need to consider these questions to make up their minds where they stood, for long before the Peninsular Campaign was launched they had done so. Their case against McClellan was strengthened early in March by the incident of the "Quaker guns." McClellan had refused to move against Joseph E. Johnston at Manassas for fear that his force was too large and too well entrenched. But in preparation for the Peninsular Campaign McClellan did agree to a limited advance toward Manassas. When the Union forces reached the presumably fortified area, they found logs painted black, to be mistaken for guns, and not a rebel soldier in sight. For the first, but not the last, time McClellan had allowed an inferior enemy force to slip away.

Thus in those early months of 1862 there was little for the Radicals to be optimistic about. Of the Cabinet members, Julian wrote in his diary, Salmon P. Chase was the only one who "talked like a man." There were suspicions, too, that Mrs. Lincoln, who came from a slave state and a slave-owning family, was influencing the President. Mrs. Lincoln, Julian recorded, "absolutely rules her husband, even in his official concerns, when she chooses. . . . Lincoln is the despicable tool of his own wife."[12]

Amidst the Radical gloom, however, there was one ray of hope, the appointment of Edwin M. Stanton to succeed the incompetent Simon Cameron as Secretary of War. Even though Cameron had made belated overtures

12 Julian's Journal, February 22, 1862, quoted in *ibid.*, 42n.

for Radical friendship, the Radicals were delighted with Stanton's appointment. Despite the fact that he had been a Democrat and had served briefly in Buchanan's Cabinet, they saw in him an ally against McClellan; their estimate turned out to be correct.

The contest between Lincoln and the Radicals over McClellan transcends in its importance the question of the General's competency or incompetency, for he soon became a symbol in the minds of various groups who were concerned about the meaning and the conduct of the war. The regular army officers saw in McClellan's demise, with some reason, the transfer of control of military matters from the hands of professionals trained at West Point to a group of meddling politicians. But to the Radicals McClellan posed a constant threat to the supremacy of the Republican party and to the antislavery movement now struggling for its final triumph. To the soldiers of the Army of the Potomac "Little Mac" meant that there was still some romance about the grim business of warfare in which they were engaged. Lincoln, the embattled President, was caught in the middle, looking for a general who could win victories and enable him to restore the Union, with or without slavery.

As we look back on these events from the vantage point of a century we can see that the Radicals, not always perhaps for the right reasons, were correct in their evaluation of McClellan. If Lincoln had known more about McClellan's role in the Union victories at Philippi and Rich Mountain it is doubtful that he would have been given command of the Army of the Potomac or made over-all commander of the Union armies. For in these engagements the General had displayed those same habits of hesitation and overestimation of enemy strength that characterized nearly all of his later performances.

These early battles were won in spite of McClellan, and the reputation that he gained from them rested more on his pompous communiques than on his fighting qualities. Granting that McClellan performed a needed task of organization and that he repaired the morale of the army, the sort of contribution to the war effort that he was equipped to make could only be transitory. Moreover, McClellan, by his own actions, gave added substance to the Radical charges against him. Imperiously he blamed the administration for the failure of the Peninsular Campaign, and in advising Lincoln, without the President's solicitation, on political matters, he overstepped the boundary between civilian and military authority and thereby violated one of the first axioms of the successful American military commander. Only thirty-five years old when called to Washington, McClellan lacked the experience requisite for the great responsibilities thrust upon him.

As Bruce Catton says, after Antietam the romance was gone and the war was no longer McClellan's kind of war, if it had ever been. Even those soldiers who sorrowed at his departure and who may have talked of mutiny knew that there was something inexorable about his removal.[13]

While the Radicals labored to be rid of McClellan, they did not overlook the necessity of grooming another general more to their liking to take his place. The logical choice still seemed to be Frémont. Three times during January Frémont met with the committee. The environment created for him could hardly have been more friendly, and every opportunity was given him to exonerate himself of the charges that had been made against him.

[13] Bruce Catton, *Mr. Lincoln's Army* (Doubleday & Co., Garden City, New York, 1951), 322-39.

In these hearings Julian took a more active part than usual. He questioned Frémont in such a way as to show the necessity of his proclamation freeing the slaves and that a Congressional committee which had investigated his handling of army contracts had dealt too harshly with him. Lincoln's wise decision not to give Frémont another important command only spurred Julian on to further efforts in behalf of the General. In the committee, on the floor of Congress, and through personal appeals to the President, Julian labored for the restoration of Frémont to a responsible command. But the best that he and the other Radicals could do was to have the General assigned to the Mountain Department in Western Virginia, an inglorious post in which he did not distinguish himself.[14]

Important as was the work of the Committee on the Conduct of the War in making emancipation a war aim and in ridding the army of incompetent commanders, there was even more important antislavery work to be done in Congress through actual legislation. Here Julian's antislavery star shone more brightly than as a committeeman. Among the unsettled matters with which Congress might deal were the continued existence of slavery in the territories and in the District of Columbia and the Fugitive Slave laws of 1793 and 1850, which still remained on the statute books. More immediate was the problem of establishing a policy for slaves who were making their way into the Union lines.

14 *Report of the Joint Committee on the Conduct of the War* (3 vols. 37 Congress, 3 session, Senate Report No. 108, Washington, D. C., 1863), 3:32 ff., 156-86; Williams, *Lincoln and the Radicals,* 106-9. On May 1, 1862, Jessie Benton Frémont wrote to Julian to come to the rescue of her husband. "Won't you," she wrote, "with all the force of one knowing the truth refuse to assist these slanderers. . . . It is not one man they are striking at but a representative of a clean policy against slavery." Giddings-Julian Papers.

Even before the end of 1861 Julian struck out at the policy of the administration, announced in an order by Gen. Henry W. Halleck, who succeeded Frémont in the West, not to admit any more slaves into the Union lines and to restore to their owners those who had come. Julian cited a specific case in which a slave had wandered into the area occupied by an Indiana regiment. The regimental commander had rejected the master's demand that the slave be returned, but was subsequently overruled by the Secretary of War. To Julian it seemed clear that the established policy of the administration was not only to reject escaped slaves but to serve as slave catchers for the South.[15]

A month later Julian was ready to present a more fully developed argument, which he did in one of his major speeches of the session, on slavery as a cause of the war. He was in agreement, he said, with the moderate view that the war was being fought over the question of the supremacy of the Union—"Government or no Government." But his understanding of this theory rested on a different premise than that of the moderates. "I admit it," he said, "but I say the *previous* question is slavery or freedom; or rather, it is the same question, stated in different words. Slavery and treason, in this struggle, are identical. It is slavery which to-day has the government by the throat, and thus thrusts upon us the issue of its life or death." For those who might have been hesitant to alter the war aims as stated by the administration and by Congress in the Crittenden Resolution, Julian cited the American Revolution as an example to be followed. Although it was not the first intention of the founding fathers to fight for independence, they had soon found that it was imperative to do so. Look-

---

[15] *Congressional Globe,* 37 Congress, 2 session, 59.

ing ahead to the final victory, Julian argued, "The rebels have demanded a 'reconstruction' on the basis of slavery; let us give them a 'reconstruction' on the basis of freedom. Let us convert the rebel States into conquered provinces, remanding them to the *status* of mere Territories, and governing them as such in our discretion." More than three years before the end of the war, then, Julian had taken his stand on one of the most difficult questions relating to reconstruction and had presented a theory that would be given more notoriety by better-known Radicals, such as Thaddeus Stevens and Charles Sumner.

In addition to the ideological reasons for waging war against slavery, Julian argued, there were very practical military and diplomatic reasons. In providing a reservoir of labor which released more southern men to serve in the armed forces slavery was a great military asset to the South, and as long as the administration protected the "Peculiar Institution" foreign leaders, such as Lord John Russell, would be justified in defining the conflict as a war merely "for independence on the part of the South, and for power on the part of the North."

Julian was willing to make one concession to the Slave Power, however—for him a rather remarkable one: He would pay to every loyal slaveholder the "fairly-assessed value of his slaves . . . not as *compensation,* for no man should receive pay for robbing another of his earnings, and plundering him of his humanity; but as a means of facilitating a settlement of our troubles, and securing a lasting peace. . . ."[16] This was not only a concession to the South but also to Abraham Lincoln, in method if not in principle. Lincoln had devised a plan

16 *Congressional Globe,* 37 Congress, 2 session, 327-32; Julian, *Speeches on Political Questions,* 154-80.

by which the border slave states were to carry out a compensated emancipation with financial aid from the Federal government. Such a policy, the President believed, would shorten the war and provide a method of emancipation that would not violate the principle that slavery was a state institution which must be abolished by the states themselves. The rejection of this plan by the border states was one of Lincoln's most bitter disappointments of the war years.

Julian's speech was acclaimed in Radical circles and was widely circulated throughout the North. Gerrit Smith ordered several hundred copies for his own use, and the Washington *Republican* stated that twenty thousand copies had been distributed and that a new edition was being published. Greeley's New York *Tribune* described the speech as a "closely-reasoned effort" and recommended a careful reading of it, for few speeches of the session would compare favorably with it. Joseph Medill, Radical owner and editor of the Chicago *Tribune,* was full of praise, and wrote to Julian, "I love your way of talking—no mincing mouthing or apologizing to the Oligarchy. Would to God all our Republicans were of your stamp!"[17]

As the session progressed, the growing power of the Radicals became more evident. They succeeded in preventing the readoption of the Crittenden Resolution, and by April they had accomplished the abolition of slavery in the District of Columbia and in the territories. To army regulations they added a new article of war prohibiting the military from returning slaves to their masters. However, they learned to their intense anger

17 Centreville *Indiana True Republican,* February 6, 20, 1862; New York *Tribune,* January 17, 1862; Medill to Julian, February 8, 1862, Giddings-Julian Papers, Library of Congress.

that the President never officially communicated the
order to the generals.[18]

The most significant Radical legislation of the session
was the second Confiscation Act, adopted July 17, after
a prolonged debate of more than two months. As originally framed the act provided for the confiscation of all
property of persons in rebellion against the United
States. President Lincoln would not accept it in this
form and succeeded in forcing Congress to accept modi-
fications, which provided that the law not be retroactive
and that the forfeiture of real property not extend
beyond the natural life of the owner.[19] Some Radicals saw
the President's act as a slap at Congress and an indication that he intended to reduce legislative power and to
carry on the war without Congress. Julian recalled that
Ben Wade said that "the country was going to hell, and
that the scenes witnessed in the French Revolution were
nothing in comparison with what we should see here."
Julian was more annoyed, however, by Lincoln's ideas
about confiscation than by the struggle for dominance
between the President and Congress. He saw a direct
connection between a war for emancipation and public
land policy and looked forward to the day when the
freedmen would be living as independent, land-owning
farmers on the confiscated lands of former planters. Julian regarded Lincoln's rejection of permanent confiscation as "anti-republican discrimination between real
and personal property when the nation was struggling

18 Williams, *Lincoln and the Radicals,* 60, 159-62.

19 *Ibid.,* 163-68. Despite the chagrin felt by the Radicals at their surrender to the President on two points, they could regard the act as a
substantial triumph. If it had been enforced, it would have freed practi-
cally every slave in the South, and one clause provided what the Radicals
had earlier sought—that the slaves of rebels should be free on entering
the Union lines and prohibiting the military from returning them to
their masters.

for its life against a rebellious aristocracy founded on the monopoly of land and the ownership of negroes. . . ."[20]

During the debate on confiscation Julian presented the second of his prepared speeches of the session, one that was also to be his keynote for the approaching election of 1862. He felt that this speech was a factor in his re-election in a year of many conservative victories. His major point was that Congress had the constitutional power to confiscate the property of rebels, a power that he took so much for granted that it was really not a debatable question; only by the "infectious influence of slavery in giving us false views of the Constitution" had it ever been seriously questioned. In direct proportion to their love of slavery, Julian exhorted, did men partake of the "never-ending gabble about the sacredness of the Constitution. . . . No class of men . . . have so much to say about the Constitution as those who are known to sympathize with Jefferson Davis and the pirate crew at his heels." Julian explained that he favored the Confiscation Act in spite of its inadequacies and because it, like the measure of a year earlier, was "in the right direction." He was "glad to see any advance step taken by Congress," for such measures only reaffirmed the "logic of events" which he was sure would lead to the ultimate victory of the antislavery cause.[21]

During the first eight months of 1862 Congress enacted other important measures that were less radical than the Confiscation Act. Julian was proud to join with other Republicans in passing the Homestead Act, a belated triumph for land reformers who had favored such a measure for thirty years. He voted for a bond issue of $500,000,000 for the issuance of greenbacks to the amount

---

20 Julian, *Political Recollections*, 219-20.
21 Julian, *Speeches on Political Questions*, 181-91; *Congressional Globe,* 37 Congress, 1 session, 184-86.

of $450,000,000 and for another tariff increase. Since Julian regarded these as war measures, his votes in favor of them are not an accurate indication of his thinking about either protection or finance. (His ideas on economic matters will become clearer when we observe him as a Congressman during the Reconstruction period and when we examine his role as a member of the Liberal Republican Movement of 1872.) His vote in favor of the Pacific railroad bill is interesting in the light of his subsequent role as a leading opponent of land grants to railroads.

The only important measure of the session that Julian opposed was the Morrill Act, which provided Federal aid to the states through grants of public lands for the establishment of agricultural and mechanical colleges. In voting against this bill Julian differed with a number of Radicals, including Ben Wade who introduced the bill in the Senate. Ironically, in opposing this measure Julian was taking a stand similar to that of southern leaders such as Jefferson Davis and James L. M. Mason, who had blocked its passage in the Senate in 1858, when it had passed the House. Already Julian was developing those ideas that were to make him a purist on public land policy. The only proper disposition of the public lands, in his view, was to distribute them in small plots to actual settlers who would cultivate them, and above all to prevent these lands from falling into the clutches of speculators. Apparently Julian did not yet see the speculative possibilities in either the Homestead or the Pacific railroad measures, but the opportunities that the Morrill Act afforded speculators loomed, for him, much too ominously.[22]

22 Paul W. Gates, "Western Opposition to the Agricultural College Act," in *Indiana Magazine of History*, 37 (1941):103-36. See particularly pages 125-26.

IV

While Congress debated and legislated on such matters as tariffs, Pacific railroads, and confiscation, there was renewed military activity. In the West a relatively unknown general named Ulysses S. Grant stirred hope in northern breasts when, in February, 1862, his vigorous action resulted in the capture of Forts Henry and Donelson, two Confederate strongholds in Tennessee. After that the Union army made its way on down the Mississippi Valley until, on April 6, the Confederates rudely checked it at Shiloh. It would be another year, and more, before the Mississippi corridor would come wholly under the control of the Union forces, but in Grant the North had found that rare specimen—a general who could win victories.

Meanwhile, McClellan had moved his army down the Chesapeake Bay and by early April was making his way slowly up the peninsula toward Richmond.

As Julian watched and waited he became more and more convinced that the nation's agonies lay in incompetent army leadership and in executive lethargy and lack of fortitude. In his journal he recorded his innermost feelings: "There is no generalship in this war on our side, and no policy."[23] As June passed into July the series of bloody battles, the "Seven Days," was fought; the last was Malvern Hill, on July 1, 1862, and with it the ill-fated Peninsular Campaign ended. Richmond was still in Confederate hands and Robert E. Lee was now in command of the southern army in Virginia. "The President sleeps on," wrote Julian; "The truth is the President is on no side, nor in the middle, having no policy or no will."[24]

[23] Julian's Journal, May 18, 1862, quoted in Engstrom, George Washington Julian, 29.
[24] Julian's Journal, July 8, 13, 1862, quoted in *ibid.*, 29, 43.

But Lincoln had decided to take a hand. He paid a visit to the army on the peninsula and asked many questions of officers and men in order to make up his own mind what to do about the army and about McClellan. His declining faith in his commanding general was not renewed when McClellan, meeting him at Harrison's Landing, handed him a letter filled with advice about how to deal with Congress, warning him against his arbitrary arrests, and criticizing his surrender to the Radicals in the matter of confiscation. This was the last straw. Lincoln retaliated by ordering a general reorganization with Henry W. Halleck as general in chief of the Union armies and Gen. John Pope, the choice of the Radicals, in command of the Virginia Theater. And over McClellan's strenuous objections, Lincoln made the decision to withdraw the army from the peninsula.

Even in the midst of Julian's anger and frustration there was that recurring ambivalence in his feelings about Lincoln. He wrote that he could not dislike him if he would, "for he is so kindly and straight forward and his very presence inspires good will."[25] Just before returning home after the adjournment of Congress, Julian visited Lincoln and informed him that he was going to assure the people of his state that the President would "co-operate with Congress in vigorously carrying out the measures we had inaugurated for the purpose of crushing the rebellion, and that now the quickest and hardest blows were to be dealt." Lincoln protested that much of the Radical criticism of him was unwarranted, but he made no objection to Julian's proposed statement to his constituents. Back in Indiana, Julian carried out his promise by announcing that an entire change in policy was resolved on in Washington.[26]

[25] Julian's Journal, July 4, 1862, quoted in Engstrom, George Washington Julian, 44.
[26] Julian, *Political Recollections,* 220.

As Julian looked toward Indiana and the campaign of 1862, he had some misgivings about his chances of reelection. In his journal he noted that the contest was certain to be a hard one and that, considering his radicalism, "a victory with any majority at all will be a very decided triumph."[27] There was ample reason for his concern. In fact, the campaign in the fifth district had been going on for some months before the adjournment of Congress, with a renewal of the argument between the pro-Julian and anti-Julian factions over the method to be used to nominate the Congressional candidate. The former succeeded in getting a resolution adopted by the Republican central committee for a popular primary such as that of 1860. This time the anti-Julian men refused to go along; a primary, they argued, would be "injurious and mischievous" and might destroy the unity that was so essential to the war effort. They demanded a nominating convention, to meet in September, rather than a primary in March or April, as the proper way to nominate a candidate. Despite this protest the townships proceeded to hold their primaries, and it soon became clear that Julian was the popular choice. Whether or not a convention was held would make no difference, since the delegates would go to it with instructions to vote for him.[28]

Julian soon discovered, also, that secession and civil war had not eliminated "fusionism" from Hoosier politics. Party leaders still feared that even the name Republican might drive prospective followers away, and so the name Union party was frequently used. Men of all po-

27 Julian's Journal, July 4, 1862, quoted in Engstrom, *George Washington Julian*, 30.

28 Clarke, *Julian*, 243-44; Centreville *Indiana True Republican*, February 20, March 6, 13, June 26, July 10, August 14, 21, 28, 1862; Richmond *Palladium*, March 8, April 6, August 1, 1862; Indianapolis *Daily Journal*, August 14, 27, 1862.

174   *George Washington Julian*

litical creeds and affiliations were invited to join the fold, if only they believed in the Constitution and favored a vigorous prosecution of the war in order to preserve the Union. The party platform praised the brave soldiers fighting for their state and nation and contained a statement of war aims closely paralleling President Lincoln's doctrine of the preceding year. (The *True Republican* pointed out, quite correctly, that the first plank in the Hoosier Republican platform was essentially the Crittenden Resolution, which had been rejected by the last session of Congress.) Democrats were branded as disunionists and traitors, but there was no mention of slavery. At the state convention Governor Morton personally gave an open-armed greeting to any and all who favored a vigorous prosecution of the war.[29]

Again the party regulars denounced Julian for not being a true party man and for continuing to embrace "one idea" which, they feared, was more apt to destroy than to save the Union. The incumbent Congressman from the fifth district had done nothing since taking his seat in Congress, the argument went, to further the Union cause. In fact, said the *Palladium*, all Julian had done was to "electioneer for a return to his seat . . . by causing to be printed a large number of copies of that '*same old speech*,' on the eternal negro question, and sending them to every man, woman, and child throughout the District."[30] Slavery and the Negro, according to the *Palladium*, had no relation to the war, except perhaps incidentally:

Let the whole negro question be settled as a *military one.* If the negro is in the way directly of stopping this rebellion,

[29] Foulke, *Morton*, 205; Indianapolis *Daily Journal*, June 19, 1862; Centreville *Indiana True Republican*, June 26, 1862.
[30] Richmond *Palladium*, October 3, 1862.

knock the negro out of the way. If slavery is killed as an incident of this war against rebellion, let slavery be killed. The only condition upon which our support of this administration is predicated, is, that it will *stop the rebellion.*[31]

Interest in Julian's campaign for re-election spread beyond the fifth district. Letters from all parts of the state either praising or condemning him appeared in the local papers; and other letters flowed out of the "Burnt District" to the Indianapolis organs describing the candidate either as an indispensable man in Congress or representing him as an incompetent.

The *Palladium* finally acknowledged that Julian was the party's Congressional candidate, but only as the "result of *gross frauds* practiced in the townships." Whereas in 1860 the *Palladium,* speaking for the Holloway-Morton combination, had given belated and reluctant support to Julian as the party candidate, in 1862 it opposed him throughout the campaign.[32]

Julian's re-election in October was contrary to the general trend. In Indiana the Democratic party easily elected its candidates for state offices, regained control of the legislature, and carried seven of the eleven Congressional districts. Results were similar in six other states, including New York, Pennsylvania, Ohio, and Illinois; and the Republicans nearly lost control of the House of Representatives. Thus Julian was not indulging in mere braggadocio when he wrote some years later of his election in 1862: "My triumph had no taint of compromise in it, and nothing saved me but perfect courage and absolute defiance of my foes."[33]

[31] *Ibid.,* May 31, 1862.
[32] *Ibid.,* August 1, 15, 29, September 12, 1862; Indianapolis *Daily Journal,* July 29, August 5, 30, 1862.
[33] Julian, *Political Recollections,* 216.

Congressmen returned to Washington in December, 1862, amidst forebodings of disaster for the Union. The military situation was probably worse than when they had departed in July. General Pope, whose boasting and show of confidence had so impressed the Committee on the Conduct of the War, had shown in his first effort against the enemy that he was even more unfit than McClellan. After the disastrous defeat in the second battle of Manassas (August 29-30) Lincoln recalled "Little Mac" to bring some order to a chaotic situation and to protect Washington, which was now seriously threatened. At Antietam, on September 17, McClellan succeeded in stopping Lee's invasion of the North, but characteristically he failed to take advantage of an opportunity to annihilate the Confederate Army. When after two months McClellan had still not advanced against Lee, Lincoln again relieved him. This time his successor was Gen. Ambrose Burnside, who took the post very reluctantly after admitting that he lacked the ability to command an army.

In spite of this depressing state of affairs the situation, from the Radical point of view, was far from hopeless. Although Lincoln had removed McClellan for military rather than political reasons, Radicals could interpret his departure as a victory over the President. To be sure, Burnside was a West Pointer and a close friend of McClellan's, and it was to be expected that he would continue McClellan's policies. But Burnside was not, and would never be, a symbolic personification of the opposition to the Jacobin clique, and he lacked the mesmeric power of "Little Mac" with the army. With Burnside in command, there was little likelihood of a *coup*.

Also, there was another removal from high military command that pleased the Radicals almost as much as

McClellan's demise. This one involved Gen. Don Carlos Buell, in command of the Ohio Department. Buell, too, was a West Pointer who resembled McClellan in his organizational ability and lack of aggressiveness as a combat leader. He, too, had been long a target of the Radical fire. Buell's removal was all the more gratifying because his successor, Gen. William S. Rosecrans, was a Radical favorite.

In the realm of politics, too, it appeared that the Republican reverses in the recent election might be advantageous to the Radicals, for they could be attributed to the soft policy of the administration toward slavery and to the incompetence of moderates in the President's Cabinet. Indeed, the Radicals saw in the situation the distinct possibility of a reorganization of the Cabinet in which they, as influential legislative leaders, would have a hand. If they could force the dismissal of Secretary of State William Seward, there would be ample reason for Radical optimism. Salmon P. Chase, Secretary of the Treasury and Radical spokesman, might then become the dominant voice in the administration.

Since the beginning of the campaign Julian had been of the opinion that the use of the term "Union" for "Republican" was a harmful delusion, implying that "we were fighting for a political abstraction called the Union, and not for the destruction of slavery." When he returned to Washington in December, he was "glad to find this fact generally admitted, and my earnest opposition to it fully justified by the judgment of Republican members of Congress."[34]

Most encouraging of all was Lincoln's decision, which he had made as early as July, to issue an emancipation proclamation. On the advice of Seward, the President

34 Julian, *Political Recollections,* 224.

had postponed its announcement until after a northern military victory, lest the proclamation be interpreted as a move of desperation during the troubled summer of 1862. The Battle of Antietam was hardly the sort of victory which Lincoln awaited. But if Lee's army of northern Virginia had not been defeated, it had been stopped in its invasion of the North, and Lincoln decided that the time had come. According to his preliminary proclamation issued on September 22, he would on January 1, 1863, declare free the slaves in all states or portions of states still in rebellion. As critics of the President were quick to point out, such a proclamation would not free a single slave. In the border states and in areas under Federal control where emancipation might have been accomplished the President did not claim the power to act. What, then, did the emancipation proclamation accomplish? What was Lincoln's purpose in issuing it? Had he changed his mind about the war aims, or was he retreating from the Radical attack? Was the proclamation a clever act of dissimulation on the part of the President?

Without attempting a full analysis of the complicated question of Lincoln's attitudes toward the Negro and slavery, which is not within the scope of this book, it does seem valid to conclude that the emancipation proclamation was not, in Lincoln's mind, antithetical to his plan of voluntary, compensated emancipation by the states. Nor is there evidence to support the charge made by some Southerners that Lincoln was trying to foment a servile insurrection in the South. By his own admission, however, the proclamation was issued because of military necessity. It would ultimately end any possibility of British recognition of the Southern Confederacy. And from this point on the Negro was to have a more important role in the achievement of a northern victory. In

OLIVER P. MORTON

CARL SCHURZ

brief, without altering the methods which Lincoln thought to be proper for the abolition of slavery, the proclamation was a kind of public avowal of that truth which the President asserted more forthrightly in his second inaugural:

One eighth of the whole population was colored slaves, not distributed generally over the Union, but localized in the Southern part of it. These slaves constituted a peculiar and powerful interest. All knew that this interest was, somehow, the cause of the war.[35]

The Radicals were aware, of course, of the defects of the proclamation as an instrument of emancipation, but they were pleased with Lincoln's decision. They were concerned, however, that Lincoln might not issue the final proclamation, and it was with apprehension that they awaited January 1, 1863. In his *Recollections* Julian recalls the vigil kept by a number of Radicals on that critical day: "On New Year's day I joined the immense throng of callers at the White House, but did not enjoy the delay of the President in issuing his Proclamation of Emancipation. It came late in the day, and brought relief to multitudes of anxious people."[36]

With the coming of the New Year the Radicals felt that the political and military situation was favorable to their effort to bring about a reorganization of the Cabinet, but for the nonce the emancipation proclamation was all the Radicals were able to get from the President. They were unable to turn political reverses and military defeats into a complete radical victory. William Seward would remain as Secretary of State.

After this disappointing failure, the Radicals again turned their fire on the President and his moderate

35 Basler, *et al.* (eds.), *Collected Works of Abraham Lincoln,* 8:332.
36 Julian, *Political Recollections,* 226.

policies. Julian was in the forefront of the attack. From Giddings came the admonition to make a speech that would "shake that old capitol." On February 18, 1863, Julian obliged with his most vigorous oratorical effort in Congress up to that time. Therein Julian reaffirmed his doctrine of the war as a conflict against slavery, called for the arming of the slaves, the confiscation of all property belonging to traitors (Southerners in rebellion), and the distribution of southern plantation lands among the Negroes. Democratic policy, he said, dominated the administration. For the President he had some severe words of warning:

I speak respectfully, but earnestly, when I say that the President must stand by his friends, if he expects his friends to stand by him. He must point the door to every pampered pro-slavery rat in any of his public cribs, and bestow the offices and honors at his disposal upon those who believe in the Republican idea. . . . This is a slaveholders' rebellion. The rebellion, in fact, is "slavery in arms," and therefore no man who believes in slavery is fit for any high command. The war is not a war of sections, but of ideas; and we need, and must have, military leaders who will conduct it in the light of this truth. To the want of such leaders must be attributed the delays and disasters of the struggle thus far.[37]

37 Giddings to Julian, January 18, 1863, Giddings-Julian Papers; *Congressional Globe*, 37 Congress, 3 session, 1064-69 (for quotation see p. 1068); Julian, *Speeches on Political Questions*, 192-211 (for quotation see p. 205).

LOOKING TOWARD
RECONSTRUCTION

⬦⬦⬦⬦⬦⬦⬦⬦⬦⬦⬦⬦

As everybody now knows, 1863 was the crucial year of the war, after which the South's chances of winning were negligible. But at the beginning of the year Northerners had little cause for optimism. Vicksburg had not been taken, and the Mississippi corridor was not yet controlled by the North. Lee had not yet been repulsed at Gettysburg. During the last weeks of 1862 the North had suffered a disastrous defeat at Fredericksburg, one of the most futile and tragic battles of American military history, in which General Burnside demonstrated the correctness of his evaluation of himself as an army commander. Also, the Republican political setbacks of 1862 were followed by predictions of a resurgent Democratic party with Gen. George B. McClellan a likely presidential candidate.

How was it, then, that Julian could report, "Everybody feels that the rebellion is on its last legs, and that we are soon to emerge gloriously from the horrid strife into which our country has been plunged by the madness of treason"? Perhaps it was the elemental optimism of the reformer who never believes that his cause can be lost. Or perhaps it was his close association with the Committee on the Conduct of the War in preparing its report which, Julian said, would be "perfectly overwhelming" to General McClellan.[1]

At this time Julian tried again to persuade the President to reinstate General Frémont in a responsible military command, but again Lincoln refused, with more firmness and finality than before. While trying to help a friend, Julian observed with satisfaction the embarrassment of an enemy, David Holloway, whose administration as Commissioner of the Patent Office was being investigated by a committee of Congress.[2]

After the adjournment of Congress Julian had no desire to remain in Washington, where winter hung on and an epidemic of smallpox had broken out.[3] After a brief visit in Centreville, he returned to the capital and then went on to Philadelphia, where he visited James and Lucretia Mott, whom he had not seen for thirteen years. Their aged appearance shocked and saddened him. In Philadelphia he also visited the Union League whose members, formerly wealthy and conservative Whigs, Julian was encouraged to find responding "to the most radical utterances." He was confident that with their help the Republicans would carry Pennsylvania at the next election. His next stop was New York where he visited the Frémonts and spoke with the General at a mass meeting. He also called on William Cullen Bryant, and he enjoyed warm hospitality at Peterboro, the estate

1 Julian's Journal, April 3, 1863, quoted in Engstrom, George Washington Julian, 31-32; Centreville *Indiana True Republican*, March 26, April 9, 1863; New York *Daily Tribune*, March 24, 1863; Williams, *Lincoln and the Radicals*, 236.

2 Centreville *Indiana True Republican*, March 26, April 9, 1863; Julian, *Political Recollections*, 229-30; Williams, *Lincoln and the Radicals*, 279.

3 Centreville *Indiana True Republican*, April 9, 1863; Margaret Leech, *Reveille in Washington, 1860-1865* (New York, 1941), 249, 251.

of Gerrit Smith. The highlight of the visit was one of Smith's famous breakfasts attended by many local friends, with Julian as the honored guest of the occasion. On April 20 he was back in Centreville.[4]

That summer northern spirits were raised by Grant's capture of Vicksburg and the repulse of Lee at Gettysburg, but Indiana and Ohio were suddenly confronted with more immediate contact with the war. On July 8, Gen. John Hunt Morgan crossed the Ohio River from Kentucky into Indiana to launch a raid that carried him on into Ohio before he was finally captured. Governor Morton, fearing for the safety of Indianapolis, called on all able-bodied men to come to the defense of the state. Julian volunteered and spent eight days in the army. His volunteer unit went first to Indianapolis and then to Cincinnati where the Buckeyes, confident that Ohio could defend herself, gave it a cool reception. The editors of the Richmond *Telegram,* a newspaper usually unfavorable to Julian, admitted their admiration for the Congressman when they saw him "going through the 'evolutions' " of military drill.[5]

Following this episode Julian entered into the political campaign of 1863. After a few speeches in Indiana he went to the Western Reserve district of Ohio to campaign against Clement L. Vallandigham in his contest for governor. In October also he spoke in Iowa.[6]

4 Centreville *Indiana True Republican,* April 16, 1863; Clarke, *Julian,* 246.

5 Julian's Journal, July 20, 1863, quoted in Engstrom, George Washington Julian, 32; Centreville *Indiana True Republican,* July 23, 30, 1863; Julian, *Political Recollections,* 232-33; Wallace, *Autobiography,* 2:656-61.

6 Centreville *Indiana True Republican,* August 13, 27, September 10, 17, 24, October 1, 8, 1863; Julian, *Political Recollections,* 234-36; Clarke, *Julian,* 247; Williams, *Lincoln and the Radicals,* 293.

II

The death of Anne Julian in 1860 was the first of a series of bereavements that Julian had to face in the years between 1860 and 1865. Before the end of the war two of the three sons born to him and Anne would die. The end came for little Louis Henry, nine years old, on October 16, 1863. Edward Channing's death came eighteen months later. Julian's diary, letters, and newspaper writings do not truly reflect the impact of these bereavements. Nor did they seem to affect his work in Congress. But apparently he did suffer intensely. In the later years of his life he talked at great length with his daughter, Grace, child of his second marriage, of these loved ones. Little "Louie" was probably Julian's favorite child. Grace wrote that it was hard for her to realize that she had never seen the little boy, "so habitually was he in my father's thoughts and conversation."[7] Julian's perseverance with his work at such a time was a demonstration of an indomitable will. As we have seen, he felt keenly the inadequacy of his own early training and education, and his tendency was to live through his sons. He wanted to give them the advantages he had missed and the opportunity to develop into more confident and happier men than he was. Lacking the pontifical confidence of a Sumner or the crude forcefulness of a Wade, Julian was shaken by the inevitable rebuffs and shocks of public life. Close and affectionate family relationships served as a cushion to help him absorb them. The death of a son or a wife was more than a temporary shock that time would eventually eradicate.

It was at this time, in the summer of 1863, when Julian may have been ripe for matrimonial plucking, that he renewed his acquaintance with Laura Giddings, the

7 Clarke, *Julian*, 248; Clarke, "Julian: Some Impressions," in *Indiana Magazine of History*, 2:64.

youngest daughter of his political godfather, whom he had met two years earlier in Washington. They were married the following December. Although she was twenty-two years younger than George, Laura was a poised and mature woman. She acted as nurse and companion for her ailing father, who died in May, 1864. When Julian's health failed a year or two after the marriage, she transferred her attentions from father to husband. She also became George's personal secretary and adviser. She was not pretty, as George's first wife had been, but she had been to college at Antioch and Oberlin,[8] and she was a woman of considerable charm. In Julian, she found a combination of lover, sage, father, and son, and she was devoted to him. She gave him the sympathy and understanding he always needed, and she was always ready with the fulsome praise on which he throve almost as a child. Two children, Grace and Paul, were born of the marriage. Ironically, George was to survive Laura by fifteen years.

III

When Julian returned to Washington in December, 1863, for the opening of the Thirty-eighth Congress, he immediately reopened his campaign against slavery. Unsuccessfully, he urged the repeal of the Fugitive Slave laws of 1793 and of 1850.[9]

Soon he was active again in the work of the Committee on the Conduct of the War. In May, 1864, the committee visited returning prisoners of war at Annapolis. The experience was a shocking one for Julian. Later he wrote

[8] Clarke, "Some Impressions," in *Indiana Magazine of History,* 2:67; Centreville *Indiana True Republican,* January 7, 1864; Clarke, *Julian,* 247-48.

[9] *Congressional Globe,* 38 Congress, 1 session, 20, 22.

that he was never "so touched by any spectacle of human suffering"; the soldiers he saw there were "living skeletons" in the last stages of life who looked at the committee members "with an expression of beseeching tenderness and submission which no words could describe." When he examined one of the men, Julian wrote, "I was perfectly unmanned by my tears; and on retiring from the tent to give them vent I encountered Senator Wade, who had fled from the work, and was sobbing like a child."[10] When the committee took testimony, Julian seemed most interested in the food that the Confederates had provided for the prisoners. He particularly wished to show the falsity of the rebel claim that northern prisoners received the same food as southern soldiers. The answer he sought finally came from an army surgeon who testified that Confederate troops could not have made the marches they had made or fought as they had fought without better care and food than the prisoners received.[11]

Midway in the session Julian had a heated exchange in the House with Representative Samuel S. Cox of Ohio. It began when Speaker Colfax left the chair to offer a resolution for the expulsion from the House of Alexander Long of Ohio who, he charged, had given aid to the rebellion by declaring himself in favor of southern independence. Cox came to Long's defense, and in his argument asked why no motion had been made to expel Julian, who had blasphemed the Constitution. Julian, said Cox, was guilty of treason in his statement that *"nothing, not even the Constitution, must be allowed to hold back . . . the Government in blasting the power of the rebels forever."* Cox had misrepresented him, Julian

10 Julian, *Political Recollections*, 239.

11 Frank Moore (ed.), *The Rebellion Record: A Diary of American Events* (12 vols., New York, 1861-69), 8:80-96.

said, as he proceeded to state his views on the Constitution: The document was made for the people, not the people for it; "our fathers were not fools but wise men, who armed the nation with the power to crush its foes as well as to protect its friends. . . . If it were necessary to save the life of the nation to depart from the letter of the Constitution I would . . . blast the power of the rebellion forever by the strong hand of war." Cox replied that the "life of the nation" was "bound up with the Constitution." Julian then seized the initiative and asked Cox, "if the salvation of the nation's life required the violation of the letter of the Constitution," would you be willing to save it at that cost? Several times Cox answered evasively and each time Julian fired the question again. Finally Cox answered that for no "conceivable purpose" would he violate the Constitution. Julian was framing another question when the objections of several Democrats were sustained and he was forced to take his seat.[12]

IV

At least fifteen months before the end of the war, despite continued combat and mounting losses, men began to ponder the problems that would face postwar America. What was the status of the seceded states, and how would they be brought back into the Union? Would the freedman be a full-fledged citizen enjoying the civil rights guaranteed under the Constitution? What was to be done about economic problems such as the tariff, banking and currency, grants to railroads, and public land policy, all of which had been drastically affected by the war?

Julian was interested in all these matters, but his appointment as chairman of the Committee on Public

12 *Congressional Globe,* 38 Congress, 1 session, 1510.

Lands gave him an opportunity to do his most effective and most important work as a Congressman. The crusade for land reform, which had been put aside but never really abandoned, now took on new meaning for him because of its connection with the condition of the Negro. Only by a drastic reform of the whole land system in the South, Julian believed, could the emancipated slaves be truly free. (Developments in southern agriculture during and following Reconstruction would bear out his fears, for freedmen and poor whites became the serfs in a semifeudal system of tenancy and debt.) But Julian was not merely interested in the emancipation of slaves; he would also destroy the landed aristocracy of the South, and punish it for the rebellion.

Indeed, the place of land reform in Reconstruction composes one of the most fascinating chapters in the history of those unhappy years; it is also one of the most enlightening. As long as Republicans viewed land legislation as a means of remolding and of controlling the South, Julian received powerful backing and achieved some success. But when this program came into conflict with other interests—railroads, lumber, iron—whose overwhelming growth was one of the legacies of the war, Julian found himself fighting almost alone.[13] Also, he soon discovered that public land policy could not be limited to the South.

The protection of settlers in California or Kansas against the ravages of speculators and railroad barons became as important to him as the emancipation of the slaves. By the time Julian's Congressional career ended, in 1871, his crusade was headed in a new direction.

13 Centreville *Indiana True Republican,* December 17, 1863; New York *Daily Tribune,* December 15, 1863; Paul W. Gates, "Federal Land Policy in the South, 1866-1888," in *Journal of Southern History,* 6 (1940): 305 ff.

Twice during the month of February, 1864, Julian reported bills from the Committee on Public Lands to provide homesteads for veterans on confiscated southern lands; both were sent back to the committee. On March 18, the consideration in the House of a Senate bill providing land bounties for soldiers gave Julian another opportunity to present his bill. It provided for a free homestead of eighty acres for men who had served in the naval or military services for two years and forty acres for all those who had aided in putting down the rebellion either as servicemen or laborers. To make it a genuine homestead bill instead of a land-bounty measure, a residence of five years on the land was required for confirmation of the title. Negroes were to have equal rights with whites to the land, and ownership was to extend to the widow or heir of the original settler.

William S. Holman, Indiana Democrat and also a leading land reformer, criticized Julian for being more mindful of the rights of Negroes than of the welfare of soldiers. Here was manifested two important facets of the complicated land reform question after the Civil War: the contest between homesteaders and those favoring bounty lands for soldiers, and the role of the Negro in reconstruction. Julian's speech, following the presentation of his bill, marked the beginning of a seven-year contest in Congress over land policy; a contest in which he was to be one of the central figures.

The speech began with a tribute to the homestead policy and an assertion that if it had been adopted when first proposed in Jackson's administration the war might have been avoided. But the homestead bill adopted just two years previously was already threatened. The chief argument of those who would overthrow the policy, said Julian, was the financial necessity of selling the public domain instead of giving it to settlers. But the greatest

encroachments came from the enormous grants of land
to railroads and to the states for the establishment of
schools and colleges. Speculators were "hovering over
the public domain, picking and culling large tracts of
the best lands, and thus cheating the Government out
of their productive wealth, and the poor man out of a
home. . . . "

In reply to those who would pay the public debt out
of the revenue of public land sales, Julian explained that
there was only one way to pay the debt: "to give homes
to the millions who need them, and at the same time
coin their labor into national wealth, by marrying it to
the virgin soil which woos the cultivator."[14]

In this reaffirmation of his old agrarian philosophy,
Julian gave evidence that the revolutionary changes of
the war years had left him relatively unimpressed. Or,
if he was aware of these changes, he saw no need for
new and different governmental policies to deal with
them. The proper role of government, according to
Julian, was one of prevention; monopoly and speculation
ought to be curbed and the individual protected in his
personal and property rights. But Julian, as many of
his contemporaries, did not envision a government undertaking centralized national planning to match the
increasing centralization in industry or commerce. It was
natural that Julian, and men like him, should have found
it difficult to adapt their thinking to fit the new kind
of country in which they found themselves after the
Civil War, a country vastly different from the bucolic
land in which they had been born and educated. Yet such
atavistic thinking must also be taken into account in ex-

14 *Congressional Globe,* 38 Congress, 1 session, 668, 874, 1185-90;
Julian, *Speeches on Political Questions,* 214-15; Robbins, *Our Landed
Heritage,* 214.

plaining those aspects of American development after the Civil War that were disruptive, or even tragic.

Julian next turned to the question of the legality of the confiscation of southern lands:

Resting our case on the law of nations and the laws of war, we are not compelled to seek the land of the rebel through a trial . . . in the county in which the offense was committed, and in which both court and jury may be in sympathy with the accused. . . . The war powers of the Government, as asserted and defined in the . . . Confiscation Act of July 17, 1862, point to a remedy as sweeping as it is just, namely, the military seizure, condemnation, and sale of the real estate of traitors and their abettors.[15]

The Federal government, Julian argued, was faced with two clear alternatives: to seize the land and hold it "in trust for the people" or to allow it to fall into the hands of speculators and thus to "become the basis of new and frightful monopolies." If the second alternative were adopted the southern slaveholder would merely be replaced by the ". . . grasping monopolist of the North, whose dominion over the freedmen and poor whites [would] be more galling than slavery itself." The proprietors of the great estates would be ". . . feudal lords, while the poor [would] have no feudal rights." In contrast, he painted a roseate picture of the future if his policy were followed: immigrants would flock into the South to cultivate the rich lands there; railroads would be built to connect all parts of the country; there would be prosperity of a kind unknown before. In conclusion Julian pleaded, "Mr. Speaker, nothing can atone for the woes and sorrows of this war but the thorough reorganization of society in these revolted States. Now is the

15 *Congressional Globe,* 38 Congress, 1 session, 1186; Julian, *Speeches on Political Questions,* 217-18.

time to begin this work. We must not only cut up slavery, root and branch, but we must see to it that these teeming regions shall be studded over with small farms and tilled by free men."[16]

Friends and antislavery sympathizers received the speech warmly. One enthusiastic admirer wrote that Julian's bill was the "grandest & most statesman-like . . . ever carried through the Congress of the United States; indeed, . . . through any legislative body on the globe." Julian's speech was "the *tallest* specimen of forensic eloquence that [he had] ever read."[17] Gerrit Smith wrote in a more restrained tone: "I like all your speeches but a better one than this I believe you never made."[18] From Lydia Maria Child came one of her frequent long letters. She agreed with Julian that "the individualizing of the masses [was] the ultimate end of *all* reforms," and she was in sympathy with the spirit of his speech, but she was skeptical of some of his proposed methods. She believed that men were "generally injured by having property *given* to them. They don't prize it so highly, keep it so carefully, or improve it so diligently, as they do when they take some pains to obtain it." To receive gifts might impair ". . . the strength and dignity of character. Whosoever would be a *man* must *earn*."[19]

During the two months after his introduction of the bill Julian fought for its adoption. On May 4, failing in an attempt to have it voted on, he stated his fear that "its magnitude is seen but dimly, or not perceived at all, by many who should give it their zealous support."

16 *Congressional Globe*, 38 Congress, 1 session, 1187-88; Julian, *Speeches on Political Questions*, 220-24.
17 John Pierpont, Washington, D. C., to Julian, March 22, 1864, Giddings-Julian Papers.
18 Gerrit Smith to Julian, March 25, 1864, Giddings-Julian Papers.
19 L. Maria Child to Julian, March 27, 1864, Giddings-Julian Papers.

On May 11, Julian forced debate on the bill again, and the next day it was voted on. The final debate led Julian into one of the hottest exchanges he ever experienced in the House of Representatives. Fernando Wood of New York, a peace Democrat, objected to the bill on the ground that it was "an obstruction to the restoration of the Union." Julian replied that he could not comprehend how the confiscation of lands belonging to men like Toombs of Georgia and Jacob Thompson of Mississippi could have such an effect. He agreed that it might obstruct the restoration of the old Union in the era of Democratic dominance, but not "a Union of regenerated States, resting upon the basis of free labor and the rights of man." When Wood expressed his fear that there was a "nigger" in the bill, Robert Mallory of Kentucky entered the discussion. He asked Julian whether the bill was not "one of a series of acts . . . to work out the entire equality, social and political, of the negro with the white man." Julian replied that the bill meant just what it said; he was confident that, under this "new dispensation," the social relationship between Negroes and whites would work itself out. "I believe in doing justice to the negro," he continued, "in guarding his rights, and in giving him fair play in fighting his own battle, leaving his social position to be determined by his own conduct, and the conditions of life in which he may be placed." As for the African domination which some Congressmen seemed to fear, Julian could see no possibility of it.

Mallory asked more prodding questions: What did Julian think of Negro suffrage? Julian replied that when the Negro had been converted from a chattel to a man the states would probably deal fairly with the question of suffrage, but he could not regard as unwise a policy

that granted suffrage to the Negroes. Still Mallory was
not satisfied, and urged a more complete explanation
of Negro equality. Julian now lashed out at the Kentuck-
ian. He admitted that Republicans had had various kinds
of dealings with Negroes:

But no such intimate relations exist between them as we find
existing between them and the Democrats of the South. . . .
The slave mothers and slave masters of the South are brought
on to the level of equality in its most loathsome forms. In
some of the rebel states I believe the number of mulattoes
is nearly equal to the number of Democratic voters. . . . The
gentleman cannot deny this, unless he can show that these
mulattoes sprouted up from the soil, or were rained down
from the clouds, or reported their presence through some
other miracle.[20]

Glowingly the Radical Washington *Chronicle* described
the futile efforts of Wood and Mallory to embarrass Julian: "Both were signally foiled, and the latter received
a 'setting down' which he and the public generally will
be apt to remember for as long as he lives."[21]

Julian's bill passed in the House by a close vote that
generally followed party lines, but it was never given
consideration in the Senate. His fight for confiscation did
not end, however, with this defeat. For a time it seemed
that the bill's essential parts would be included in the
Republican platform in 1864. They had the approval of
the powerful Union League, whose convention met in
Baltimore concurrently with the Republican convention.
The national convention's subcommittee on resolutions
agreed to include them, but the general committee struck
them out. The refusal of President Lincoln to use his

[20] *Congressional Globe,* 38 Congress, 1 session, 2108, 2233, 2249-52.
[21] Washington (D. C.) *Chronicle,* quoted in Centreville *Indiana True Republican,* May 26, 1864.

executive power to abolish the fee of southern landholders was also a strong obstacle to its adoption. Julian regarded this as one of Lincoln's gravest mistakes in the management of the war. Later Julian enjoyed some success in opening up the public lands of southern states for homestead settlement, but the failure of his bill in 1864 doomed confiscation as an element of post-Civil War public land policy.[22]

V

When Julian returned to Indiana after the adjournment of Congress in July, he was already the Congressional nominee of the Union party in his district. The fact that his opponent was Gen. Sol Meredith, a wounded hero returned from the war, did not make the campaign any gentler than in former years. Its seismic rumblings were heard outside the "Burnt District." In mid-March the Eaton, Ohio, *Register* reported, "We are sorry to observe the biennial squabble over the nomination of Rep. representative in the 'Burnt District,' has commenced again with more than its usual fury and venom."[23] Meredith's January announcement of his candidacy brought forth immediate comment, pro and con. The *True Republican* contended that Meredith's only hope for the nomination lay in the repeal of the popular primary. It predicted that, in spite of his ravings against it, the primary would prevail as the means of nominating the candidate and that the man who received the majority of the "whole unadulterated Union vote, without regard to county or township lines . . . will be nominated, and 'the gates of hell will not prevail against' him at the gen-

22 Julian, *Political Recollections,* 242-43; Robbins, *Our Landed Heritage,* 210-11.
23 Centreville *Indiana True Republican,* March 24, 1864.

eral election. . . ." The *Palladium* denied that Meredith was opposed to the popular vote system and predicted that under it he would win the nomination by a two thousand majority.[24]

On February 25 the *True Republican* published Julian's letter announcing his candidacy. Here he asserted that the popular primary was the fairest and most economical method of nomination and that only a man who feared the people would object to it. But Julian wanted to impose one restriction: only those men who were in favor of a vigorous prosecution of the war and who refused to be identified with the pro-slavery Democracy should be permitted to vote. Because Julian would not be free from Congressional duties to take part in the canvass, he enjoined his friends to take charge of it and "to see to it that justice and fair dealing . . . not be sacrificed through any lack of zeal and energy on their part." In warning them of the methods his enemies would use, he cited the previous election in which "the most extraordinary combinations were formed, disowning all honor and manhood in their methods of warfare, and giving themselves to their work with zeal which could scarcely have been exceeded if I had betrayed the country to its enemies."[25]

Julian's friends had begun to act even before the announcement of his candidacy. When they introduced resolutions favorable to him at the Wayne County Union convention, a near riot resulted. Meredith and his followers created such a disturbance that the resolutions were never discussed. There followed a prolonged controversy over what had actually happened at the con-

24 Centreville *Indiana True Republican,* January 21, February 4, 18, 1864; Richmond *Palladium,* February 24, 1864.
25 Centreville *Indiana True Republican,* February 25, 1864.

vention. The Julian men claimed that Meredith had personally precipitated the disturbance.[26] Meredith men asserted that Julian's followers had tried to railroad through a set of resolutions favorable to their candidate with no pretense of following proper parliamentary procedure. Here was evidence, they said, that Julian was "organizing a party within the Republican party, having for its main object the continuance of himself in Congress during the term of his natural life; and as incident thereto, the control of all county offices, and of the political affairs generally in the district."[27]

The Indianapolis *Journal* described the fifth district campaign as one whose contestants had abused one another with the most "unseemly bitterness" and recommended abandonment of the popular primary.[28] Julian also expressed regret that the campaign had not been conducted with "moderation, fairness, and good temper, on all sides," but he asserted that if Meredith had remained at his post of duty, as he (Julian) had done, the bitterness and invective would have been avoided. He hoped the people would not consider abandoning the primary because of "the angry contentions of the late contest."[29]

Even though Julian won the nomination in the primary on April 4, Holloway's *Palladium* refused to recognize him as the candidate. Only after the intervention of President Lincoln did the *Palladium* give Julian passive approval. Twice during the campaign Julian went to Lincoln to discuss the political situation in his district. His first objective was to bring about Holloway's dismis-

26 *Ibid.*, February 18, 1864.
27 Richmond *Palladium*, March 2, 1864.
28 Indianapolis *Daily Journal*, April 5, 6, 1864.
29 Centreville *Indiana True Republican*, April 21, 1864.

sal as Commissioner of Patents; failing at that, he sought the President's intervention to force Holloway to recognize his candidacy. After receiving a petition from a number of Senators and Representatives asking for Holloway's removal, Lincoln ordered him to support Julian or to give up his office. Thus, on July 6, there appeared in the *Palladium* the endorsement: "For Congress in Opposition to a 'Copperhead,' GEORGE W. JULIAN."[30]

During the campaign Julian's enemies also accused him of being implicated in the movement to secure the Republican presidential nomination for Salmon P. Chase. Julian had only withdrawn from the movement, said the *Palladium,* when it became clear to him that sentiment in the fifth district favored Lincoln. The following day the *True Republican* came out with a categorical denial: "Let no man be deceived by the loud and persistent lie of the Meredith organs, that G. W. Julian is opposed to Mr. Lincoln. Every form and modification of that story is a base and unfounded falsehood." Soon afterward Julian issued a public explanation of his connection with the Chase movement. He admitted that he had been appointed to a committee working for Chase's nomination, but he said that he had disavowed the movement immediately and had had no further connection with the committee. Disappointed Chase men also attacked Julian; one wrote to the *Palladium* castigating him as a "cowardly hypocrite and political demagogue" who had abandoned the radical cause.[31]

30 Richmond *Palladium,* July 6, 1864; Centreville *Indiana True Republican,* July 14, 1864; Indianapolis *Daily State Sentinel,* June 25, 1864; Julian, *Political Recollections,* 244-45. A letter to the Indianapolis *Sentinel* stated that Julian also had asked Lincoln to order Meredith back to duty with the army.

31 Centreville *Indiana True Republican,* March 3, 24, 1864; Richmond *Palladium,* March 2, 22, 1864; Julian, *Political Recollections,* 237-38; Clarke, *Julian,* 250-51.

Julian was even less friendly to the Cleveland convention of Radicals who nominated John C. Frémont for President and adopted a platform that called for the abolition of slavery by constitutional amendment and the confiscation of slaveholders' property. This was the program Julian had fought for in Congress, the program he had demanded that the Lincoln administration adopt. Where was the Julian of old—of the 1850's —who had demanded that his party forget about immediate victory and concentrate on fostering a program undiluted by "fusionism"? Was he the victim of "Old Abe's" personal magnetism? Was the reformer in Congress suddenly transformed into a vacillating opportunist when he stepped onto the hustings? Or were the stakes in the campaign simply different from those of an earlier time in Indiana?

An explanation of Julian's decision to support Lincoln instead of a more radical candidate must take into consideration all these questions. Certainly the reformer had not been transformed into a mere scheming politician, bent only on election to office as an end in itself. But Julian did have an unquenchable thirst for political life, and he was beginning to believe that he had a mission in Congress; this feeling grew stronger as he became more deeply involved in the land reform movement. It was essential that he remain in Congress in order to institute and to carry through his projected reforms. If expediency forced one to support a moderate, it was fortunate that it was "Old Abe" rather than a less honest or appealing man. But the greatest force holding Julian and other Radicals within the Union party was the fear of a Democratic victory and the possibility that something less than total victory over the slavocracy might be the result. The increasing demands for a negotiated peace were anathema to Radicals, and the Democratic nomination of McClellan for President gave a great boost to Republican unity. When Lincoln finally agreed to make Cabinet changes favorable to the Radicals, there was no longer any doubt where the majority of them would stand. Thus Julian did not wait this time, as did some other Radicals, for developments late in the campaign. From the very beginning he saw the practicability if not the inevitability of Lincoln's nomination.

After the *Palladium* ceased its fire on Julian, there was more unity among the factions of the Hoosier Union party than there had been since 1856. During the months of August and September, Julian went on a campaign tour under the direction of the Indiana central committee. In a number of speeches, with that of September 27 in Indianapolis as the climax, Julian scored McClellan as a traitor and as the "lightest and shallowest man in the United States." Repeatedly he called for the "earnest support of Governor Morton and the Union ticket" in opposition to "plotters of treason and coworkers of rebellion." Julian joined in the refrain of Morton and his henchmen that Democrats were traitors and that Lincoln and Morton must be returned to office in order to prevent insurrection in Indiana.[32]

The result was a Union triumph of unexpected proportions. Morton was re-elected, the Unionists regained control of the legislature and elected eight of the eleven Congressmen, and Lincoln carried Indiana by a twenty thousand majority. Julian, too, enjoyed the fruits of victory. He was elected by a seven thousand majority,

[32] Centreville *Indiana True Republican,* August 18, September 8, 1864; Indianapolis *Daily Journal,* September 24, 28, 1864; Indianapolis *Daily Gazette,* September 28, 1864; Clarke, *Julian,* 258-59; Stampp, *Indiana Politics,* 217-54.

the largest in any Congressional election in the "Burnt District" up to that time.[33]

VI

In December, 1864, President Lincoln greeted the returning Congress with an annual message that gladdened the hearts of Radicals. He promised to stand by the Emancipation Proclamation and even to demand emancipation of the slaves as a *sine qua non* for peace with the Confederacy; he also agreed to the abolition of slavery by constitutional amendment. Julian thought the message "a grand document compared with his previous ones" and was convinced at last that "Old Abe" understood that the people were radical.[34] But before long the conservative and radical factions were fighting again, this time over the question of Reconstruction.

In December, 1863, Lincoln had devised a plan for an easy return of the southern states to the Union. It provided that they could proceed with the organization of governments, which would receive executive recognition when 10 per cent of the voters of 1860 had taken an oath of loyalty to the Union. By July, 1864, the occupied states of Louisiana and Arkansas had complied, and their representatives were seeking admission to Congress. To block the President's plan the Radicals pushed through Congress the Wade-Davis bill which provided, among other things, that a majority of prewar voters must take the oath. When at the end of the session the President gave the bill a

---

33 Centreville *Indiana True Republican*, October 27, 1864; Harbison, "Indiana Republicans and the Re-election of Lincoln," in *Indiana Magazine of History*, 34:61.

34 Julian's Journal, December 7, 1864, quoted in Engstrom, George Washington Julian, 38-39; James D. Richardson (ed.), *A Compilation of the Messages and Papers of the Presidents, 1789-1897* (10 vols., Washington, D. C., 1896-99), 6:252.

"pocket veto," the Radicals were furious. They retaliated with the "Wade-Davis Manifesto," an excoriating rebuke of the President for his Reconstruction policy and for his refusal to sign the Wade-Davis bill. Except for the approaching presidential election the battle between Lincoln and the Radicals would probably have been fought out to a finish at that time. Instead, it was postponed to the last few months of the war and of Lincoln's life.

Meanwhile, Lincoln proceeded with his plan, and when Congress convened in December four states were preparing to return to the Union under its provisions. No longer satisfied with their own Wade-Davis bill, the Radicals were now determined on a complete regeneration of the South. The first step was to prevent the new southern Congressmen from being seated, which they succeeded in doing.

It was in the atmosphere of renewed hostility between the President and the Radicals that Julian made his last speech against the Lincoln administration. "Radicalism," he asserted, "has saved our nation from the political damnation and ruin to which Conservatism would certainly have consigned it." Only through a new and radical policy could the administration "vindicate its wisdom, command the respect and gratitude of the people, and save it[self] from humiliation and disgrace." In returning Lincoln to the Presidency, Julian contended, the people had

. . . voted for liberating and arming the slaves of the South to crush out a slaveholders' rebellion. They voted that the Republic shall live, and that whatever is necessary to save its life shall be done. They voted that slavery shall be eternally doomed, and future rebellions thus made impossible. They voted, not that Abraham Lincoln can save the country, but that *they* can save it, with him as their servant.

He ended with a tribute to the abolitionists who had overcome enormous opposition in their long and arduous fight for human freedom. When the nation was threatened with a ". . . lapse from the grand ideas of our revolutionary era, [the abolitionists] began to 'cry aloud and spare not,' and they never ceased or slackened their labors."[35]

As 1864 ended Julian went again with the Committee on the Conduct of the War to investigate the military fiascoes at Petersburg, Virginia, and Fort Fisher, North Carolina. But before the end of January he had returned to the national capital.

January 31, 1865, was certainly one of the most gratifying and thrilling days of Julian's Congressional career. On that day the House passed the Thirteenth Amendment to the Constitution. The abolition of slavery was for Julian the culmination of a twenty-year crusade. In his diary he described it as the "greatest event of the century"; the scenes in the House "beggared description. . . . Some embraced one another, others wept like children." Julian thanked God that his name would be recorded in a place where it would be honored "as those of the signers of the Declaration of Independence."[36] Later he wrote that he felt as if he "had been born into a new life, and that the world was overflowing with beauty and joy. . . ."[37] Soon afterward the first Negro ever to do so preached a sermon in the House of Representatives, and the first Negro was admitted to practice at the bar of the Supreme Court. Julian wrote, "The world *does* move."[38]

[35] "George W. Julian's Journal—The Assassination of Lincoln," in *Indiana Magazine of History*, 11 (1915):328; *Congressional Globe*, 38 Congress, 2 session, 654; Julian, *Speeches on Political Questions*, 229-44.

[36] "George W. Julian's Journal," in *Indiana Magazine of History*, 11:327.

[37] Julian, *Political Recollections*, 249-52.

[38] "George W. Julian's Journal," in *Indiana Magazine of History*, 11:328.

VII

With the Negro now virtually assured of his freedom under the Constitution, Julian could return again to that other crusade which he had postponed but never abandoned—the land reform movement. Perhaps for the first time the legislation he now sponsored had no direct connection with slavery. Even before the end of the war Julian was moving, as a reformer, in a different direction. Relevant to it were some of his concepts on monetary questions.

The bill which Julian reported from the Public Lands Committee early in February, 1865, prescribed a policy for public lands containing precious metals. His purpose was to apply the principle of individual ownership to these lands in place of the existing policy of leasing. The lands were to be sold in forty-acre plots with a minimum price based on location and mineral value. Each purchaser was to take an oath of loyalty to the United States; no foreigners were eligible except those who expressed their intention of becoming United States citizens. The gold and silver extracted was to be coined in United States mints located in districts where the metal was mined. Julian argued that his bill would bring more revenue into Federal government coffers than the old leasing system, that it would enhance the value of the lands because owners would improve them where leasers would not, that it would be more difficult for owners than for lessees to escape taxation. It would also check the nomadic tendencies of the miners and thus protect the institution of the family, which Julian regarded as being the very "foundation of the State, the peculiar institution of God." To those who feared the growth of monopolies under his plan Julian explained that he was opposed to monopoly in principle; hence he opposed government monopoly as well as private monopoly. Moreover, he feared the development in the United States of a feudalistic land system similar to that in the European countries.[39]

In preparing the bill and the accompanying speech Julian consulted with Hugh McCulloch, Comptroller of the Currency and soon to be Secretary of the Treasury. Horace Greeley and John Wilson, former Commissioner of the Land Office, whom Julian considered the best expert on land matters in the country, also helped him. Coin, said Julian, was the only safe medium of exchange, a concept accepted throughout the civilized world and beyond dispute. Julian now deplored the policy of the government in not adopting, in 1862, a vigorous taxing program instead of issuing paper money. The solution to the nation's monetary ills, he argued, was a greater quantity of precious metals, and his bill would stimulate increased production. He strongly implied—and quoted the Secretary of the Interior to sustain his argument— that if his bill had been in operation in 1862, the production of gold could have been increased fourfold.[40]

While much of Julian's program for dealing with mineral lands was predicated on his old ideas about individual landowners, there were other possible reasons for his sudden interest in monetary affairs: he had become an investor in government securities, and one of his chief advisers was Hugh McCulloch. Just a month before the mineral lands speech Julian had invested, "on

[39] *Congressional Globe,* 38 Congress, 2 session, 684-87; Julian, *Speeches on Political Questions,* 245-46, 255-59; Julian, *Political Recollections,* 281-92.

[40] "George W. Julian's Journal," in *Indiana Magazine of History,* 11:325-26; Julian, *Speeches on Political Questions,* 246-47; Hugh McCulloch, *Men and Measures of Half a Century* (New York, 1888), 163-209, 243-57.

the advice of financial friends," $1,800 in seven-thirty bonds, an investment that brought his total holdings in stocks and bonds to $6,000. Although this was no fabulous sum, he looked forward to saving nearly all his salary for the next two years.[41] From that time on, especially after he left Congress, Julian became more and more critical of "inflationary" monetary policy.

Julian's bill did not pass the Thirty-eighth Congress. But the following year a mineral land bill was adopted; its provision that local custom was to prevail in the establishment of claims and that litigation was to be carried on in the local instead of Federal courts virtually destroyed any control that the Federal government might have exerted.[42] Thus even the limited role of the government in surveying lands and in establishing claims to them was out of step with the "Gilded Age's" concept of *laissez faire*.

VIII

Julian did not remain in Washington for the whole of the short session. Late in February he was called away by the illness of Edward Channing, his oldest son. The boy died, at the age of nineteen, soon after Julian reached him in Iowa, where he was visiting his grandmother. He accompanied Edward's body back to Centreville for the burial.[43]

Late in March Julian returned to Washington to find the city deserted by government officials but office seekers much in evidence. Within a fortnight he was off to

---

[41] "George W. Julian's Journal," in *Indiana Magazine of History*, 11:325.

[42] Julian, *Political Recollections*, 281-88; Robbins, *Our Landed Heritage*, 221-22.

[43] "George W. Julian's Journal," in *Indiana Magazine of History*, 11:329; Centreville *Indiana True Republican*, March 16, 1865.

New York to attend a Unitarian meeting. En route news came of the fall of Richmond. There was great gaiety on the train and a grand celebration upon arrival in New York. Following the meeting Julian went to the home of the Frémonts. The General had retired, but Julian had a visit with Mrs. Frémont, who denounced the "pretended radical and anti-Lincoln men" who had deserted her husband after the Cleveland convention. "Jessie rages at all sorts of people," Julian recorded, "especially at Greeley, Beecher, and Garrison."[44]

On April 6, Julian returned to Washington, but four days later he was off on another journey, this time to the South. The trip was a project of the War Committeemen who planned to go down the Chesapeake Bay to Fortress Monroe and Richmond; later they were to go on to Fort Fisher and then to Charleston. When they reached Richmond, they heard news that changed their minds about going on farther: Lincoln had negotiated an agreement with certain Virginians whereby he was to give recognition to the state's existing government in return for Virginia's abandonment of the rebellion.[45] The Committeemen took the President's action as a declaration of war upon the Radicals, and spurred on by Wade and Chandler they returned to Washington. Julian would have preferred to go on to Charleston, but later he agreed that the decision to return was a wise one.

During the one day spent in the Confederate capital the Committee made a thorough excursion of the city. They visited Jeff Davis' quarters, then occupied by Gen. Godfrey Weitzel, the Union commander. Next they

---

44 "George W. Julian's Journal," in *Indiana Magazine of History,* 11:329-30; Centreville *Indiana True Republican,* April 6, 13, 20, 1865.

45 Williams, *Lincoln and the Radicals,* 370; Lincoln to General Weitzel, April 6, 1865, Benjamin F. Wade Papers, Library of Congress.

visited the Capitol, which Julian thought did not compare with the modern state capitols in the North. He
was interested in the Capitol library, but he found the
books there mostly English and French and thought they
"showed the monarchial tastes of the 'first families.'"
They found Libby Prison occupied by rebel soldiers
who, Julian thought, were the "most filthy and im-
bruted looking wretches" he had ever seen.

Julian noticed in the Richmond *Whig* an invitation
by General Weitzel asking Confederate leaders to attend
a conference with him. Indignantly he wrote that it
was a "dastardly and infamous proposition to treat with
leading rebels instead of hanging them." The sight of
southern "officers, in full uniform, defiantly strutting the
streets" was equally exasperating. His description of
General Weitzel indicated that he had not forgotten his
study of phrenology years earlier. "General Weitzel looks
the soldier all over," he wrote. "His head is a German
one, not intelligent in its frontal appearance, but fully
developed in the 'driving powers.'"[46]

The Committee returned to Washington on April 14.
That night President Lincoln was assassinated. The
next afternoon Julian spent in caucus with a group of
Radicals, including Wade, Chandler, and Covode of the
Committee on the Conduct of the War. Among the plans
they discussed was one for a new and more radical
Cabinet that they hoped to urge upon President Andrew
Johnson. Julian liked the radicalism of these men and
shared their feelings that Lincoln's death was a godsend
to their cause. In his diary he wrote: "The dastardly attack upon Lincoln and Seward, the great leaders in the
policy of mercy, puts to flight utterly every vestige of

[46] "George W. Julian's Journal," in *Indiana Magazine of History,*
11:331-33; Centreville *Indiana True Republican,* April 27, 1865.

humanitarian weakness, and makes it seem that justice shall be done and the righteous ends of the war made sure. The government could not have survived the policy upon which it had entered."[47]

Two days after Lincoln's assassination the War Committee met with President Johnson. Wade expressed to the President the Committee's confidence in him: "Johnson, we have faith in you. By the Gods, there will be no trouble now in running the government." Johnson replied, "We must make treason *infamous,* and punish and impoverish the traitors." Julian also counted on Johnson, for whatever the former Democrat Johnson might think of the Republican party, he regarded the war as a people's war and would "demand justice against the rebel conspirators."[48]

Not long after Lincoln's death the Committee members turned to another investigation, the last one of importance they would make. It concerned the activities of Gen. William T. Sherman, whose army had dealt the last blow to the Confederacy. From a conversation with Lincoln a month earlier Sherman had got the impression that he had been given the authority to deal with Gen. Joseph E. Johnston in any way that would

[47] "George W. Julian's Journal," in *Indiana Magazine of History,* 11:334-35; Clarke, *Julian,* 272-74. Despite the evident satisfaction Julian took in being a member of the Committee on the Conduct of the War, he was not always comfortable in the company of men such as Wade and Chandler, whose coarseness and profanity he found "intolerably disgusting." He also had been repelled by Zachary Taylor's bad grammar, as he was now by President Johnson's. He found Grant's drinking offensive. Perhaps Julian should not be classified as a patrician, but he appears to have considered himself one. Such men, however radical they may have been ideologically, were not always in tune with the ethos of post-Civil War America.

[48] "George W. Julian's Journal," in *Indiana Magazine of History,* 11:335-36; Centreville *Indiana True Republican,* April 27, 1865.

hasten the end of the war. On April 18, Sherman's opportunity came to use his newly won powers, for on that
day General Johnston offered to surrender all remaining
southern armies in return for a lenient peace. Sherman
agreed and promised a general amnesty and executive
recognition of the state governments then in existence in
the South. When news of this agreement reached Washington it caused a furor. Instead of the instantaneous approval that Sherman expected, he received a personal
visit from General Grant who brought him instructions
to revoke his order. This was the work of the Radicals
through their spokesman in the Cabinet, Edwin M. Stanton. Not content with the mere revocation of the order,
the Radicals insisted that the Committee on the Conduct
of the War investigate Sherman's negotiation of the
"treaty."

In accounts to his newspaper Julian expressed himself
freely about Sherman: The General's "surrender is . . .
so perfectly monstrous that everybody is bewildered in
the attempt to find an adequate explanation." Sherman's insanity was the kind "so often born of ambition,
which . . . made fools of the wisest . . . statesmen."
Because he had lived in Louisiana, Julian argued, Sherman believed in slavery; he was ambitious to be President; his wife, a Catholic, had abetted his "natural leaning toward aristocracy" and had given him "hierarchal
ideas." But before the end of the investigation Julian
eased up on Sherman and wrote to the *True Republican*
admitting that the General "had a substantial defence in
the authority and instructions of President Lincoln."[49]

As Julian wound up his work with the Committee, he
concluded that the Lincoln administration had settled
scarcely any of the great questions of the war. He

[49] Centreville *Indiana True Republican*, May 4, 11, 18, 1865.

thought it imperative to confiscate southern lands and to adopt a policy to help the "swarms of helpless contrabands turned adrift" by the war. Johnson would have the "opportunity and the honor of sharing in the adjustment" of these problems. Julian was disappointed that treason trials had not been started—for this he blamed Attorney General James Speed, of Kentucky. Yet he did not despair altogether of the Johnson administration. Of one thing Julian seemed certain: "Radicalism will not be expelled from the Cabinet, but will rule the Administration."[50]

IX

On May 29, 1865, President Johnson issued a proclamation pardoning all Southerners except those who had held Confederate offices and those whose taxable property was valued at more than $20,000. On the same day he appointed William W. Holden provisional governor of North Carolina and announced a plan of reconstruction for that state which was subsequently to be applied to other seceded states. In effect, it was a reassertion of Lincoln's lenient policy. The provisional governors were to supervise the re-establishment of loyal state governments. Men who had taken an amnesty oath were to serve as delegates to state conventions convened for the purpose of establishing new governments. When this was done and new officials were elected, the provisional governors were to retire from the scene and the states were to resume their place in the Union. To the astonishment of the Radicals, there was nothing in the plan to suggest that Johnson intended to act on his pronouncement of a few weeks earlier that treason was odius and traitors must be punished. The plan did not even have a provision

[50] *Ibid.*, May 11, 18, 25, 1865.

for the confiscation of southern property (except slaves), and it said nothing about Negro suffrage, which the President had decided to leave to the states. Nor had Johnson consulted with Congress in devising his plan. In fact, he hoped to take advantage of the fact that Congress was not in session and to have the seceded states back in the Union when Congress convened the following December.[51]

The announcement of the President's plan ended the courtship between him and the Radicals almost before it had begun; each side had grievously miscalculated in its assessment of the other, and a contest was taking shape between them, the first skirmishes of which occurred during the summer and autumn of 1865. One of these was in Indiana in the form of a prolonged debate between Morton and Julian over Reconstruction, with particular emphasis on the question of Negro suffrage.

In regard to the political status of the seceded states, Morton's view was that because the crime of treason was an individual one, the Federal government had no legal power to punish the people of a state collectively.[52] It was a potent argument, but one which the Radicals could answer with some logic. They argued that the South ought to be treated as a conquered nation, whose states could be remanded to the condition of territories. After all, the South had established a national Confederate government and had sought recognition as a nation by foreign powers. Both sides had handled prisoners of war as belligerent nations, and the North had blockaded the South as one nation blockades another.

51 Richardson (ed.), *Messages and Papers of the Presidents*, 6:310-14; J. G. Randall and David Donald, *The Civil War and Reconstruction* (Boston, 1961), 559-62.

52 "George W. Julian's Journal," in *Indiana Magazine of History*, 11:337; Julian, *Political Recollections*, 262.

But the Radicals did not leave the argument there. They went on to say that Southerners had engaged in a treasonable uprising against the United States and that individual men ought to be tried for treason. To maintain both positions and still be consistent was difficult. Yet this is what many Radicals, including Julian, tried to do.

Hoosiers were concerned about Reconstruction in general and about Negro suffrage in particular; and thus the stage was set for the revival of the Morton-Julian feud. Some thought that the Negro, having demonstrated his fitness by his contribution to the war effort, should be granted the franchise immediately. Others favored granting it because of their fear of a resurgence of southern political power. Still others, including some of Morton's followers, favored a constitutional amendment which would leave the question up to the states.[53] Julian, too, had hoped that, after the defeat of the South and the emancipation of the slaves through constitutional amendment, the southern states would acquiesce in Negro suffrage without interference from the Federal government.

The announcement of Johnson's plan and the actions of southern states under it convinced Julian that the Federal government must now insure the vote for the Negro as a part of its general plan of Reconstruction. He entered the Hoosier debate in August, 1865, with speeches among his own constituents, whom he found not to be of one mind on the subject. The crusading spirit in him was aroused, and he carried on with a determination and élan which is reflected in his description of the campaign in his *Political Recollections:*

In the beginning of the canvass I . . . found a considerable portion of my old anti-slavery friends unprepared to follow

[53] Indianapolis *Daily Journal,* July 7, 10, 1865.

me; but feeling perfectly sure I was right, and that I could revolutionize the general opinion, I entered upon the work, and prosecuted it with all my might for nearly four months. My task was an arduous one, but I found the people steadily yielding up their prejudices, and ready to lay hold of the truth when fairly and dispassionately presented, while the soldiers were among the first to accept my teachings.[54]

Soon Julian was advocating, in addition to Negro suffrage, the punishment of rebels and the confiscation of their lands.[55]

Before a month had passed Morton invaded Julian territory with a powerful speech delivered at Richmond. He asserted that the people had put themselves on record as favoring the Lincoln-Johnson plan of Reconstruction by their re-election of Lincoln in 1864. Again he stated his thesis that a state could not secede from the Union, and thus he rejected the conquered-nation concept of the Radicals. Turning to Negro suffrage, he pointed out that the Radicals had not provided for it in their own Wade-Davis bill; and of the Julian men he asked the question: How could anybody from Indiana, a state whose limitations on the Negro were well known, ask Congress for a bill assuring Negro suffrage in the South? Morton's solution was to give the Negro a few years to become prepared for the franchise through the acquisition of property and the process of education. He also favored a constitutional amendment to base the representation in the House of Representatives on the number of voters in the states instead of on the total population.[56]

54 Julian, *Political Recollections,* 264-65; Clarke, *Julian,* 274-91.
55 Centreville *Indiana True Republican,* September 7, 1865.
56 Indianapolis *Daily Journal,* October 2, 1865; Foulke, *Morton,* 1:446-52.

There was nothing unreasonable or ardently conservative about Morton's views concerning the Negro in Reconstruction. The chief weakness of his approach lay in the absence of any method of preparing the Negro to take his place as a citizen. Commenting on his speech, the *True Republican* asked some penetrating questions: How was it possible for the freedman to acquire property and education and to learn about the exercise of political power "if in the absolute power of [his] white oppressors? . . . To *prepare* him by committing him to the tender mercies of his old masters, who hate him . . . more bitterly than ever before, is as unnatural and as cruel as committing the lamb to the tender mercies of the wolf."[57]

Yet within a year Morton was performing one of his accustomed somersaults by becoming a strong advocate of immediate Negro suffrage and a leader in the Radical ranks. Even so, he had posed at least one question for Julian to grapple with, one that he eventually had to answer: Why did Julian recommend Negro suffrage in the South and not in Indiana? His answer suggests that Julian's reforming impulse stemmed at least as much from his desire for punitive measures against the South as from humanitarianism toward individual Negroes. His reply to Morton was simply that Indiana had not been one of the states in rebellion.[58]

However, by the end of October Julian had become enough of a threat to the Morton forces to call forth the kind of attack which the Governor reserved for those recalcitrants who insisted on resisting his power in Indiana. Julian's speech in Lafayette was the final provocation. The Indianapolis *Journal* stated that while Julian

[57] Centreville *Indiana True Republican*, October 5, 1865.
[58] Julian, *Speeches on Political Questions*, 281-82.

remained in his own district it felt no disposition to fight him, but now with the extension of his mendacious campaign against Morton throughout the state the time had come to act. In spite of vigorous and repeated denials from people who heard the Lafayette speech that Julian had said anything personal against Morton, the campaign against the "Burnt District" Congressman continued.[59]

Julian climaxed his campaign with his Indianapolis speech on November 17. The legislature was in session at the time and tendered to him the use of its hall by the adoption of a resolution requesting that he be very explicit in expressing his views on the Johnson policy. Julian opened the speech with a denial that he had made a personal attack on either Morton or Johnson. He then stated that he was not sure exactly what the President's policy was, but he would be very specific on what he regarded as the important issues facing the country. He reiterated his stand for Negro suffrage in the South, for the confiscation of southern lands, and for the execution of Jeff Davis, Robert E. Lee, and other southern leaders.[60]

Later Julian claimed that Republican leaders had sought a reconciliation between him and Morton at this time. Writing of the matter in his *Political Recollections,* he said, "If I had been willing to subordinate my political convictions and sense of duty to his ambitions, peace could at once have been restored; but . . . this was impossible."[61] The Julian-Morton rivalry was, indeed, a contest between two irreconcilables, both capable of

59 Indianapolis *Daily Journal,* November 3, 8, 10, 1865; Centreville *Indiana True Republican,* November 9, 16, 1865.

60 Julian, *Speeches on Political Questions.* 262-90.

61 Julian, *Political Recollections,* 271.

extraordinary hatred, both politically ambitious, both enthralled by the plaudits of followers; but Julian was animated by the vision of himself as a crusader for the right, while Morton saw himself as the type of practical political leader indispensable to the proper functioning of the American political system.

After the Indianapolis speech, the harshness of the attack on Julian by the Morton forces increased. The Indianapolis *Journal* did not carry the speech, but printed lengthy descriptions of Julian as a disorganizer, a misanthrope, a creature with "the temper of a hedgehog, the adhesiveness of a barnacle, the vanity of a peacock, the vindictiveness of a Corsican, the hypocracy of Aminadab Sleek and the duplicity of the devil." Julian, in a rejoinder, claimed that he "rather enjoyed these paroxysms of malignity. . . ."[62] The Democratic Indianapolis *Herald* judged the contest one between two "ineffably mean" men whose programs did not differ very much, but with Julian easily superior to Morton in talents and in his openness and frankness. The *Herald* also believed that in spite of Morton's power, Julian would be the ultimate victor: ". . . while there is no difference . . . between MORTON and JULIAN except in the form of words, still they apparently place themselves in the attitude toward each other of the Girondins and the Jacobins in the French revolution." Said the *Herald*, ". . . the JULIAN Jacobins will first apply the guillotine to the political necks of the Morton . . . Girondins."[63]

Hoosiers had not yet witnessed the end of the Morton-Julian contest of 1865. The finale occurred on November 27, when Sol Meredith attacked Julian in the Richmond

62 Indianapolis *Daily Journal*, November 18, 19, 22, 25, 1865; Julian, *Political Recollections*, 268; Clarke, *Julian*, 291-92.
63 Indianapolis *Daily Herald*, November 20, 1865.

railway station. Meredith apparently held Julian responsible for his dismissal from his command in Paducah, Kentucky, the preceding spring. He also blamed him for the publication of certain newspaper accounts of his relief from command on the basis of incompetency. From the confused reports of the attack a few verifiable facts emerge. Meredith knocked Julian down and whipped him with a cowhide whip. Julian's injuries were not so serious as they at first appeared. Meredith was dragged into court on charges of assault and battery, but the case was dropped without establishing his innocence or guilt.[64] Most significant, perhaps, was the fact that the Meredith-Julian affair mirrored some of the feelings involved in the irrepressible conflict between the Morton and the Julian factions in Indiana.

[64] Indianapolis *Daily Gazette*, November 29, December 4, 5, 1865; Richmond *Palladium*, March 23, 30, December 7, 1865; Centreville *Indiana True Republican*, May 11, November 23, December 14, 1865; Indianapolis *Daily Journal*, November 29, 1865; Clarke, *Julian*, 292-95; Sol Meredith, *Defense against False Charges and Infamous Slanders of George W. Julian* (Indianapolis, 1866).

Julian recalled Meredith's attack on him at the time of the latter's death in 1875: "As to his brutal and cowardly attack on me at Richmond ten years ago it is due to truth to say that it was largely inspired by Morton, who counseled it a few days before in a crowd of Meredith's friends. This leaked out afterwards. . . . If Meredith had killed me he [Morton] would have been morally & legally guilty as an accessory to murder." Julian's Journal, November 1, 1875, Indiana Division, Indiana State Library.

VORTEX OF RADICAL
RECONSTRUCTION

⬦⬦⬦⬦⬦⬦⬦⬦⬦⬦⬦⬦

As the year 1865 drew to a close, hopes for a reunited Republican party faded and before two months of the new year had passed several events deepened the cleavage. On February 19, 1866, President Johnson vetoed the Radical-sponsored bill to continue the Freedmen's Bureau; and on Washington's birthday he followed up with an attack on the Radicals in his best frontier political style. He accused Radicals, by name, of plotting to assassinate him and of seeking the destruction of traditional American government. Late in March he vetoed Senator Lyman Trumbull's Civil Rights bill. The approaching Congressional election, it was quite clear, was going to be a contest between Johnson and the Radicals for control of the government. Politicians spurned any discussion of the important issues of Reconstruction awaiting solution and stumped the country in a campaign filled with claptrap and invective.

As the contest between Johnson and the Radicals became more intense, the President welcomed the support of Democrats and thereby made himself vulnerable to the Radical's denunciation of him as a traitor. "Waving the bloody shirt" was a potent political weapon in 1866, and it remained so for many years.

The Radicals, particularly, resorted to every conceivable strategy in order to assure victory. The newly organized Grand Army of the Republic brought its power into the Radical camp. When the President personally entered the campaign, he was greeted by audiences sprinkled with hecklers who goaded him into undignified conduct. The presence of General Grant on the President's "swing around the circle" also proved to be a great liability. Time and again the silent military commander was made the hero of the occasion at the expense of the humiliated chief executive.

In Indiana Julian found himself in a somewhat anomalous political situation. Governor Morton had come over to the side of the Radicals, greatly strengthening them in the Hoosier state, but the old Morton faction in the "Burnt District" still opposed Julian's nomination. Julian managed, however, to retain control of the local party machinery in his district and thus was assured the use of the popular primary again. After a campaign of demagoguery and "waving the bloody shirt," quite in tune with the time, he again received the nomination. Although he remained in Washington until after the primary, Julian's friends and his political organ did yeoman service on his behalf. Said the *True Republican* ". . . every Copperhead in the land would rejoice in the defeat of Mr. Julian. . . . There is not a traitor in the South [who] would not thrill with a joy only second to that which he experienced at the veto of the Freedmen's Bureau Bill, should this district fail to return Mr. Julian to Congress." According to that organ, the only significant issue of the campaign was whether the rebels would regain control of the southern state governments.[1]

1 Richmond *Palladium*, February 15, 1866; Richmond *Indiana True Republican*, March 29, 1866.

In spite of rumors that the anti-Julian faction in the Republican party would support his Democratic opponent in the October election, Julian won by a majority of nearly two thousand votes. But fear of defeat through disunity had its effect on the Republican campaign tactics in the "Burnt District." The Wayne County party convention even refused to have a plank in its platform for the repeal of the thirteenth section of the Indiana constitution, with its limitations on the rights of Negroes. The *True Republican* offered an explanation: "Men may differ from each other upon all these questions and still be good Union men. And we cannot afford to drive away a single voter from our ranks because he opposes this or that measure. . . ."[2]

The Indianapolis *Daily Journal* also deprecated the "animated" and "acrimonious" canvass in the fifth district: "We have no strength to spare, and it will be a calamity if our majority in that district is frittered away by controversies over individual grievances."[3]

Following the October election Hoosier Republicans turned their attention to the selection of a United States Senator to replace the retiring Henry S. Lane. Morton was the logical candidate. As war governor he had gained notoriety and had built up a powerful political machine. It was becoming customary for men who had been elected governor or lieutenant governor to step into Senate vacancies. The Indianapolis *Journal*, assuming that Morton was in, expressed reluctance even to discuss the senatorial question. This aloof attitude brought a sharp blast of criticism from several Hoosier newspapers. The Madison *Courier*, long an anti-Morton organ in southern Indiana, came out openly for Julian. The Richmond

2 Richmond *Indiana True Republican*, February 15, April 19, 1866.
3 Indianapolis *Journal*, April 6, 1866.

Telegram, which had never been a Julian advocate, scolded the Mortonites for their assumption that Oliver had an automatic claim to the senatorship. Democrats, always ready to aggravate Republican factionalism, touted Julian as the real Republican leader in Indiana. As early as May, 1866, the Indianapolis *Herald* had predicted that if the Morton faction succeeded in defeating Julian in the fifth district, he was certain to be a strong contender in the Senate race.[4]

As the January date for the senatorial election approached, Morton's opponents raised another objection to his election. They said that he was not eligible for the senatorship under the Indiana constitution, which stated that "neither the Governor nor the Lieutenant Governor [was] eligible to *any other office* during the term for which he shall have been elected." But no mere constitutional obstacle was to deny him the senatorship; Morton, who was experienced in taking such hurdles, overpowered the opposition and went on to the United States Senate.[5]

Although Julian was to win one more election to Congress, in 1868, his political strength in his district declined after 1866. This was in part due to the redistricting of the state by the General Assembly in 1867. Julian's district, which again became the fourth, was

4 Indianapolis *Gazette*, October 26, 1866; Indianapolis *Herald*, May 19, 26, 1866; Richmond *Palladium*, November 22, 1866; Richmond *Indiana True Republican*, November 8, 15, December 20, 1866.

5 Richmond *Indiana True Republican*, December 27, 1866, January 3, 10, 1867; Indianapolis *Journal*, December 18, 1866; New York *Tribune*, January 11, 12, 1867. In running for governor in 1864 Morton had violated the spirit, if not the letter, of another constitutional provision, designed to prevent a governor from having more than one consecutive term. Morton evaded the provision on the technicality that he had not been elected governor, but lieutenant governor, in 1860. Nevertheless, he had served a full term as governor.

gerrymandered in such a way that three loyal Julian counties were replaced by four less- friendly ones. Julian blamed Morton and his satellites. It was an outright attempt, he cried, to "legislate your Representative out of Congress, all other expedients having signally failed."[6]

The pattern of his last successful candidacy, in 1868, was different from those of previous years. Formerly the significant contest had been for the nomination, after which his election was almost a certainty. This time the nomination came fairly easily by a Republican convention, but the election was close and bitterly contested. As early as January, 1868, the opposition newspapers in the district began their biennial chant that the Republicans would nominate a new man in April.[7] In the weeks that followed, some of Julian's friends became alarmed and pleaded with him to come home to enter the campaign personally. In the press Julian made an ardent appeal for Republicans to stand by him. To leave Washington at that time of crisis, he said, would be irresponsible. From the capital he appealed to all "fair-minded Republicans" not to allow him to be "stricken down while endeavoring faithfully to serve them."[8] In his private correspondence he showed his awareness of the

6 Indianapolis *Journal*, May 1, 1868; New York *Times*, May 10, 1868; Richmond *Indiana True Republican*, February 28, March 7, 1867, May 7, 1868; Julian, *Political Recollections*, 303; Richmond *Indiana Radical*, December 24, 1868. On July 2, 1868, the name of the *Indiana True Republican* was changed to the *Indiana Radical*. An act of February 20, 1867, redistricted the state, placing the counties of Shelby, Rush, Franklin, Union, Fayette, Wayne, and Hancock in the fourth district. *Laws of Indiana*, 1867, p. 108.

7 Indianapolis *Journal*, January 15, 1868; Richmond *Palladium*, January 2, 1868.

8 Julian to Laura Julian, March 27, 1868, and Julian to his constituents, January, 1868, Julian Papers; Indianapolis *Journal*, April 4, 1868; Richmond *Indiana True Republican*, April 2, 1868.

political advantage of remaining away from Indiana: "I think remaining at my post will aid me as much as returning home & laboring there personally." Presumably one of the duties that kept him in Washington was his recent appointment to the committee to prepare the articles of impeachment for the trial of the President. Of the appointment Julian wrote to Laura: "I am of course pleased with this & it will help me at home."[9]

There were other reasons, too, for Julian's ebbing political strength. With each re-election his enemies could more effectively accuse him of trying to perpetuate himself in office. His appeals that he not be sacrificed, his assertion that only he could truly serve the "Burnt District," gave some substance to the accusation that he had come to regard himself as an indispensable man. Moreover, his health had begun to break during the war years, and by 1868 it was apparent to all that he was a sick man. He was physically unable to complete some of his speeches in the campaign that year; other engagements he was unable to fulfill at all.[10]

Julian's election over his Democratic opponent, John Reid, in 1868 was made possible only by the Board of Canvassers of Wayne County in disallowing the vote of one Richmond precinct. Reid took the case to the House of Representatives where the decision went ultimately in favor of Julian. There were glaring inconsistencies in the election in Richmond's south poll, and Julian brought forth ample evidence to show that the ballot

9 Julian to Laura Julian, February 24, 25, March 23, 24, 1868, Julian Papers; Richmond *Palladium*, February 13, 1868.

10 Indianapolis *Journal*, August 31, 1868; Richmond *Indiana Radical*, August 27, 1868. Ague was a common disease in the nineteenth century, and its symptoms suggest that it was probably malaria. Its recurring pattern suggests that this is the malady from which Julian suffered.

box had been tampered with, that it had been moved from the polling place to another precinct, and that it had been left unguarded several times after the voting began and before the final count.[11]

II

Julian's last two terms in Congress spanned the years of the most complete dominance of the Radical wing of the Republican party over the conservatives. The victory of 1866 made the Radicals' power incontrovertible. Indeed, in the decade following the Civil War, Radicalism and Republicanism became virtually indistinguishable. True, the Radicals did not succeed in the accomplishment of all their goals. They did not remake the South in the image of the North; they did not plant the Republican party there on any permanent basis; they did not even secure permanently the freedmen's rights and privileges as citizens. But the Radical Republicans increased the power of the Republican party and helped it to dominate the American political scene for the better part of the next seventy years. Julian was a witness to, and a participant in, the great Radical triumph.

What were the elements of the Radicals' triumph over Andrew Johnson and over the Democracy? Following the election of 1866, they proceeded to overthrow the President's program of Reconstruction and to replace it with one of their own. The southern states did not return to the Union under anything remotely approaching the lenient Lincoln-Johnson plan. Instead, the Radicals divided the South into five military districts with a major general in command of each. They deprived

11 Richmond *Indiana Radical,* October 15, 22, December 3, 1868; New York *Times,* October 16, 1868; New York *Tribune,* October 16, 24, 1868; John S. Reed [Reid] vs. George W. Julian, *House Reports,* 41 Congress, 2 session, No. 116 (Papers in Contested Election).

the Confederate leaders of all control of the southern state governments, and only after "loyal" men were in charge of those governments were the southern states allowed to return to the Union.

Two amendments were added to the Constitution during the Radical regime: one to establish the fact of citizenship of the freedmen and the other to insure the franchise to male Negro citizens of voting age.

Under Radical control the Republican party also made secure its wartime economic program. The protective tariff, advocated during the war as a necessary revenue measure, was maintained, and the party successfully defied those who made increasing demands for easier currency and credit. This trend in monetary policy had its culmination at the turn of the century in the legal establishment of the gold standard.

In the impeachment of President Johnson in 1868 the Radicals, quite possibly, came near to overturning the American system of checks and balances in the Federal government and replacing it with what might have developed into a parliamentary system similar to that of Great Britain. While the Radicals fought the President they cultivated the nation's greatest military hero. Failing through impeachment to remove Johnson from the Presidency, they had Grant groomed and ready to be their standard-bearer in 1868. Thus, through the time-honored electoral processes they extended their dominance from the legislative branch of the government to the executive branch as well.

Where did Julian fit into the vortex of Radical reconstruction? In what ways did he try to shape policies, and how successful was he? What was the effect of it all on him?

Two significant forerunners of the Fifteenth Amendment were the bills that passed Congress for Negro

suffrage in the District of Columbia and in the territories of the United States. Julian was probably their
strongest and most persistent advocate in the House of
Representatives. One of his first acts in the Thirty-ninth
Congress was to introduce, in December, 1865, a bill for
Negro suffrage in the national capital. When it came up
for consideration a month later, Julian was ready with
an effective speech in its favor. He demanded the ballot
for the Negro in the District "on the broad ground of
absolute [natural] right." Eloquently he answered those
who opposed Negro suffrage because the Negro lacked
education. The gist of Julian's argument was that there
was too much emphasis on mechanical qualifications
such as education and too little emphasis on moral
qualifications. Quoting John Stuart Mill, he said, "It is
not necessary that the many should, in themselves, be
perfectly wise; it is sufficient if they be duly sensible of
the value of superior wisdom." Julian did not oppose
all limitations on voting, but he held that the ubiquitous
demand for "education" was too nebulous. "If pen-
manship must be made the avenue to the ballot," he
said, "I fear several honorable gentlemen on this floor
will be disfranchised."[12]

The passage of the bill put Julian in a radiant mood
reminiscent of his reaction to the passage of the Thirteenth Amendment. To Laura he wrote, "Oh! how I
wish you were here so that we could go into each others
arms in one dear glorious embrace! My Child! I can't
tell you how happy I am."[13]

---

[12] Julian to Laura Julian, February 17, 1866, Julian Papers; Indianapolis *Journal*, December 11, 1865; New York *Tribune*, December 12, 1865;
Congressional Globe, 39 Congress, 1 session, 255-59; Julian, *Speeches on
Political Questions*, 291-308; Clarke, *Julian*, 295-97.
[13] Julian to Laura Julian, January 18, 1866, Julian Papers.

Before the end of the session Julian had introduced and fought through to adoption a resolution calling on the Judiciary Committee to consider a bill for Negro suffrage in the territories and forbidding the admission of any state into the Union whose constitution did not give the Negro the vote.[14] In the following session the territorial suffrage bill passed, and under the Reconstruction acts southern states were also required to provide for Negro suffrage before being readmitted to the Union. These suffrage provisions were, in Julian's mind, significant steps in the direction of the "thorough" Reconstruction he envisioned for the South. Even so, he could not agree to the second section of the Fourteenth Amendment, which prescribed a proportionate decrease in the representation of any state denying the vote to any portion of the population. The natural right to the ballot should not be compromised by a constitutional provision which could be used to deprive the Negro of his vote. For a time the ratification of the Fourteenth Amendment by the southern states was proposed as a satisfactory *quid pro quo* for their readmission into the Union. As Julian saw it, only "rebel desperation" in rejecting this proposition had saved the Negro.[15]

Julian finally accepted the Fourteenth Amendment, as well as the Thirteenth and Fifteenth, as the final constitutional guarantees that could be obtained for the freedmen. With the adoption of the Reconstruction amendments his long crusade against slavery ended. But his career as a reformer was far from being finished.

Back in the 1840's, around the time of his adoption of abolitionism, Julian had become interested in woman's

14 *Congressional Globe*, 39 Congress, 1 session, 2429, 2509; Richmond *Indiana True Republican*, January 17, 1867.
15 Julian, *Political Recollections*, 304.

rights, but he had not been active in the movement. In his *Political Recollections* he explained his irresolution: for the sake of the Negro he had accepted Lincoln's philosophy of "one war at a time." But with the Negro question "fairly out of the way, [he] was prepared to enlist actively in the next grand movement in behalf of the sacredness and equality of human rights."[16] Before leaving Congress Julian proposed a constitutional amendment, modeled after the Fifteenth Amendment, for the establishment of woman suffrage. His Congressional colleagues disdainfully rejected this proposal. On this issue Julian was simply too far ahead of his time. He was hurt by the rebuff though the plaudits of his female admirers rang in his ears.

There were more practical and more immediate questions to be settled, such as the handling of the huge national debt left by the Civil War. In spite of the intricacies of such a question, its relation to the fundamental change that America was undergoing from an agrarian to an industrial nation, Julian and some others could take a stand on this question which they believed was in the direction of reform. They were convinced that those who differed were motivated simply by greed or self-interest. In 1865, the public debt stood at $2,758,000,000 held in a variety of government securities. Its management and the establishment of a monetary policy were among the most vexatious problems of the Reconstruction era. Foremost was the question of redemption of bonds— whether to redeem them in gold or in legal tender currency—and the related question of withdrawing the greenbacks from circulation. One of the first acts of Congress after the election of Grant was the passage of a resolution that government obligations be paid in coin.

16 *Ibid.*, 328.

"Sound money" versus "cheap money" was not, however, an issue between the Radical and Conservative wings of the Republican party. Some Radicals were for cheap money, some for sound money, some clung to the orthodox concept of an earlier era in advocating hard money. Two such ardent Radicals as Julian and Thaddeus Stevens could be far apart on monetary questions. Julian leaned toward the contraction, hard money school of Hugh McCulloch, whereas Stevens favored the redemption of bonds in greenbacks.

Julian was no expert in economic questions, and he seldom participated in the debates on bills and resolutions dealing with money. On one or two occasions, however, he made his views known. After 1868, his interest in monetary affairs steadily increased until, by the end of his Congressional career, they were of great concern to him. On January 21, 1869, he introduced a resolution instructing the Committee on Banking and Currency to inquire into the expediency of paying all existing and future government contracts in gold "on the basis of the relative value of gold and United States notes."[17] A few days later, while arguing for the sale of mineral lands, he advocated a speedy return to the specie redemption of greenbacks.[18] These two complementary propositions would appear to place Julian firmly on the "sound money" side of the question.

Julian's columns in the *True Republican* indicate some abstruseness in his thinking on matters of monetary policy. In trying to solve monetary problems he thought that men ought to look for guidance to the "instinct of the masses" rather than to "any fine theories of finance."[19] But the small farmers whose guardian and

17 New York *Times,* January 21, 1869.
18 Julian, *Speeches on Political Questions,* 415-31.
19 Richmond *Indiana True Republican,* July 9, 1868.

champion he considered himself to be were generally in opposition to sound money. It was this very group that supported the "Ohio Idea" of George H. Pendleton. Indeed, Julian could hardly have been thinking of the little man in the region from which he came, for in the Old Northwest sound money politicians were forced to compromise between their own beliefs and the demand for greenbacks from their constituents.[20]

On the related tariff question Julian's thinking was more consistent. From the beginning of his political life he had been an advocate of free trade. Nothing—not even the Civil War and Reconstruction—changed his ideas on this subject. After the war he was ready whenever the occasion rose to thwart the "lobby manufacturing interest" in its demands for still higher protective tariffs.[21]

In the spring of 1866 Julian spoke to a workingmen's meeting at the Washington Navy Yard. He received a friendly response, for only a few weeks earlier he had introduced a bill to fix eight hours as the maximum labor per day for all workers "employed by or under the authority of the Government of the United States." To the Navy Yard gathering Julian spoke of the eight-hour movement as a "natural, if not inevitable" development. The growing dignity of labor was another natural phenomenon in the progress toward an ideal human society. Julian's homestead policy, he told his audience, was

20 Politicians such as John Sherman of Ohio and Oliver P. Morton were fearful that a too rapid contraction of the currency might result in a business depression. Hence they opposed the policies of Secretary McCulloch and recommended a gradual reduction of the debt and the establishment of a future date for the redemption of greenbacks. Such a program was incorporated into the Resumption Act of 1875. See Foulke, *Morton*, 2:65-102; Chester M. Destler, *American Radicalism, 1865-1901* (New London, Conn., 1946), 32-49; McCulloch, *Men and Measures*, 163-480.

21 Richmond *Indiana True Republican*, March 7, 1867.

merely a corollary of the larger movement for the rights of labor, as well as a "death blow at the black power of the South."[22] Perhaps if Julian had remained in Congress he would have been a more persistent and more persuasive advocate of labor. As it was, however, his interest was short-lived. He could be an advocate of fair wages and hours for the individual laborer, but he failed to understand the forces leading to the organization of labor as a means of coping with the increasing concentration of business and industry. In this he was, of course, not alone in the post-Civil War era.

III

Radical Republicans might differ on such matters as tariffs and monetary policy, but after 1866 there was one article of their faith on which no heterodoxy was permitted: their condemnation of President Andrew Johnson. The election of 1866 had ended any effective control Johnson might have had over the adoption or operation of the Radicals' legislative program; still the culminating act of the contest between them and the President was impeachment. For different reasons Radicals demanded the removal of Johnson. Some were determined to end the regime of Hugh McCulloch in the Treasury Department. Others found that Johnson was making inroads into their local political machines by removal of innumerable local officials. Still others apparently had no such specific reasons, and Julian was one of these. It is conceivable that the campaign against Johnson was a necessary unifying force during the Re-

22 William T. Jessup to Julian, March 27, 1867, Julian Papers; Richmond *Indiana True Republican*, May 3, 1866, July 2, 1868; *Congressional Globe*, 39 Congress, 1 session, 1331; Julian, *Political Recollections*, 274-75; Clarke, *Julian*, 300.

construction period, a force such as the war and emancipation had been.

For Julian the continued presence of Andrew Johnson
in the White House was a symbol of the failure of the
war as an instrument of achieving Radical goals. His animus seems to have come chiefly from feelings of revenge
toward a traitor to the cause. With avid interest he
watched every step toward impeachment, and in some
of them he personally participated. In the early months
of 1867 we find him writing home of the study of the
question of impeachment by the House Judiciary Committee, and expressing chagrin at the reluctance of
some Republicans to proceed with it. Soon, however,
he wrote of encouraging rumors coming from the secret
meetings of the Committee to the effect that men were
now beginning to see the wisdom of impeachment. Without impeachment, Julian wrote, "nothing [can] be done
for the loyal cause in the South." Having one day seen
the President briefly, he wrote in the *True Republican:* "His passions have left their foot prints on his features and revealed more and more the *animal* predominance in the man. . . . His eye is that of venom. . . ." Soon
he was able to write more jubilantly: "I entertain no
doubt whatsoever that impeachment has become inevitable, and that it will be successful."[23]

Thus, a year before Andrew Johnson's trial for high
crimes and misdemeanors Julian was one of those in the
front rank of the impeachment movement. He craved
to be one of the House managers of impeachment along
with Stevens, Ben Butler, John A. Logan, and other
Radicals. But he had to be satisfied with the more dubi-

[23] Richmond *Indiana True Republican,* January 17, February 14,
March 14, 1867.

ous honor of serving on the House committee of seven that prepared the articles of impeachment.[24]

When the President's case was brought before the Senate in February, 1868, Julian wanted Laura to join him in Washington to witness "this grand trial." Family responsibilities held Laura at home, but George kept her informed of events in the national capital. He described the excitment at the opening of the trial as comparable only to that at the first battle of Bull Run. Through March and well into April his optimism persisted. On April 21, he wrote, "Impeachment is all right. 'Have no alarm,' tell the folks it is a sure thing." But within a fortnight Julian's mood had changed, and he was writing that there was a "fearful impression that impeachement [would] fail." And if that happened, "God help the country. . . . " As the day of decision approached "an awful gloom" descended upon the Radicals. "To the surprise & great consternation of every body on our side," Julian lamented, "the President is likely to be acquitted. It makes me *chilly*. . . ." When the trial was over, Julian gave vent to his anger in a bitter attack on all those responsible for the evil deed: the seven Republican Senators who had voted against conviction were betrayers of the Radical cause; their deed had made them "a blessed riddance" to that cause and "unworthy any longer to serve" it.

Chief Justice Chase, who had presided judiciously at the trial, Julian regarded as the most shameful recreant of all. Johnson had wined and dined him, said Julian, and the Chief Justice had been duped. Then he, in turn, had influenced "Grimes, Fessenden, and the other recreant Senators." As the impeachment trial began to fade into the past, Julian embellished his ex-

24 Clarke, *Julian*, 308-9.

planation of the acquittal with another fanciful idea; the "whisky ring," he now said, was largely responsible.[25] "Bluff Ben" Wade was probably the man most disappointed by Johnson's acquittal. As president pro tempore of the Senate he was next in line for the White House. Rumor had it that he was packed and ready to move in, and people were speculating about who would be in his Cabinet. Several newspapers picked Julian as the probable choice for Secretary of the Interior. Julian insisted that he had no intention of accepting the post if it was offered to him, but to Laura he expressed his gratification at being considered for it. The confidence in him seemed to "reveal the fact of [his] supposed competence & integrity in the matter of managing that Department."[26]

Fifteen years later, when in the secure embrace of the Democratic party, Julian wrote somewhat apologetically his reflections on the impeachment of Andrew Johnson. The excitement of those days, he recalled, was "perfectly overmastering."

Passion ruled the hour, and constantly strengthened the tendency to one-sidedness and exaggeration. . . . The judicial spirit was everywhere wanting, and the elevation of Senator Wade to the Presidency in the midst of so much passion and tumult, and with the peculiar political surroundings which the event foreshadowed, would have been, to say the least, a very questionable experiment for the country.[27]

From these reflections of events in which Julian played a prominent and active part comes no trace of self-

[25] Julian to Laura Julian, February 15, 22, 29, April 21, May 5, 11, 1868; Laura Julian to Julian, March 15, 1868, Julian Papers; Richmond *Indiana True Republican*, May 21, 28, June 4, 1868.
[26] Julian to Laura Julian, March 12, April 28, 1868, Julian Papers.
[27] Julian, *Political Recollections*, 317-19.

examination. His complete reversal concerning the impeachment raises no question with him as to the dangers and shortcomings of interpreting problems in the affairs of men as battles between good and evil, between right and wrong. Rather, Julian was, characteristically, making a case for himself as a Democrat and setting out to prove that in his current battle he was still aligned with the forces of good against the forces of evil.

IV

As a member of Congress, two primary objectives shaped Julian's concept of a correct Reconstruction policy: the punishment of rebel leaders and the remaking of the South into a land of small independent farmers.

When he returned, in December, 1865, for the opening of the Thirty-ninth Congress, he brought with him the same zeal for the punishment of rebel leaders that he had displayed in the recent debates at home. From January to April, 1866, he demanded, without effect, the adoption of a resolution for the speedy trial of Jefferson Davis and his execution *if* found guilty.[28] Near the end of April, Julian made a desperate final plea. If any man owed fidelity to the Union, he insisted, that man was Jefferson Davis. He had been educated at public expense, "honors and emoluments of office" had been showered upon him. Hence his treason was no mere accident or temporary lapse of judgment; it was premeditated. And the "spared life" of Robert E. Lee, Julian continued, had "outraged the honest claims of the gallows ever since his surrender." In its treatment of criminals no state in the Union, no civilized country, sanc-

28 Italics are the author's. As first introduced, Julian's resolution read that Davis should be executed "when found guilty." He was persuaded to change the wording.

tioned "the sickly magnanimity and misapplied humanity of this nation in dealing with its leading traitors."[29]
Northerners who, like Julian, insisted that Southerners
suffer retribution had to be satisfied with the trial and
execution of one inconspicuous southern junior officer.
The victim was Capt. Henry Wirz, whose offense was
that he had commanded Andersonville prison where
thousands of northern soldiers perished from starvation,
disease, and improper care. Lacking food, medical sup-
plies, and personnel, Wirz probably performed his un-
pleasant duties about as well as could have been expected under the circumstances. His predicament aroused
Julian's sympathy even for this rebel. To the *True Republican* he wrote, "Why should so small an offender be
singled out, like poor Wirz, and made to suffer, when
the whole policy of the Government has been that of a
most sickly humanitarianism, sparing even the most
flagitious villains of this or any age?"[30]

Even though Julian was a strong advocate of the
"state-suicide" theory of Reconstruction, within the
framework of that theory his ideas differed markedly
from those of some other Radical leaders. Giving southern
states the status of territories, in Julian's view, should
not be designed to bring them back into the Union as
states in the shortest possible time, even with loyal
governments. He also regarded the establishment of
military governments in the South as very unwise. He
preferred civil governments in the southern territories under the control of loyal Southerners, including Negroes,
with the military ready to back up these governments
whenever it might become necessary. In December, 1866,

29 *Congressional Globe*, 39 Congress, 1 session, 138, 482, 2282-85;
Richmond *Indiana True Republican*, May 17, 1866.
30 *Ibid.*, July 25, 1867.

he introduced a bill embracing these ideas, but it was referred to the Committee on Territories, where it rested.[31]

A month later, in his speech, "Regeneration before Reconstruction," he made the most forceful and most in-
cisive presentation of his views. After lamenting that
"not a single rebel [had] yet expiated his crime on the
gallows," Julian proceeded to set forth what he regarded
as a proper Reconstruction policy. Even if the rebel
population were disfranchised, he would not advocate a
quick return of the southern states to the Union, for
there would still lurk the danger of a resurgent landed
aristocracy. Only "the strong arm of power, outstretched
from the central authority . . . in Washington" could
make the South

safe for the freedmen . . ., safe for her loyal white men, safe
for emigrants from the Old World and from the Northern
States to go and dwell there; safe for Northern capital and
labor, Northern energy and enterprise, and Northern ideas
to set up their habitation in peace, and thus form a Christian
civilization and a living democracy amid the ruins of the
past. . . . The political and social regeneration of the country
made desolate by treason is the prime necessity of the hour,
and it is preliminary to any reconstruction of States. Years of
careful pupilage under the authority of the nation may be
found necessary, and Congress alone must decide when and
upon what conditions the tie rudely broken by treason shall
be restored.[32]

Reluctantly Julian voted for the "Military Bill" that
eventually emerged from the Joint Committee on Reconstruction, but not until the adoption of an amend-

---

[31] *Congressional Globe,* 39 Congress, 2 session, 133; Indianapolis *Daily
Journal,* December 15, 1866; New York *Times,* December 15, 1866; New
York *Tribune,* December 15, 1866; Richmond *Indiana True Republican,*
December 6, 20, 1866.

[32] *Congressional Globe,* 39 Congress, 2 session, Appendix, 77-80; Julian,
Speeches on Political Questions, 348-60.

ment making Negro suffrage one of the conditions of readmission. To turn the South over to major generals, Julian believed, was an admission that Congress was incompetent to handle a matter over which it had constitutional power.[33]

Still another serious flaw that Julian found in the "Military Bill" was the implication that the President, not Congress, was to control the South, for the President was commander-in-chief of the armed forces, and the rebel in the White House was certain to "do everything in his power to render it a failure." But the bill had one conceivable advantage: it would inevitably bring "fresh conflicts" between President and Congress that would advance the impeachment movement.[34]

Perhaps Julian's Quaker upbringing caused his deep and consistent distrust of army officers in any civilian office. "Old Zach" Taylor's military career had been one of the most serious counts against him as a presidential candidate; nor did Grant, according to Julian, have any qualifications for the presidency. Indeed, while Congress was engaged in working out a Reconstruction program Julian proposed a resolution providing for an investigation by the Committee on Military Affairs into the advisability of abolishing the regular army altogether and of replacing it with a militia composed of volunteer regiments.[35]

V

The problem of devising and implementing a land policy that would be workable in the postwar era re-

33 New York *Tribune,* January 29, 1867; Richmond *Indiana True Republican,* January 24, February 14, 21, 1867; Julian, *Political Recollections,* 308.

34 Richmond *Indiana True Republican,* February 28, 1867.

35 *Congressional Globe,* 39 Congress, 1 session, 2859.

mained an acute one. Certainly the homestead concept, which had been enacted into law in 1862, the parceling out of land in 160-acre plots to those who would occupy and cultivate it, was inadequate and unrealistic. The failure of the Homestead Act in some measure symbolizes economic change and the transfer of political power in the late nineteenth century. Between 1862, when the Homestead bill was passed, and 1890, the population of the United States increased by some thirty-two millions; but the number of entries perfected under the Homestead Act was less than two million. During that period the railroads sold more land to settlers—at an average price of $5.00 per acre—than the settlers took up under the Homestead Act.

Speculators continued to get their slice of the public domain in various and sundry ways; among the more prominent were through the commutation clause of the Homestead Act, the purchase of soldiers' land bounties, and swampland legislation. Swamplands and overflow lands were supposed to be unfit for settlement and cultivation, and thus the Federal government granted them to the states to make whatever use could be made of them. But the term "swampland" was never adequately defined, and often the Federal land officers merely accepted the findings of state land agents. The end result was that vast acreages of arable land passed from the states into the hands of railroads or speculators who sold it to settlers for whatever they could get.

In Congress Julian became the leader of a little group of recalcitrants who tried to stem the tide of land speculation. Julian, the fiercest Cerberus of all, placed himself at the gates of the public domain to guard it for the actual settlers from those who would encroach upon it. His ultimate failure was a manifestation of the demise of the Jeffersonian ideal of a nation of independent farmers. For the "Gilded Age" brought with it not only the predominance of industry; it brought radical changes for those who remained on the farm. By 1900 more than 35 per cent of American farmers were actual tenants, and many more—under the burden of mortgages —were virtual tenants.[36]

Julian's objective was to establish a policy of disposing of the public domain exclusively to actual settlers under homestead and pre-emption laws. It appears that his goal was to make this a permanent policy applicable to any territory that the United States might acquire in the future; during his last year in Congress, for example, he tried repeatedly to get a bill adopted to extend the pre-emption and homestead laws to the newly acquired territory of Alaska.[37]

In his role of protector of the public domain Julian was forced to oppose the almost irresistible political pressure of organized Union Army veterans. The Grand Army of the Republic was one of the Republican party's greatest sources of strength; refusal to pay due deference to it was an act of real political courage.

By 1866 petitions were flowing into Congress demanding a land bounty for veterans. Soon a provision for it was brought before the House. Summoning his best oratorical powers, Julian opposed it. In the past, he

[36] Paul W. Gates, "The Homestead Law in an Incongruous Land System," in *American Historical Review*, 41 (1935-36):657; Gates, "Federal Land Policy in the South," in *Journal of Southern History*, 6:306-7; Benjamin H. Hibbard, *A History of the Public Land Policies* (New York, 1939), 270-78; Smith, *Virgin Land*, 190-94.

[37] George W. Julian, "Our Land Policy," in *Atlantic Monthly*, 43 (1879):325-37; *Congressional Globe*, 40 Congress, 2 session, 4081; 41 Congress, 1 session, 72-73; 41 Congress, 2 session, 2290; 41 Congress, 3 session, 972-74; New York *Times*, March 16, 1869; New York *Tribune*, January 15, 1868.

argued, land bounties had always resulted in land speculation, and they were certain to do so again if the bill
passed. Even though the measure made lands granted
under the bounty unassignable, Julian believed that there
would be irresistible pressure to change this provision.
In place of land bounties Julian offered a bill for the
payment of a cash bounty of eight and one-third dollars
for each month of military service. It was referred to the
House Military Committee from which it finally emerged
and became known as "General Schenck's Bill." Repeatedly it passed the House always to fail in the Senate.
But neither did the land bounty bill pass so long as
Julian remained in Congress.[38]

Julian's earlier failure to have the plantation lands of
Southerners confiscated was not the end of his effort
to establish southern Negroes on homesteads. In the five
public land states of the South there were approximately
46,000,000 acres of public lands that had long been open
to entry at $1.25 per acre. If these lands were opened for
homesteaders in plots of eighty acres, a considerable
number of farms might be established. Julian took the
lead in the movement which resulted in the adoption of
a Southern Homestead bill, legislation through which
Congress came closest to establishing a program for the
economic welfare of the freedmen. Before its final passage in 1866 Julian succeeded in having the bill amended
so as to prevent occupation of the land by any person
who had "borne arms against the United States or given
aid and comfort to its enemies." An Iowa Congressman
thought this provision too restrictive; he could see no

38 Richmond *Indiana True Republican,* April 23, 1868; New York
Tribune, December 5, 1866; Julian, *Political Recollections,* 277-80; Julian,
Speeches on Political Questions, 385-98; Robbins, *Our Landed Heritage,*
215-16; Clarke, *Julian,* 298-99.

ZACHARIAH CHANDLER

BENJAMIN WADE

advantage in depriving former rebels of an opportunity to make a living. But Julian refused to agree to the eligibility even of those Southerners who had been pardoned.[39] Julian's plan for regeneration was not tempered with benevolence even toward the southern poor whites who had fought for the Confederacy. Even so, the choice between punishing rebels or remodeling the South into a land of small independent farmers must have been a difficult one for him to make.[40]

The Southern Homestead Act remained on the statute books for ten years, but the failure of Radical Reconstruction doomed it. Its repeal came with the compromise between southern redeemers and northern Republicans, in 1877, that brought the formal end of Reconstruction and the election of Rutherford B. Hayes to the Presidency.[41]

On March 6, 1868, Julian delivered a long and carefully prepared speech designed to instruct his fellow Congressmen in the intricacies of land monopoly. Patiently and in great detail he explained how the homestead policy was being jeopardized by railroad grants, swampland grants, agricultural college grants, grants to eleemosynary institutions, soldiers' land bounties, and so on. He proposed as a solution the adoption of legislation to prevent any disposal of public land except under the pre-emption and homestead acts. Land granted to rail-

[39] *Congressional Globe,* 39 Congress, 1 session, 715-18, 748; 39 Congress, 2 session, 1660-61; Gates, "Federal Land Policy in the South," in *Journal of Southern History,* 6:303-8; Robbins, *Our Landed Heritage,* 212-13; Clarke, *Julian,* 299.

[40] The author has treated this question in somewhat greater detail in an article, "George W. Julian: Abolitionist Land Reformer," in *Agricultural History,* 29 (1955):108-15.

[41] Gates, "Federal Land Policy in the South," in *Journal of Southern History,* 6:311-12; C. Vann Woodward, *Reunion and Reaction . . .* (Boston, 1951), *passim.*

roads was to be sold to actual settlers at the maximum price of $2.50 per acre. Opposition to this particular bill came primarily from the representatives of Michigan lumbering districts who argued that it would ruin the lumber industry and stimulate, rather than check, land speculation. They wanted no restriction on grants to railroads or on the sale of public lands.

It was this sort of fight that brought expressions of support for the chairman of the Land Committee. Again and again the *True Republican* published letters from settlers and farmers all over the West urging Julian to continue his campaign against land monoply. The greatest tribute came from the Chicago *Tribune* whose only complaint was that the bill did not go far enough, and that it ought to have provided for government regulation of freight and passenger rates on all railroads with land grants.[42] The *Tribune's* statements reflected the growth of some new concepts concerning the place of the Federal government in an industrial nation. But Julian had little sympathy with, or understanding of, such ideas. His ardent advocacy of governmental control of monopoly was not tainted with any suggestion that the government embark on a policy of extensive business regulation or planning. His appeals for adoption of his land measures continued to be couched in the language of the Jeffersonian ideal and reflected the habit of Julian and others to turn back to the ethos and the values of their youth for their solutions to problems of the post-Civil War years. Citing such authorities as John Stuart Mill, Vattel, and Sismondi, Julian still spoke of the culti-

---

42 *Congressional Globe,* 40 Congress, 3 session, 958-59; Richmond *Indiana True Republican,* May 7, 1868; New York *Tribune,* February 9, 1869; Julian, *Speeches on Political Questions,* 365-84; Gates, "Homestead Law in an Incongruous Land System," in *American Historical Review,* 41:677-78.

vation of the soil as the natural employment of man and the basis of the independent citizenry of small farmers that he believed indispensable to "comfort, security, confidence in the future . . . happiness, and virtue."[43]

His bill to restrict the disposal of public lands to actual settlers failed to pass. The House did adopt a powerless resolution with the same recommendation but after showing its good intentions it refused to pass the bill itself.

Still another check that Julian tried to place on land monopoly was the establishment of regulations for handling lands ceded to the United States as a result of Indian "treaties." As the Indians moved into reservations the Federal government compensated them for the lands vacated, but in many cases the government turned over the negotiations to private corporations who secured the land for themselves. In this way the railroads came into possession of some of the best lands being opened. Although Julian failed in his efforts to have a law passed requiring the Indians to deal only with the Federal government or with actual settlers, his work did not go entirely unrewarded. Probably his greatest triumph was the blocking of the Osage Indian treaty, which would have handed over to the Leavenworth, Lawrence, and Galveston Railroad of Kansas eight million acres of land at about twenty cents an acre. Although the Senate refused to agree to Julian's joint resolution opposing this treaty, the resolution aroused so much opposition to it that the Senate refused to ratify.[44]

[43] Julian, *Speeches on Political Questions*, 367-71; Riddleberger, "George W. Julian: Abolitionist Land Reformer," in *Agricultural History*, 29:111.

[44] *Congressional Globe*, 40 Congress, 2 session, 1705, 2753, 2816; 41 Congress, 1 session, 512, 513, 516; New York *Times*, March 7, 1868, April 6, 1869; New York *Tribune*, June 27, 29, 1868, April 6, 1869; Julian, "Our

Through railroad legislation Julian also attempted to implement a homestead policy for the South. In 1856, Congress had granted five million acres of land to five southern states to aid in the construction of railroads. In the summer of 1867 Julian began a campaign in Congress to force the forfeiture of these lands to the Federal government and to open them for settlement under the Homestead Act. The following year his bill passed the House, but in the Senate the Committee on Public Lands refused to report it.[45]

There was heated controversy over the southern railroad bill in the House. Julian's most effective opponent was John Chanler of New York, ably assisted by Fernando Wood and Stephen Taber from the same state.[46] On Julian's side were Thomas Williams of Pennsylvania, the Illinois Radical, Elihu B. Washburne, and Ignatius Donnelly of Minnesota who later became famous as one of the leaders of the Populist movement. And a Hoosier Democrat, William S. Holman—although not conspicuous in the debates on the southern railroad bill—became the most valiant fighter of all against railroad and land monopoly. He was still in Congress in 1876, and led the futile battle against repeal of the Southern Homestead Act.

From the time Julian introduced the bill for forfeiture of southern railroad lands until the House passed it, Chanler sniped at him. He repeatedly called the Hoosier

Land Policy," in *Atlantic Monthly*, 43:331-32; Gates, "Homestead Law in an Incongruous Land System," in *American Historical Review*, 41:660-61, 676-77.

45 New York *Tribune*, July 6, 1867; Gates, "Federal Land Policy in the South," in *Journal of Southern History*, 6:308; Robbins, *Our Landed Heritage*, 212-13.

46 Taber was a dissenting member of the House Committee on Public Lands, of which Julian was chairman. Frequently he would present a minority report on resolutions or bills reported out of the Committee.

to a point of order, or accused him of destroying vested interests in property. There were several angry exchanges between the two men. On one occasion an Indianapolis correspondent dropped in on Julian to find him stripped to the waist and receiving instructions from a boxing teacher, who was ready to bet on Julian against Chanler.[47]

Although generally faithful in his role of protector of the small farmer against land monopolists and railroads, Julian had one or two lapses. In 1853 the states of Arkansas and Missouri had been given a land grant to aid in the construction of a railroad; this was implemented in 1866 by further legislation, with the deadline set for beginning construction in three years. The Little Rock and Fort Smith Railroad Company was organized in 1867 to carry out the construction. In April, 1869, during the House consideration of a Senate bill to extend the time for the company to complete the first section of twenty miles, Julian proposed an amendment that the lands granted by the original act should be sold only to actual settlers in quantities not greater than 160 acres to one purchaser, at a price not to exceed $2.50. The bill and amendment passed. A year later bills were introduced in both the House and Senate to repeal the proviso regarding the sale of the lands. The report of the House Committee on Public Lands, which accompanied the House bill, explained that inasmuch as the time for beginning construction should have been interpreted as 1870 (three years after the organization of the company) it was not fair to impose in 1869 any condi-

47 *Congressional Globe*, 40 Congress, 1 session, 615-17; 40 Congress, 2 session, 95, 310-12, 694-97, 806-14, 833-44, 985; New York *Times*, January 31, February 1, 6, 1868; New York *Tribune*, December 10, 1867; Richmond *Palladium*, February 13, 1868.

tion regarding the sale of the land that was not in the
original bill. Julian's support of the repeal came as a
surprise to his colleagues. John F. Farnsworth, of Illinois,
asked Julian what harm the proviso would do. Julian's
answer was that perhaps it would do no harm. "Then let
it be," said Farnsworth. Julian replied: "Perhaps it will
do no harm. But it may breed trouble and doubt, and
affect the credit of the railroad company. It may perhaps lead to litigation; and we thought it ought to be
removed in justice to all parties." "So it is for the benefit
of the corporation," Farnsworth interjected. Julian replied,
"We are legislating to undo what we ought never to have
done. The gentleman knows I am not the champion of
railroad corporations." "We [the Committee on Public
Lands] have examined the question of law, and because
we regarded it as clear that our power to attach this
condition did not exist we ask that it be removed from
the statute-book." The clause was repealed by a vote of
109 to 38, Julian voting for repeal.[48]

VI

It may appear from the foregoing that Julian's land
policies were always corollaries to his Reconstruction
policies. But this was not the case. He was interested
in problems of public land policy per se, wherever they
might arise.

California land matters had a peculiar fascination for
him, and he became as deeply involved in them as he did
in land questions pertaining to the South and Reconstruction. Numerous bills were presented requesting grants
of land for railroads in California and on the Pacific Coast,
which he almost invariably opposed. Frequently he tried

48 New York *Tribune*, April 10, 1869; *Congressional Globe*, 41 Congress, 1 session, 701-3; 41 Congress, 2 session, 1698-99.

to have these bills referred to his Committee on Public Lands, where they would remain without being voted on. Thus there were frequent contests to have bills referred to some other committee, and there were sharp debates between Julian and certain California Representatives, particularly John Bidwell and William Higby.[49]

In 1870 Julian was one of a group of lawyers who prepared a brief for Levi H. Whitney, the defendant in the case of *Frisbie* v. *Whitney* before the Supreme Court. The case involved the rights of pre-emptors on the Suscol Ranch, a Mexican land grant in California. In 1862 the ranch had been transferred to the United States as public land. Although Whitney had gone through no legal proceedings to establish his title, Julian thought that he was entitled to it under the pre-emption laws by the mere act of settling on it.

In 1866 Julian brought to Congress the case of Whitney and other settlers and tried, unsuccessfully, to have a bill passed establishing their claims. Whitney then turned to litigation, and the Supreme Court of the District of Columbia confirmed his claim. John B. Frisbie appealed the case to the United States Supreme Court where Julian appeared as one of three attorneys for the defendant. The decision of the lower court was reversed. Julian regarded the decision as favoring land grabbers and monopolists and against actual settlers, and labeled it the "Dred Scott decision of the American Pioneer."[50]

[49] *Ibid.*, 39 Congress, 1 session, 1725, 3267-68, 3298; 39 Congress, 2 session, 1696-1700.

[50] Julian to Laura Julian, July 7, 22, 1866, November 23, 1867, Julian Papers; *Congressional Globe*, 39 Congress, I session, 2957, 3590-95, 3650-55; 9 Wallace 187-97; Julian, "Our Land Policy," in *Atlantic Monthly*, 43:334; Julian, *Political Recollections*, 298-301; Julian's Journal, March 27, 1870, Indiana Division, Indiana State Library.

More significant was the Yosemite Valley case. It also involved pre-emptors' rights, but it carried an additional connotation of public versus private interests. Newspapers, East and West, discussed it, and Julian, as chairman of the Committee on Public Lands, was one of the important public figures involved in it.

It began in 1864, when Congress granted the Yosemite Valley to the state of California to be preserved as a public park. Soon after the grant was made two settlers, J. M. Hutchings and J. C. Lamon, claimed legal title to quarter sections of land in the Valley under the pre-emption laws. They appealed to the California legislature and received satisfaction when the legislature passed a bill granting each man 160 acres of land, subject to the ratification of Congress. When the bill came before Congress, Julian became the chief proponent for speedy ratification; he succeeded in getting it through the House, but it failed in the Senate. For two years Julian argued the case of the Californians in Congress.

Finally, in 1872, the case came before the Supreme Court, with Julian acting as legal counsel for Hutchings. In ruling against the settlers, the court rested its decision on two related propositions: first, that "mere settlement" on the land did not give the settler a vested interest in it nor did it deprive Congress of power to grant it to another party, in this case the state of California; and second, that the private interests of individuals could not contravene the public interest.

Another relevant question was the date of Hutchings' settlement on the Yosemite lands. Julian contended that he had settled there years before the grant was made in 1864; others said that he had moved there only a few weeks before. The court accepted the evidence of the side opposing Julian. The question of time of settlement was indeed significant, for it shed light on the question of whether Hutchings was a mere speculator or a bona fide settler. If he had been on the land several years before 1864, it would have been easier to make a case for him as a genuine settler; if he had gone there only a few weeks before the land grant, he could be shown up as a speculator seeking a remunerative monopoly on hotel accommodations, tolls, and concessions in a public park.

The Yosemite case led Julian into a prolonged controversy with Horace Greeley in the New York *Tribune*. Primarily, Greeley's argument was that the public interest must supersede the private interest and that a confirmation of the Californians' claim could lead to a dangerous precedent under which any squatter might forestall the application of the right of eminent domain, and the Federal government might be prevented from establishing necessary military and other installations.

Josiah Dwight Whitney—geologist, metallurgist, commissioner of Yosemite park, and Harvard professor—brought the weight of his prestige and knowledge into the contest against Julian. He made a convincing argument for the public against the private interest, but he did not stop there. As a firsthand observer he declared that Hutchings and Lamon had settled in the Valley only a few weeks before Congress made the grant. He pointed out, also, that Julian had been mistaken in his statement that the two men had spent thousands of dollars in improvements on their lands. According to Whitney, they merely had taken over the installations of an earlier settler.

When Julian visited California in the summer of 1869, the San Francisco *Bulletin* expressed the belief that when he and other Congressmen saw the Yosemite Valley they would understand the importance of keeping it "wholly a public property, so that it could never be shorn of any of its natural charm or made a means of imposition upon the traveler, like Niagara and other famous natural wonders in other parts of the country."[51]

Actually, James Hutchings was neither a typical land speculator nor a poor settler dependent on his small holding of land for a living. He was a California publisher and artist whose initial interest in the Yosemite Valley was primarily aesthetic. His failure to secure the quarter section of land caused him no great discomfort or inconvenience.[52]

VII

Life for a Congressman in Washington during Reconstruction was not merely a series of battles on the floor of the House or conferences in committee rooms. It had its lighter side, too. Occasionally Julian enjoyed a scintillating social gathering. Once he went to a party at the French Minister's house that he found "dazzling to the eye and charming to the senses [and] . . . French all over." The house of Speaker Colfax, Vice-President after 1868, continued to be a center of social life, and Julian was a fairly regular attendant at the Thursday evening gatherings there. Occasionally he went to the parlor readings of Julia Ward Howe, and less frequently to the spiritualist meetings of Mrs. Cora Daniels.

[51] Julian's Journal, January 24, 1870; Julian to Laura Julian, July 3, 14, 1868, Julian Papers; New York *Tribune*, June 24, July 2, 10, 17, 21, 24, 30, 1868, March 23, 1869; Richmond *Indiana Radical*, July 22, 1869, February 3, 1870; *Congressional Globe*, 40 Congress, 2 session, 2585, 2816-17; 41 Congress, 1 session, 194; 41 Congress, 2 session, 2726, 5129-32; 15 Wallace 77-94; Julian, "Our Land Policy," in *Atlantic Monthly*, 43:334-35; Whitney biography in *Dictionary of American Biography*, 20:161-63.

[52] Carl P. Russell, *One Hundred Years in Yosemite* . . . (Berkeley, Calif., 1947), 50-57, 149-52.

There were a few favorite plays that he never missed when they came to town, such as *Rip Van Winkle,* with Joseph Jefferson in the leading role, and *King Lear* with Edwin Forrest playing the lead. He also enjoyed Maggie Mitchel in *Fanchon.* Although political life curtailed his reading somewhat, he never gave it up completely, and when Laura visited him they read together as he and Anne had done years earlier. During his last few years in Congress he read, among other things, Buckle's *Essays* and de Tocqueville's *Democracy in America.* During the Reconstruction years his columns in the *True Republican* became less frequent, but he never stopped writing them altogether.[53]

The arrival of a son in July, 1867, brought Julian great elation for a time. He thought of naming the boy John Bright. "How do you like it?" he asked Laura. "In these days of sturdy radicalism & in view of John Bright's character as a reformer & a Quaker will it not be appropriate?" But eventually the boy was named Paul, "after the first apostle."[54] George's high spirits following Paul's arrival did not last long; the baby was a difficult one, and Laura's recovery after the birth was slow and precarious. Julian was worried about her, but he had to remain away from her for months at a time.

The following November Julian's mother died. She was an old woman, and he expected her death; but it

[53] Richmond *Indiana True Republican,* January 24, 1867; Julian to Laura Julian, November 23, 1867, Julian Papers; New York *Times,* January 11, 1866; Julian's Journal, February 11, March 6, 1866, quoted in Claude G. Bowers, *The Tragic Era . . .* (Cambridge, Mass., 1929), 97-99. Regrettably portions of Julian's Journal were destroyed, presumably by his daughter, Mrs. Grace Julian Clarke. Bowers was able to use the Journal while it was still intact.

[54] Julian to Laura Julian, July 8, 9, 1867; Mollie Giddings to Julian, September 23, 1867, Julian Papers.

was more of a shock than he had anticipated. Full of self-reproach, he poured out his feelings to Laura: He had been "too much engrossed with self" and had "forsaken" his mother in her old age. He conjured up a picture of himself as an old man about to die and deserted by his children. A few days later his daughter Grace, who was born in 1865 and whom he idolized, was taken sick with a childhood malady and Julian feared that she too would be lost to him.[55]

Julian's health through the war years had never been good, and the strain of political life aggravated his illnesses. He suffered from a terrible insomnia that left him enervated and unfit for his work and resulted in more frequent absences from Congress. By the summer of 1869 he could endure it no longer. The time had come for a long vacation and a complete change. In this state of mind he could hardly have chosen a worse place to go for rest and relaxation than to California. The journal that he kept during the trip shows his continuing concern about land matters, from the Kankakee swamplands in northern Indiana to the valleys of California. Wyoming, he found, needed water and timber, and "a policy that shall rid it of Indian outrages. . . . The failure of my bill extending our land laws over their territory was likewise unfortunate." Salt Lake City delighted him, and he was generous in his praise of the accomplishments of the Mormons. He regarded polygamy as "a system of unmitigated sensuality & lust on the part of the men, & of degradation & superstition on the part of the women," and was pleased to find only about a twentieth of the Mormons were polygamists. He predicted its practice would gradually die out. The Mormons

[55] Julian to Laura Julian, November 24, December 3, 1867, Julian Papers.

though "exceedingly superstitious" were, he thought, "practical and worldly people."

The high point of the California visit was to be the Yosemite Valley. "I felt bound to see the valley," he wrote, "not only because of its wonderful features but on account of my special connection with the preemption grievance pertaining to it which is now before Congress." Twice Julian went to Yosemite, but each time he became deathly ill with extreme chills, fever, and insomnia. Vividly he described his reactions: "I shall never forget it, or the resolution I then made to live a better life if spared to escape from this valley of beauty & wonder, which had become to me a prison of despair."

Back home Julian's health was worse than ever, and his fears and anxieties were intensified. His life was becoming a "frightful burden," he wrote. "I see that I must soon lay it down or become insane if I cannot get sleep. This thought is most dreadful. I am only fairly launched upon my life-work, & this world & its cares and calls never before have had so strong a hold on me. But I greatly fear it is now too late for help."[56]

Julian's reactions to the Yosemite venture seem to be those of a man so emotionally disturbed and so involved with the duties of his office that he was unable to extricate himself. Probably he needed more than ever, in these latter years of his political career, to identify himself with virile Radicalism; and we find him repeatedly proclaiming his faith in the cause. He must have shared the sentiments expressed in a letter to the *True Republican* holding that all progress from the time of Moses, Christ, and Confucius to the time of Abraham Lincoln had been the work of radicals and that among con-

[56] Julian's Journal, June 13, 17, August 11, October 4, 1869, Julian Papers.

servatives were to be found the tyrants of history. Julian seemed convinced that only the hampering interference of conservatives had prevented the Radicals from solving difficult postwar problems.[57]

A decade after he had left Congress Julian could still write that his Congressional career had been a "perfect illustration" of his faith in the ultimate emancipation of men from all forms of servitude. "The rights of man are sacred," he proclaimed, "whether trampled down by Southern slave-drivers, the monopolists of the soil, the grinding power of corporate wealth, the legalized robbery of a protective tariff, or the power of concentrated capital in alliance with labor-saving machinery."[58]

Yet, whatever Julian may have said about radicalism and reform during his last five years in Congress, his reforming zeal was diminishing. Perhaps the explanation can be found in his growing affluence. Although he was not a wealthy man, he could now afford some of the physical comforts and social contacts of a man of affairs. Occasionally he even invested in the stocks and bonds of railroads whose practices he condemned.[59] Perhaps it was simply that Julian was growing older. More basic, perhaps, was the fact that the reform movement in America was no longer driven forward by the force that characterized it in the prewar years.

In any case, as Julian ended his Congressional career there were signs that the metamorphosis of the Radical Republican was well under way.

57 Richmond *Indiana True Republican*, February 27, 1868.

58 Julian, *Political Recollections*, 322-23.

59 Julian's Journal, July 13, 1870, Julian Papers; Julian, *Speeches on Political Questions*, 456-60.

FROM RADICAL
TO LIBERAL

◇◇◇◇◇◇◇◇◇◇◇◇◇◇◇◇◇◇◇◇

On February 27, 1870, Lydia Maria Child, the indefatigable scribe, wrote to her friend Wendell Phillips, editor of the *Anti-Slavery Standard:* "Do write one of your rousing editorials about the election of Geo. W. Julian. I am dreadfully afraid his enemies will defeat him. It would be such a loss to the cause of freedom, that I want to move heaven and earth to prevent it; and that *forthwith.*"[1] Phillips responded, on March 12, with a ringing appeal. The nation, he pleaded, simply could not spare the services of such a man at so critical a time.

During the war, [Julian's] service to the loyal cause has been invaluable. Watchful, hopeful, uncompromising, far-sighted, patient of labor, always at his post, fearless, and with the most thorough comprehension of the whole nature of our epoch, no man in Congress has outrun him in purpose, and only one or two in the opportunity to serve the Negro and the Union— Liberty and Justice.

The herculean effort to defeat Julian, said Phillips, came from a distressed "army of rapacious land lobbyists, and certain Senators and Representatives of the Western Speculating Ring, whose enmity he [had] earned by

---

[1] Lydia Maria Child to Wendell Phillips, February 27, 1870, Giddings-Julian Papers, Library of Congress.

thwarting many of their monopolizing schemes and shame-less frauds." Julian, he concluded, was an honor to his native state, whose fame rested on a few such outstanding men rather than on many able men.[2]

Settlers in Kansas and California also appealed to the people of the "Burnt District" to return Julian to Con-gress. In great detail the Kansans related how he had protected them from land speculators and railroad mag-nates. In Washington the *Civil Service Journal* listed Julian among the Congressmen who deserved the sup-port of labor, for he was one of those Republicans who refused to follow his party's trend toward merging with "organized capital." A Negro convention in Newport, Indiana, also adopted resolutions endorsing his renomi-nation.[3]

Along with this widespread support, there was op-position to Julian's nomination from some unexpected quarters. Horace Greeley did not favor his return to Congress. When Julian wrote asking him to say a friendly word in his behalf, Greeley replied by citing two important reasons for his opposition: Julian was one of the few abolitionists who still refused to adopt a "kindly, generous, magnanimous disposition toward the beaten, broken-down Rebels"; and he was a free trader who re-peatedly opposed protective tariff measures.[4] The Cin-cinnati *Gazette*, with a large circulation in eastern Indiana, was also an effective force in bringing about Julian's defeat.[5]

From closer home came mounting evidence that many of his constituents had had enough of him. The Shelby-

2 Richmond *Indiana Radical*, March 24, 1870; Clarke, *Julian*, 329.
3 Richmond *Indiana Radical*, February 24, March 24, 1870.
4 Julian's Journal, March 6, 27, 1870; Clarke, *Julian*, 332-33; Greeley to Julian, March 7, 1870, Giddings-Julian Papers.
5 Richmond *Indiana Radical*, March 3, 1870.

ville *Republican* announced that its "day of labor in the interest of this selfish and vindictive man" was over; now George and the other Julians would "have to work out their own salvation." Nor was this the bitterest denunciation. A letter signed "Nigger Hater" prophesied that when he died Julian would go to a "still more burnt district" than the one he represented in Congress, for he was a "black-hearted old abolitionist" who had cheated his way back into Congress in 1868. Another critic wrote to the *Palladium* that Julian had lost his interest in the masses; others saw a martyr complex developing in him and believed that he had lost his usefulness as a Congressman.[6]

Meanwhile, Julian worried through his next-to-last session in Congress. Frequently he went to New York for treatment of his sleeplessness and fevers; somewhat whimsically he described the medication that Dr. Hammond, his New York physician, administered to him: "The Dr. increased my Bromide of potasseum to 45 grains three times per day, prescribing along with this 3 pills daily chiefly composed of phosphorus, 3 drops of Hemlock thrice daily, and a teaspoonful 3 times a day of a mixture of quinine, phosphoric acid, & stricknine; to which he added a teaspoonful 3 times a day of cad-bar oil. Still I did not sleep, and I now think it is no wonder."[7]

Julian's journal portrays a man vacillating between fear that his days in Congress would end long before he was ready to retire and the earnest desire to put the burdens of his Congressional career behind him. Sometimes he felt confident of victory; at other times he feared that "the enemy would demolish me." His answer to the

6 *Ibid.*, February 10, March 31, 1870; Richmond *Palladium*, March 8, 1870.
7 Julian's Journal, January 3, 1870.

old election-year query: Would he support the Republican nominee, whoever he may be? was in the affirmative, but it carried a qualification: "If my constituents believe they can find a new man who can serve them with more ability than I can, in whose hands great and vital interests will be more certainly secure, and who will be more zealously faithful to his trust than I have been to mine, then, of course, they will nominate him as my successor; and they will find me joining them in the use of every honorable endeavor to elect him."[8]

When Julian was defeated in the spring primary by Jeremiah M. Wilson of Connersville, he called publicly for party unity behind the new candidate, but his feelings were still mixed. "I never brought myself to believe I would be defeated," he wrote, but when he received the word he "felt all at once a great load lifted" from him. "Up to this time," he continued, "it had seemed to me impossible to live out of Congress, but now my defeat seemed to me a perfect Godsend, & that I had been mad in attempting the fight in my miserably nervous condition." Within a fortnight his mood changed again, and he wrote of feeling "very keenly the great injustice done me after so many years of hard & faithful service. . . . I have felt at times inexpressibly grieved that my constituents should have allowed me to be sacrificed at a time when my triumph should have been signal, & when I am far more needed . . . than ever before. . . ." He had no expectation that the new Congressman would distinguish himself, and was optimistic about being returned to Congress in the election of 1872. Some of Julian's old reformer friends shared his view of himself.

8 Julian's Journal, February 9, 20, March 27, 1870; Julian to Franklin County Convention, January 31, 1870, in Richmond *Indiana Radical,* March 24, 1870.

Wendell Phillips spoke eloquently of him, and Mrs. Julia Ward Howe told an antislavery meeting in New York that his defeat was "only a furlough such as are always given to our great Generals after wearying and exhausting service."[9]

II

There is nothing to indicate that Julian was in any way implicated in the financial malpractices of the Civil War era or that he was tainted by the scandals of the Grant regime. Even so, he did not overlook the financial opportunities that came to Congressmen through contacts and professional advice. By the standards of the "Gilded Age" Julian was not wealthy, but he ended his Congressional career financially solvent and comfortable. There were several sources of income. In addition to his salary, he had acquired nearly twelve hundred acres of land in Missouri and Iowa. Ironically, Julian came into possession of all this land under the military bounty land warrant act of 1855. No records indicate what income he received from these lands, but he also owned lots in Indianapolis that probably brought in rent. In addition, George and Laura received a share of the estate of Joshua R. Giddings, and when Laura's sister Maria died, she left them bonds valued at $2,600.[10]

After 1865 Julian continued to invest in government securities; he also made loans to relatives and friends ranging from $600 to $1,500. His own account of finan-

9 Julian's Journal, April 11, 25, 1870; Richmond *Indiana Radical*, April 21, 1870. In November the vote for Congressman was extremely close and Wilson's seat was unsuccessfully disputed by his opponent, David S. Gooding.

10 S. A. Northing to Julian, March 6, 1867, and J. S. Wilson, commissioner of the General Land Office, to Julian, December 14, 1868, Julian Papers; Julian's Journal, October 30, 1871.

cial transactions in four months of 1871 shows that in July of that year he had more than $20,000 invested in five-twenty bonds at par value, as well as $5,000 in bank stock. During 1871, Julian transferred a considerable amount of his holdings from government securities to bank stock; his journal shows that on at least one occasion he sold some five-twenties at a premium of 65 per cent, and the bank stock yielded a semiannual dividend of 6 per cent.[11]

His service in Congress as chairman of the House Committee on Public Lands changed the nature of his practice of law and probably made it more lucrative. After 1870 his work was concerned chiefly with land matters. In addition to the two California pre-emption cases that went to the Supreme Court, Julian was legal counsel in a number of cases before the Commissioner of the General Land Office in the Department of the Interior, one of which involved 17,000 acres of disputed swampland in California. In the first two years after leaving Congress Julian collected nearly $5,000 in fees from swampland cases alone.[12]

III

Julian was soon to discover, also, that his defeat had not really severed his connection with politics. To be sure, his role after 1871 would be different, but the Liberal Republican movement and the resurgence of the Democratic party served to keep him on the political scene. Indeed, the Liberal Republican movement brought one of those decisive moments to Julian's life second only

11 Julian's Journal, January 15, 1870, July 5, October 9, 30, 1871; Julian to Laura Julian, December 11, 1865, July 3, 1867, Julian Papers.
12 Julian's Journal, March 16, 1873; Richmond *Julian's Radical,* January 18, 1872. The latter was the new name of the *Indiana Radical.*

in importance to his entrance into the Free Soil party in 1848. For the biographer, too, these moments are illuminating, bringing into focus as they do the mode of his thought and action.

There was much in the Liberal Republican movement that appealed naturally to Julian. It demanded mild, libertarian reforms of the kind that had interested him for thirty years. Probably only his intense and time-consuming abolitionist activities had precluded a more active roll in these lesser reform activities. Throughout his public life Julian had been a free trader; he had never been able fully to accept Republican protective tariff policies. The civil service reform demanded by the Liberals had appealed to him more and more during the preceding five or six years. He believed that the best qualified men intellectually ought to be induced to enter politics, and he considered himself one of this type. He still maintained his ideas on land reform, another plank in the Liberal platform. His abhorrence of the Grant regime, the *cause célèbre* of the Liberal Republican movement, was not of recent vintage. Although he opposed the nomination of Grant in 1868, he had reluctantly supported the General in the election. But the corruption in the administration, the Santo Domingo affair with the demotion of Charles Sumner, and the rise of Oliver P. Morton to pre-eminence in the regime, all served to make Julian's relations with it difficult.[13]

13 Although many historians of politics and reform in the post-Civil War era have dealt with the Liberal Republican movement, the best and most complete study continues to be Earle D. Ross's *The Liberal Republican Movement* (New York, 1919). Eric Goldman writes on the subject briefly but illuminatingly in his *Rendezvous with Destiny* (New York, 1952). Much interesting and pertinent material can be found in the Carl Schurz Papers, Manuscript Division, Library of Congress. Here we find that one of Julian's first favorable reactions to the movement followed an

Only on the subject of amnesty was there originally any serious conflict between Julian and the rank and file Liberals, but his attitude on this subject underwent a rather unseemly and rapid change after his defeat in 1870. In fact, it was none other than the old "Copperhead," Clement L. Vallandigham, who set the stage for Julian's initial retreat from Radicalism. Early in 1871 Vallandigham proposed a program for the Democratic party that he had first suggested three years earlier, a "New Departure" in which there was to be full acceptance of the Fourteenth and Fifteenth amendments as part of the final settlement of the war. Now there was a whole new set of problems, said Vallandigham, challenging enough for the best brains and talents in the Democratic party. These were the same issues that led to the formation of the Liberal Republican party the following year. Julian was impressed, and before the end of 1871 he had written articles recommending a similar "New Departure" for the Republican party.

Now the old Radical, who only a year earlier had been defying traitors and had demanded that Lee and Jefferson Davis be permitted no longer to cheat the gallows, suddenly called for a spirit of brotherhood toward the rebels. Gone were the chants of "sickly magnanimity" and "misapplied humanity"; the new refrain was that past differences must be forgotten or reconciled if solutions were to be found for the new problems facing the nation. Julian discovered that war leaders were ill-equipped for these new tasks; now men of vision were needed, and men of good will. Thus the Grants, Mortons, Camerons, and Conklings must go, and if the Republican party refused to purge them, a new party must be

attack on Schurz by Morton in the Senate. Julian to Schurz, February 23, 1872, Carl Schurz Papers.

formed. These were the ideas that Julian shared with other men looking toward the election of 1872.[14]

Although Julian's general acceptance of the ideas of leading Liberals and his genuine disgust with the Grant regime were important factors shaping his decision, they were by no means the only ones. The power of Morton in the Grant administration was, in a way, the culmination of the long contest for Republican dominance in Indiana. Now it was over, and Julian was the loser. At the beginning of Andrew Johnson's administration Julian's patronage had begun noticeably to suffer. After Johnson's impeachment and the election of Grant, Julian's stock rose for a time, so much so that he was able to have his brother Isaac appointed postmaster in Richmond, Indiana. But Julian's defeat in 1870, in the middle of Grant's first term, was followed by Isaac's removal from this position. This was a blow to the Julian family fortunes and to their pride, especially to George's. He was shocked and embittered when Grant appointed the editor of the *Palladium* to the postmastership.[15] These were clear signs indicating that if Julian wanted to return to politics he would have to do it in some party other than that of Grant and Morton.

In 1872 Indiana was to elect two Congressmen at large, and several months before the Republican nominating convention, which was held February 22, Julian's friends began to recommend him for one of the seats. In his journal Julian recorded that, "in response to a general

---

14 Julian's Journal, May 28, October 9, 1871; Richmond *Indiana Radical*, July 13, September 14, November 30, 1871; Julian, *Political Recollections*, 331-33.

15 Julian to Daniel D. Pratt, May 25, August 28, 1869, Daniel D. Pratt Papers, Indiana Division, Indiana State Library; Richmond *Indiana True Republican*, May 24, 1866, January 24, July 25, 1867; Richmond *Indiana Radical*, April 15, 22, 1869, April 13, September 7, 14, 1871.

expression in the state in my favor, . . . [I] finally gave my consent; but fearing I would have to scuffle for it & might be defeated, I sent a telegram the night before the convention . . . forbidding the use of my name. It turned out I would have been nominated by acclamation. I would have liked the compliment but could not consistently have accepted the nomination with my views of Grant."[16]

But this explanation of Julian's refusal to become a candidate came only after the Republican state convention had met and nominated other men. Indeed, there is evidence that Julian would have accepted the nomination if it had been offered to him and that a concerted effort was made to get it for him. As the nominating convention approached, Julian's political organ came out with articles designed to ameliorate the damage of his recent criticism of the Republican party. The *Radical* now stressed his criticism of the Democratic party, an indication that the "New Departure" was not so imperative that it could not be jettisoned if political expedience demanded it.[17]

It was reported that one of the delegates to the convention bore a letter that Julian had written to him less than two weeks earlier in which he asked the delegate to keep a close eye on developments in the convention and to act for him if the situation progressed advantageously. If the convention seemed willing to offer Julian the nomination, the intermediary was to make the fact known that George was not "clean out of politics," as rumor had it, and that he would accept the nomination

16 Julian's Journal, no date, p. 122.
17 *Ibid.*; Richmond *Indiana Radical,* November 2, 1871; Richmond *Julian's Radical,* February 15, 22, 1872; Julian, *Political Recollections,* 335-37.

as a reward for his "long and faithful public services." But if the convention under the leadership of the Mortonites showed decided opposition to Julian, the intermediary was to remain silent. Whatever the actual circumstance, Julian's name was not presented.[18]

It might be mentioned here that the day before, on February 21, Julian's name had been presented to another meeting—the National Labor Reform Convention at Columbus, Ohio. He was one of six persons receiving votes for nomination for the Presidency. Judge David Davis of Illinois was nominated and a platform was adopted endorsing civil service reform, an eight-hour day for government employees, equal rights and privileges for all citizens, and an end to land monopoly. Julian gave no recognition to the convention and maintained a discreet silence concerning the introduction of his name among the prospective party leaders.[19]

In biding his time so as to assess his political prospects before committing himself to the Liberal Republican movement, Julian was not alone. The movement cannot be properly understood if we overlook the fact that it emerged from a contest between Stalwarts and reformers within the Republican party, between the "ins" and the "outs." There were, of course, fundamental differences between these two factions which sooner or later would sunder the party, but the original purpose of the Liberals was to control the party, not to divide it. Despite their bitter criticism of Grant, there is evidence that such important leaders as Carl Schurz and Lyman Trumbull were ready to make their peace with the President and

18 Indianapolis *Daily Journal,* February 23, 30, July 1, 1872; Indianapolis *Sentinel,* February 23, 1872.

19 Richmond *Julian's Radical,* March 7, 1872; New York *Tribune,* February 23, 1872; John R. Commons, *et al., History of Labor in the United States* (4 vols. New York, 1918-35), 2:154-55.

forget the Liberal movement if by doing so they could have found a place in the regular Republican party. When Grant and his Stalwarts rudely rejected their overtures, they turned back to the Liberal movement and brought about its transformation into the Liberal Republican party.[20]

Finally, just before the opening of the Liberal Republican convention in Cincinnati on May 1, Julian wrote a letter to the Richmond Liberal Republican meeting openly committing himself to the Liberal Republican movement and against Grant. "It was morally impossible to avoid the parting of the ways . . . ," he wrote in his journal.[21] As he prepared to depart for Cincinnati he did some reflective thinking about his years in the Republican party and about the new role he was to assume. What he wrote in his journal leaves little doubt that he still saw himself as a fighter in the same old crusade, though under different colors:

> There are none of its [the Republican party's] real glories in which I have not had an honorable if not historical share. . . . My revolt now against its discipline reminds me forcibly of the trials of 1848, & I never dreamed till within the past year that I should ever again be called to face another conflict with old & dear friends. I have now, as I had then, no other alternative as an honest man. . . . In all human probability it will place me in awkward relations with the democrats, whose misdeeds I have so earnestly denounced for years, while the bitterness of many who have been among my most faithful friends will know no bounds.[22]

In joining the Liberal Republican movement Julian was working in concert with some of his comrades of the

---

[20] For a more complete analysis see Patrick W. Riddleberger, "The Break in the Radical Ranks: Liberals vs Stalwarts in the Election of 1872," in *The Journal of Negro History,* 44 (1959):136-57.

[21] Julian's Journal, April 28, 1872.

[22] *Ibid.*

abolition crusade and the land reform movement, but it was the moderate reformers of the postwar era who gave the party its tone. Horace Greeley, for example, went in because of the Grant corruptions and his belief in the necessity of amnesty for the South. Carl Schurz and Charles Francis Adams epitomized the libertarian, patrician nature of the movement, with its demand for civil service reform and free trade. From the ranks of the Radical Republicans came Lyman Trumbull whose apostasy in voting for Johnson's acquittal Julian had so bitterly attacked.

But conspicuously absent were several notable reformers who had fought the battle for the abolition of slavery and for Negro rights throughout the middle decades of the nineteenth century. Lydia Maria Child, Julian's old friend and confidant, wrote that she was hoping for the re-election of Grant, in spite of his break with Sumner.[23] Frederick Douglass clung to the Republican party as the best hope for his people. And, most conspicuous of all, Wendell Phillips worked for the re-election of Grant. Indeed, the decisions of Julian and Phillips make an interesting contrast. In 1868, when Julian had reluctantly supported Grant as the party standard-bearer, Phillips had stumped the country in opposition to his election. In 1872 the positions of the two reformers were reversed. Eschewing political office, Phillips lambasted the Liberal Republican movement as a humbug. The Cincinnati convention had ignored the demands of labor, he pointed out, and had then shown its true colors in the nomination of the protectionist Greeley, a man who could not be trusted and who had been too lenient with rebels. Grant, with all his weaknesses, was for Phillips preferable to Greeley.

23 Lydia Maria Child to Julian, January 31, 1872, Giddings-Julian Papers.

Thus the election of 1872 not only brought a break in the Republican ranks, it also forced a division among the abolitionists as well. The Liberals, faced with the dilemma of reconciling amnesty and civil rights for the Negro, chose the former, and in doing so rejected the solution suggested by Charles Sumner to combine amnesty and civil rights in the same measure. Then in their search for votes they turned to the white South where they proposed to barter civil rights for political aid. In short, the Negro was abandoned by men who only four years earlier seemed dedicated to the cause of the freedman.[24]

Julian went to the Cincinnati convention in 1872 as head of the Indiana delegation. His choice for presidential nominee, and the choice of the majority of Hoosiers, was Charles Francis Adams. Like many others, Julian was bitterly disappointed with Greeley's nomination, but he stuck with the party and fought valiantly for it in the campaign that followed.

For a brief period, when Schurz was called away from the chair to meet with the Missouri delegation, Julian presided over the convention. This was a good opportunity for the woman's rights advocates to make themselves heard. A reporter for the New York *Tribune* described Susan B. Anthony leaning on the arm of the presiding officer's chair and engaging him in a whispered but animated conversation, in spite of pronounced hissing in the hall. Her efforts were unavailing for the Liberal Republicans were politically astute enough to avoid an issue which could only have weakened them. Julian thought their attitude "toward Miss Anthony . . . was

[24] For a more detailed treatment see Patrick Riddleberger, "The Radicals' Abandonment of the Negro during Reconstruction," in *The Journal of Negro History*, 45 (1960):88-102.

all wrong, but the temper of the gathering towards women was such that nothing . . . could be done." "Almost a world of prejudice" would have to be conquered before woman suffrage could become a reality.

A determined group of Julian men in the Indiana delegation tried to make him the vice-presidential candidate, and he was convinced that their efforts would have been successful if Adams had been the presidential nominee. On the first two ballots for the Vice-Presidency Julian did receive enough votes to make him a serious contender, but the nomination finally went to B. Gratz Brown of Missouri as part of a political deal that made Greeley the presidential candidate. In spite of Julian's disappointment with the ticket, he was enthusiastic about the convention. He considered it the "grandest convention ever held in the country . . . made up of men of brains, of conscience, and of the most determined moral purpose." He was especially pleased also not to have seen "one drunk man in the convention or on the streets of the city."[25]

In June there was another incipient move to make Julian a candidate for office. The Democrats, meeting in

[25] Julian's Journal, May 7, 1872; Indianapolis *Daily Journal,* May 1-4, 1872; Indianapolis *Sentinel,* May 1-4, 1872; New York *Tribune,* May 4, 1872; Julian, *Political Recollections,* 337-52; Ross, *The Liberal Republican Movement,* 86-105. Julian's enthusiasm was not shared by all the Liberal Republican leaders. Schurz wrote a scathing letter to Greeley expressing his disappointment. "The only effect this . . . Convention had on popular sympathy and support consisted in its rising above the moral level of existing political organizations . . . nobody can read the proceedings of the convention in the light of surrounding circumstances without concluding that, on its very face, the first fruit of the great reform, so hopefully begun, was a successful piece of political huckstering and that the whole movement had been captured by politicians of the old stamp." Schurz to Greeley, May 6, 1872, in Frederic Bancroft (ed.), *Speeches, Correspondence and Political Papers of Carl Schurz* (6 vols. New York and London, 1913), 2:362-63.

state convention on June 12, considered nominating him for Congressman at large, but nothing came of it. Julian remarked on "the unbounded enthusiasm & perfect union" manifested in this meeting. "Everybody was for Greeley & the Cincinnati platform. . . . The Democratic masses," he recorded, "at last, have completely escaped from the control of their leaders and are free. Their sincerity in the [Liberal Republican] movement was perfectly demonstrated by their earnest and unmistakeable friendship for me, and their purpose to nominate me for . . . Congressman at large, which they would have done by acclamation if I had consented."[26]

By August 1, Julian was deep in the political campaign in Indiana, a campaign in which he spoke tirelessly at crossroads and metropolis in every section of the state. After six weeks of it he was weary from physical exertion and loss of sleep, and he complained of being "bored almost to death by constant political talk." Still he kept going, and by the time of the state elections in October he had made sixty-eight speeches. Toward the end his weariness abated, and he became stimulated with the campaign. Earlier he had feared that the strenuous routine might endanger his health, but now he began to fear, instead, his return to a quiet life rather than overexertion on the hustings. Since 1856 he had not experienced anything like the "perfect ovations" that he received, and they gave him unbounded confidence in victory for the Liberal Republican-Democratic alliance. "If we don't beat them," he recorded, "then no men were ever so deceived as we shall be. . . . We have preached reconcili-

26 Julian's Journal, June 15, 1872. The Indianapolis *Daily Journal* (June 20, 1872) portrayed Julian as actively seeking the nomination, but on finding his chances were impossible, he departed from Indianapolis the day before the convention, leaving behind a letter of declination.

ation & peace, & they have preached the gospel of hate; and while our men have kept in good humor & enjoyed the canvass the Grant men got mad in the start & have continued so to the end." He was confident that Thomas A. Hendricks, the former Democrat now running as coalition candidate for governor, would win by ten thousand to twenty thousand majority.[27]

The campaign demonstrated the continuing notoriety of the "Burnt District" Congressman throughout Indiana, for of all the Liberals he was the most maligned. The Morton forces made him the scapegoat of the whole Liberal Republican movement; they cited him as the living embodiment of everything evil about it: he was an apostate who always deserted his party and his friends when he failed to gain political office; time and again opposition newspapers devoted columns to episodes in Julian's career to prove this point. The Meredith affair was dragged out for another airing and given a "bloody shirt" twist that held Julian up as an abuser of courageous men who had fought for their country. Julian's illness, charged the Indianapolis *Journal,* was feigned to attract attention and sympathy where other means had failed.

The high point of the attack came on August 2, at the village of Economy in Wayne County, in a speech delivered by H. C. Fox, one of Morton's followers. Julian was not a reformer, Fox asserted, but a revolutionary who sought change only as a disturber and not as an advocate of progress. Fox also accused him of nepotism, as evidenced by the appointment of George's relatives to postmasterships in Richmond and Centreville. In

27 Julian's Journal, August 11, September 8, 22, October 8, 1872, Julian Papers; Whitelaw Reid to Julian, August 22, 1872, Giddings-Julian Papers; Indianapolis *Sentinel,* June 29, July 25, September 18, 1872.

great detail Fox reviewed Julian's political career, emphasizing those episodes that would prove his disloyalty to party and friends.[28]

There is every likelihood that such attacks on Julian were planned and instigated by Oliver P. Morton, now a Senator firmly entrenched among the Stalwarts of the Grant administration. Despite Morton's strong political position he still feared that Julian, in a close election, might wrest from him control of the state legislature. But Julian's role in the Liberal Republican movement presented Morton with an opportunity permanently to dispose of his most persistent and troublesome enemy in the Hoosier state. Nearly a year before the election Morton had written to a friend of Julian's affinity for the Liberal Republican movement: "He has taken his position himself; others have not taken it for him."[29] With Julian so accommodatingly digging his own political grave, Morton would be derelict indeed if he did not arrange for the burial.

The October election in Indiana resulted in an appalling defeat for the Liberals. The popular Hendricks was elected governor, but the Republicans elected the rest of their state ticket as well as the two Congressmen at large. Triumphantly and condescendingly the Indianapolis *Journal* extended permission to those misguided Republicans who had voted the Liberal ticket to return to the fold, but Julian and two or three others were invited to remain outside the Republican party. At some future date, taunted the *Journal*, "we may permit you

[28] Indianapolis *Daily Journal*, June 7, 19, July 1, August 7, 12, October 14, 1872; Indianapolis *Sentinel*, June 29, July 25, September 18, 1872.

[29] Morton to Simon J. Power, December 19, 1871, Oliver P. Morton Collection, Butler University Library, photostat copy in Indiana Division, Indiana State Library.

to vote for the Republican candidates for constables and real estate appraisers, but it will only be when satisfied that you have 'brought forth fruits meet for repentance.' "[30] This was the lash of Morton's party whip laid on with a vengeance.

On the heels of the local defeat in Indiana came Grant's victory in the national elections. To Julian it was "overwhelming & stunning." "The Liberals & democrats seem considerably dismayed and bewildered," he recorded in his journal, "& may charge the result to the unfortunate selection of Greeley as our candidate; but the trouble was the bourbon element in the democratic party, which was too completely demoralized to be rallied on the side of reform." Politically, the future looked dark indeed, and Morton was more firmly in the saddle than ever before. Still Julian did not completely abandon hope. The Republican party, he believed, would eventually hang itself with the rope of its own corruption; the Democratic-Liberal Republican combination was far from finished, and it would re-emerge, perhaps under a different name, with better prospects. He was certain that the people were bound to see that the Republican party was no longer their champion and that it had become the political agent of corporations, banks, and manufacturers.[31]

IV

For a while after the close of his Congressional career in the spring of 1871, Julian found real peace and contentment in his Centreville home. He spent hours at a

[30] Indianapolis *Daily Journal*, October 14, 15, 1872; New York *Daily Tribune*, October 7, November 6, 1872; Ross, *Liberal Republican Movement*, 180-82.

[31] Julian's Journal, November 5, 24, 1872.

time in his garden, building a new fence, and generally improving the appearance of the place. At last, it seemed, he had found some leisure and rest. Pleasurably he set about preparing his speeches in Congress for publication; a year later they appeared in print in a volume titled *Speeches on Political Questions.* Lydia Maria Child wrote a long and laudatory introduction, a task, she claimed, that she would not do for any other person.

Even Julian's recurring insomnia, which at times brought great despondency, did not affect his general happiness. Fred, the only surviving child of his first marriage, began to give "promise of becoming a good boy & a faithful worker." He had been a problem for his father and stepmother. The chief difficulty seemed to be that the boy did not fit into the preconceived pattern that George and Laura had created for him; he was no scholar, refused to study, and seemed to lack ambition, at least Julian's kind of ambition. Apparently he had been going through the toils of adolescence which his father never seemed to understand. But in the pleasant spring of 1871, he seemed at last to be growing up.[32]

These blissful days were not to last long. In June Laura's dying sister came to spend the remaining two months of her life with them. Her presence depressed George, and brought more bitter times in place of the gay ones: "I have had so much sickness in [my house], and so many deaths," he wrote in his journal. His own health grew worse again, perhaps because of the "contagion" of a sick person there. But "far worse" than these troubles, Julian soon discovered, was a recrudescence of "the wayward and ungracious conduct of [the] only child of my first marriage." Julian complained that he

32 Julian's Journal, April 23, 1871.

had done all that he could to save Fred, but it all seemed useless. In his relationship with this son, Julian was experiencing the "greatest trial of [his] greatly tried life."[33]

The election of 1872 brought a different sort of disappointment. Julian had hoped that his old district would demonstrate a continuing affection for him by giving the Liberal Republican candidates a big majority; instead, they voted heavily in favor of the Republicans, and Julian felt that he had been rejected politically by his own people. Brother Isaac had gone heavily into debt, so that in 1872 he was forced to stop publishing the *Radical*. The protracted battle over the location of the county seat ended with its being moved from Centreville to Richmond. Julian foresaw, as a result, a rapid decline in property values in Centreville.

Thus, as 1872 ended, Julian was thinking seriously of leaving Centreville, "and thinking of it sadly." Soon the decision was made, although, as he said, "I regret it profoundly, as I never meant to leave this land of my birth and early days and early struggles." The new house was located in Irvington, a suburb of Indianapolis where Julian looked forward to such advantages as "society, Libraries, Lectures, &c."[34]

In November, 1873, the Julian family moved into the unfinished Irvington home. But the event carried with it no great exhilaration. Upon their departure from Centreville George wrote nostalgically, "It was my home for more than thirty years. There I married the wife of my youth, and there she and the two oldest boys are buried. There I fought my political battles and into those years the chief events of my life are crowded. Near the town

33 *Ibid.*, June 16, August 27, 1871.
34 *Ibid.*, November 24, 1872, February 23, 1873. Jacob, George's brother, was one of the proprietors of Irvington.

I was born, and in its cemetery I expect my body to be laid."

Julian discovered that the carpenters who built the new house—"scalawags by nature" he called them—had overcharged him. The cost of the building was $18,000, twice as much as he had expected to pay. In his journal he despaired of the whole enterprise: "It was a fearful mistake, and places me in a false position since I had no *intention* of going into such a folly, and setting so undemocratic an example."

At the same time more bad news came from Isaac, who had gone West where family illness and his lack of business acumen had driven him more deeply into debt. A few months after his arrival in Texas his wife died. George aided him with large financial contributions.[35]

The change in Julian's physical surroundings in 1873 was accompanied by a change in his thinking. As he departed from the scene of his battles in the arenas of politics and reform, he left them behind him intellectually and spiritually as well. Although Julian was probably not altogether aware of it—he tried to convince himself otherwise—his great crusade was about over. Considering its importance to him, professionally and emotionally, during the past twenty years, there is little wonder that the metamorphosis should have had some profound effects.

[35] Julian's Journal, December 15, 1873, February 22, 1874.

FROM LIBERAL
TO DEMOCRAT

◇◈◇◈◇◈◇◈◇◈◇◈◇◈◇◈◇

THE defeat of the Liberal Republicans so altered Julian's political situation and so diminished his chances for an active public life that it might seem appropriate to end this account here, with a few additional pages summarizing the remaining years of his life. Granted, his career after 1872 was somewhat anticlimactic. But his interest in national affairs did not diminish; nor did he abandon his search for a political organization within which he could continue to work toward the goals of the reformer as he understood them in the post-Civil War era. Perhaps because he was so harshly expelled from the Republican party in 1872, he made his way during the next few years into the ranks of the Democratic party, where he was to remain, not always comfortably, during the last twenty-seven years of his life. The groping and the disappointment which were his lot during these years illuminate some aspects of the post-Reconstruction period in America and, therefore, call for more than a summary or cursory treatment.

While Julian was attempting to adjust to enforced changes in his public life, he was faced with continued difficulties in his private life. Especially grievous was the illness of his wife, which was serious enough that Julian sent her to New York for special treatment. One of the physical manifestations of her trouble was deafness, but she suffered even more from emotional disturbances. From New York she wrote letters that could have come only from the pen of a lonely and despondent woman who was fearful that the home could not function in her absence and that her children were not properly cared for. She wanted to be assured that George would not "neglect their evening stories" and that he would "bring them near" to him before they went to bed—so their dreams might be happy. Yet she did not wish George to be subjected to such woman's work. Laura seemed to feel that her very absence from home was proof enough that she was a failure as a wife. Fearing that her death was approaching, she instructed George about the differing personalities of the children and how to deal with them: Grace was selfish, but with discipline would grow into a charming woman. Paul was too trusting, and his weak eyes would need attention. But, "What I need always—and cannot live without," she pleaded, "is the blessed consciousness that *you love me.*"[1]

Evidently, Laura's difficulty was not all physical; nor was her dilemma unique. Her situation may have been that of many wives of career-minded men whose insatiable ambition precludes any love except that of self, realized in some form of public success.

Julian's son Fred also caused concern. He had been sent to Swarthmore College where he was popular with both teachers and students, but he either could not or would not abide by the college regulations, and he was soon dismissed. His enchantment with the theater drew him to Philadelphia, where he joined a theatrical group and be-

[1] Laura Julian to Julian, January 12, May 13, 14, 16, 17, 20, 22, 26, 1874, Julian Papers.

gan seriously to prepare himself for a career on the stage. His father had no faith in this project, but he did not interfere. During a trip to the East he visited with the theater manager, who confirmed his view that Fred had little if any dramatic talent. But the manager liked him and was willing to continue to work with him. Fred seems to have had that appeal which is sometimes found in the sons of public or otherwise successful men who never quite make the adjustment expected of them. Wherever he went, he seems to have attracted friends.

George's brother Isaac also continued to be a problem. His business fortunes did not improve, and Julian had to assist him. By this time a temporary rapproachement had been reached between George and his older brother, Jacob, but he, too, was in financial difficulties and Julian had to help him pay his debts by selling some of his bank stock. Moreover, with assets in the form of land and securities, George himself was hit hard by the depression which began in 1873.[2]

These pressures and tensions renewed Julian's old fears that he would lose his mind or that his health would become so bad as to incapacitate him. Although he enjoyed the reading and the intellectual pursuits that he had taken up after 1872, the need for more income and for a more active life became ever more pressing. For a time he considered returning to the practice of law; but it did not appeal to him and he was convinced that he was too far out of touch with the profession to make a living at it. Thus he accepted a position as a partner in a loan and collecting agency in Indian-

2 Julian's Journal, December 22, 1872, June 8, August 17, November 16, 1873, February 22, April 12, 1874, June 27, August 8, 1875; Julian to Laura Julian, May 13, 1874, Joseph A. Giddings to Laura Julian, January 4, 1875, Julian Papers.

apolis. This enterprise, in which he found little stimu-
lation, was short-lived. About all it produced was the
pretext for a "business" trip to the East where he spent
most of his time visiting old antislavery acquaintances,
among them Garrison and Phillips in Boston and William
Cullen Bryant in New York. While he was in Washington,
Charles Sumner, his antislavery comrade since the Free
Soil days, died, and Julian attended his funeral.[3]

Politics continued to be Julian's most absorbing interest. "Most of all my own health demands some active
employment of mind & body," he wrote. "I sometimes
long for politics again, in which I think I could be more
useful than any other work & for which I believe I am
best fitted."[4]

II

Although Julian was saddened by the magnitude of the
Liberal Republican defeat, it did not lead him into dis-
illusionment or to an immediate rejection of the idea of
a viable third party. Only with the approach of the
next presidential election did he give up hope and begin to consider the prospect of joining one of the two
major parties. Meantime, he was active among Indiana
Liberals and Democrats in a movement to create a new
party with a new name, but still embracing Liberal
Republican principles.[5]

His reluctance to return to the Republicans or to go
over to the Democrats can be explained in part by his
having adopted, as his most recent crusade, the anti-

---

3 Julian's Journal, April 12, 1874; Julian to Senator Henry B. Anthony,
dated Providence, March 26, 1874, Miscellaneous Julian Collection, Indiana Historical Society Library, Indianapolis. The letterhead is Tilford,
Julian & Co., Loan and Collection Agency, the address Indianapolis.

4 Julian's Journal, December 13, 1874.

5 *Ibid.*, March 16, May 4, 1873.

inflation movement. On the currency question the position of neither of the two major parties was satisfactory to him. More and more now he railed at "soft money lunatics" and inflationist demagoguery. Observing the Ohio campaign of 1875, where the currency question was a major issue, Julian confided to his journal that the hard money people "have all the argument & all the philosophy of the matter on their side, but the inflationists have the demagogues & fools, and these can be numerous." He was disgusted to find that some of his former comrades of the antislavery movement, Wendell Phillips and Cassius Clay among them, were stumping for "inflation and democracy." In contrast, Carl Schurz was "covering himself with glory" by campaigning for hard money.[6] Julian was so aroused by his fear of cheap money that he could even be complimentary of President Grant when, in 1874, he vetoed a bill to increase the number of greenbacks.[7]

Julian's role in the currency-reform crusade tells us more about him than his views, per se, on monetary and currency questions. It places him clearly among the patrician reformers of his era, men who, according to Eric Goldman, would reform America in the Grant era by attacking corruption from the top. They were condescending in their attitudes toward the robber barons as well as toward laborers and farmers who might thrust from the bottom against the miscarriage of American democratic ideals.[8] That before the end of Reconstruction and in the midst of an economic depression they could become deeply involved in a campaign so narrow as anti-inflation makes one wonder whether they had any

6 *Ibid.*, August 8, October 10, 1875.
7 Julian to Laura Julian, May 13, 1874, Julian Papers.
8 Goldman, *Rendezvous with Destiny*, 10-28.

real awareness of the social and economic realities of their times.

Julian's attachment to anti-inflation is especially interesting in the light of his concern about the plight of the farmer who at that very moment was organizing an inflation party as a means of contending with the forces unleashed by the Industrial Revolution. However, if Julian's understanding of the ethos of the 1870's was inadequate and his point of view narrow, he was not simply a maverick with heretical economic concepts. Rather he was on the side of most of the respectable and educated men of the time, including the professional economists, who held that currency reform, in particular the return to hard money, was a matter of first priority. In hard money they thought they had found the answer to management of the currency and other forms of economic control; thus it was an article of their continuing faith in a classical kind of *laissez faire,* which had already passed from the American scene never to return. It does not follow that Julian and the men whose ideas he shared were humbugs. If their views at this time are in any way illuminating, they suggest that these men who held them were essentially intellectual in their approach to public questions rather than humanitarian. They were too firmly committed to the conventional wisdom of their era.

When it became apparent that there would be no independent or Liberal Republican party in 1876, Julian had to decide which of the two major parties to support. Although it would be "very awkward [for him] to join the democrats in a fight against our old party friends and co-workers during the great trial of our country," it would be even more awkward to join a party dominated by such men as Grant and Morton. With the demise of the Liberal Republican party Julian's decision to become an independent Democrat was all but inevitable. To be independent was one thing, to be passive was quite another, and Julian was probably incapable of it. Once his mind was made up, Julian offered his services to the Democrats, and as he looked toward the approaching campaign he reflected, "Of course I shall be blackguarded in the old style, but feeling perfectly sure I am right I shall simply go ahead."[9]

On August 26, Julian opened his campaign with a speech at the Grand Opera House in Indianapolis. He began with a pronouncement that he appeared as an independent voter rather than as a representative of either party. Then there followed an airing of the corruptions of the Republican party under the Grant regime. A political party, he said, was not meant to be permanent. Rather, it should be thought of as a temporary organization dedicated to a set of definite goals; when these had been attained the party should cease to exist. This principle he now applied to the Republican party, which he said had outlived its usefulness.[10] Thoughtful listeners might have asked themselves what basis there was, according to this syllogism, for the existence of the Democracy. And those who recalled Hoosier politics of three decades earlier might have remembered that as a Free Soiler, Julian had predicted the demise of the Democratic

9 Julian's Journal, July 16, August 27, 1876. "The situation is very peculiar," Julian wrote as late as July 16, "& while it is true that the power of the Independent voter has been felt in putting both the old parties on their good behavior it is very questionable whether the Independent element should not have organized an Independent party, & thus have afforded a refuge for the consciences of those who have faith in neither of the existing parties."

10 Indianapolis *Daily Sentinel*, August 27, 1876; George W. Julian, *Later Speeches on Political Questions* (Indianapolis, 1889), 106-40.

party as a result of the same sort of evolution. For those who might have wondered at Julian's most recent transfer of allegiance he offered the platitudinous explanation that the war was over, that peace, order, and tranquillity were the things now needed most, and that the Democratic party could best bring about these conditions. If these words were somewhat redolent of the appeal of another oracle only a few years earlier who had pleaded, "Let us have peace," Julian was not distressed by the analogy.

In the political milieu of 1876, Julian's Indianapolis speech was just the sort of campaign document leaders in both parties were seeking. That the election would be close was conceded by all. While the Democrats indicted the Republicans with Grantism and corruption, the Republican leaders continued their "bloody shirt" attack on Democrats. In Rutherford B. Hayes and Samuel J. Tilden the two parties had brought forth innocuous men whose chief claims for support were that they were honest and that they might establish some of the mild reforms that had called forth the Liberal Republican movement four years earlier. The alignment of such men as Julian and Schurz thus took on added importance in a year when real differences between Democrats and Republicans were not always easily determined. It is hardly strange, therefore, to find among Julian's letters one from Abram S. Hewitt, the Democratic national campaign manager, in which he said, "I think the [Indianapolis speech] the most valuable and able speech that has yet been made." Hewitt apparently meant it, for within a month four hundred thousand copies had been printed as a campaign document, and before the end of the campaign two million copies had been distributed.[11]

11 Abram S. Hewitt to Julian, September 14, 1876, Julian Papers. Julian was one of a number of former Liberal Republicans who cam-

In September and October the campaign increased in tempo, and Julian entered energetically into it. He visited every region of Indiana; and, after the Hoosier election in October, in which the Democrats scored a victory, he extended his activities into Michigan, Wisconsin, and Illinois. He met Laura in Chicago, where he spoke on October 25, after which they journeyed home together for a few days' rest. On October 30 he was off again, this time for the East. His first stop was in Cincinnati and the next in Pittsburgh. He then proceeded to New York, where he expected to speak in the Cooper Institute, but Hewitt had not received his telegram accepting the invitation and had engaged another speaker. The campaign manager quickly arranged a street meeting where Julian made his last speech of the regular campaign.

In New York he dined with Tilden who impressed him favorably. Tilden recalled that the two had met at the Free Soil convention in 1848. In his journal Julian wrote of the nominee: "I found him genial, familiar, & very instructive. I saw nothing of the coldness that is generally attributed to him, & was most agreeably surprised to find him a fine looking, well-preserved old gentleman who has a first rate prospect of living ten or twenty years longer."[12]

The struggle between Republicans and Democrats for contested electoral votes in three southern states, which complicated and postponed the final decision in favor of Hayes by a Congressional electoral commission, provided the setting for an unusual episode in Julian's life— one that is enlightening as to his changing ideas and

paigned for Tilden at the behest of Hewitt. Others were Cassius M. Clay, Lyman Trumbull, Charles Francis Adams, and Henry Watterson. Allan Nevins, *Abram S. Hewitt* . . . (New York and London, 1935), 311.

12 Julian's Journal, September 10, 17, October 8, 29, December 10, 1876; Julian to Laura Julian, November 3, 1876, Julian Papers.

principles during the 1870's. For Julian was one of a group of Democrats who were chosen by Hewitt to go to New Orleans to observe the proceedings of the Louisiana Returning Board. In his journal and in letters to his wife Julian recorded some of his reactions to the South as well as to the stirring political developments. Upon arrival in New Orleans he was sanguine enough about Tilden's election to write, "I don't *believe* the enemy will dare to count him out." But before two weeks had passed Julian saw that the board was going to declare Hayes the winner in Louisiana. Immediately he began to prepare "an appeal to the people."[13]

Julian's reactions to the South during the month that he remained in New Orleans reflect a very different man indeed from the Radical crusader of only a few years earlier. Now that the slavery question was "settled," the old abolitionist displayed little concern for the problems of the freedman. His letters contain no reference to the Negro's social or economic condition. Indeed, the only reference to Negroes in his letters to his wife during this sojourn in the deep South was to describe the woeful lack of intelligence of the two who served on the returning board and to remark that the Negroes still seemed to have faith in *him*.

The five years that had elapsed since his departure from Congress had also erased his repugnance for southern Democrats, especially those in the upper social brackets. "I am in love with the South," he wrote to Laura, "as I know you would be." And after an evening of entertainment at the home of the governor-elect, a conservative Democrat, he wrote that he was "more and more pleased with the refinement of the upper ten here,

[13] Julian's Journal, December 10, 1876; Julian to Laura Julian, November 13, 20, 23, 24, 26, 1876, Julian Papers.

& the perfect ease and gracefulness with which they do everything in the department of social life."[14]

Julian made his "appeal to the people" in a speech delivered in Indianapolis on January 8, 1877, in which he sought to prove that Tilden was the legally elected President and that the Republicans were trying to steal the victory. Concentrating on the election in Louisiana, of which he had personal knowledge, he made several charges: the election board was illegally constituted; the observers sent by the Republican party refused to use their influence to bring about a fair election; the returning board offered no proof of charges that Democrats had intimidated voters at the polls. In short, a Democratic majority of eight or nine thousand had been fraudulently transformed into a Republican majority of four thousand. With bitter invective he charged the Republican high command—particularly Morton and John Sherman—with treason, and he called for "popular agitation" against it.

In stentorian phrases he concluded with a warning as to the result if the wrong was not righted:

A century ago our fathers took up arms in defense of their right to a voice in the government which dealt with their liberty, their property and their lives. We assert the same right now when we ask that the will of the people be registered as the supreme law, and that whoever may defy it by overt acts shall receive the same treatment which the nation awarded to the man who appealed from the ballot to the bayonet in 1861. Let them be warned in season by every lover of . . . liberty that millions of men will be found ready to offer their lives as hostages to the sacredness of the ballot, as the palladium of our liberty.[15]

14 Julian to Laura Julian, November 16, 27, 1876, Julian Papers.
15 Julian, *Later Speeches,* 141-75.

The speech elicited an editorial in the Cincinnati *Commercial.* Though too severe, it captured in a few phrases some of the contradictory essentials of Julian's personality:

Into it [the speech] he poured all the gall of disappointment, all the bitterness of jealousy, all the hatred of envy, all the eloquence of abuse that could originate in the brain of one of the ablest, most brilliant, meanest and most malignant of men —a man whose nature is great and small, admirable and hateful, with the brain of a man and a statesman and the soul of a cynic and misanthrope—one of the brightest, greatest, meanest of mankind.[16]

When the election was turned over to an electoral commission, Julian went to Washington where he could watch the proceedings at close range. Now it was the Democrats' turn to receive his rebuke for irresolution and lack of fight. The Democrats, Julian believed, ought to delay the commission's decision with a Congressional filibuster, and then insist on a new election. But the Democratic leaders, and especially Tilden, were not brave enough to lead the attack. An Andrew Jackson was needed, but Tilden was not such a man. Thus, said Julian, "If [the Democrats] perish utterly as a party they will have nobody to blame but themselves," for not only was Tilden pusillanimous, but his followers had proved themselves to be "cowards & idiots."

Although Julian chastised the Tilden men for their lack of energy, he, himself, refused to take an active part in the proceedings of the commission. On at least two occasions Tilden men urged Julian to make the leading argument before the commission in the case of South Carolina, but each time he refused, pleading that there was too little time to prepare his argument. He lapsed

16 Quoted in Clarke, *Julian,* 372ṇ.

into a state of mild vertigo and wrote to Laura that his Indianapolis speech had led to an overestimate of his abilities and that if he entered into the case, he was afraid that he would be unable to sustain the prevailing good opinion of himself.[17]

Julian's analysis of the political situation in Louisiana turns out to have been reasonably accurate (although conclusions about that state would not necessarily be accurate if applied to South Carolina and Florida where the other two contests occurred). Also, his fighting mood was shared by many northern Democrats who were adamant against the compromise agreed to by the southern party leaders. Not only were the northern Democrats angered at having the victory snatched away from them, some at least saw clearly that the nature of the compromise opened the floodgates for the development of monopolies in the South similar to those in the North during and after the Civil War.

One such Democrat was William S. Holman of Indiana, long a champion in the House of Representatives against railroad and land monopolies of all kinds. Holman was particularly bitter over the repeal of the Southern Homestead Act of 1866, for which Julian had battled, on the grounds that it would place the South at the mercy of lumber magnates and other northern business interests. The aims of men like Holman were to continue to apply the homestead principle, to reestablish economy in government, and to bring an end to government subsidies to railroads. They were the advocates of reform along Jeffersonian lines, which meant that all they had in common with southern Democratic Redeemers was their membership in the same political

[17] Julian's Journal, January 21, February 11, 1877; Julian to Laura Julian, February 23, 24, 25, 26, 27, 28, March 1, 1877, Julian Papers.

party.[18] Julian shared Holman's fears, and wrote to the New York *Tribune* protesting the repeal of the Southern Homestead Act.[19] He was also in essential agreement with men such as Holman on the methods and objectives of reform a decade after the end of the war. But it was personal disappointment and pique rather than his disenchantment as a reformer that more adequately explain Julian's frenetic reaction to Tilden's defeat. One searches in vain through Julian's personal correspondence and his journal for statements or reflections on the repeal of the Southern Homestead Act, the compromise that turned the fate of the southern Negro over to the white South, or other such consequences of the election. What one does find is that Julian was slated for the post of Secretary of the Interior, which now went under Hayes to another former Radical and abolitionist, Carl Schurz. "What a narrow escape I made!" Julian wrote. "I had a right to feel disappointed, for I always . . . felt that Tilden believed in me & would give me that position." The election of Rutherford B. Hayes was a bitter pill for Julian. It made him "sick at heart," and he could see "no silver lining to [the] cloud."[20]

III

The end of Julian's activities in the election of 1876-77 brought a great restlessness that left him floundering. He began to renew his prodigious reading program undertaken in 1873,[21] but even that left unsatisfied his

---

18 Woodward, *Reunion and Reaction,* 53-54.

19 Gates, "Federal Land Policy in the South, 1866-1888," in *Journal of Southern History,* 6:311.

20 Julian's Journal, March 11, 1877; Julian to Laura Julian, February 25, 1878, Julian Papers.

21 Among the books that Julian read at this time were John Stuart Mill, *On Liberty,* William E. H. Leckey's *History of the Rise and Influ-*

desire to be actively employed. Again he thought of returning to the practice of law, but he feared that, at the age of sixty, there was little chance of success; and he dreaded the humiliation of failure. For repose he turned to the past. Even before the engrossing campaign of 1876, Julian had begun to find solace in reflections on his more active years. In reading that part of his journal covering the Civil War years he was "astonished" with the amount of labor he had performed and with his "absolute surrender" of himself, "night and day," for his constituents. He recalled that he had been "perfectly spell-bound by the crisis & its demands" upon him and that he had completely disregarded his "health, personal comfort, or social enjoyment." "This dedication of myself continued through ten years," he reflected, "& ever since it ended I have been realizing more & more what a fearful load I was carrying & what a release I have found in the sweet quiet of home & private life."[22] Thus, instead of returning to the practice of law, Julian decided to occupy himself by writing his autobiography. The story of his life, he believed, would "embody matters of interest & instruction" to his progeny, particularly if they had "any concern in the struggles and trials of the poor & the lessons which they teach." At the end of five months the task was completed; Julian had worked at it five hours a day, and he had written 333 pages.[23]

ence of the Spirit of Rationalism in Europe and his *History of European Morals,* Herbert Spencer's *Universal Progress,* Darwin's *Origin of Species,* William S. Jevons on currency, Sumner's *History of American Currency,* Motley's *Rise of the Dutch Republic,* and Carlyle's *French Revolution.*

22 Julian's Journal, June 4, 1876.

23 *Ibid.,* April 17, August 5, September 16, 1877. The burning of this manuscript, along with Julian's journal covering the period before 1869, by his daughter Grace, constituted an inestimable loss to historians.

Although the autobiography was not written for publication, it ushered in a period of writing that brought
forth, during the next few years, the publication of a
number of articles as well as Julian's *Political Recollections.* Two of the articles dealt almost exclusively
with political matters. "The Death-Struggle of the Republican Party," which appeared in the *North American
Review* of March, 1878, was merely a restatement of
Julian's oft-repeated philosophy of political parties, with
the Republican party cited as the execrable example of
what happens when a political organization is permitted
to outlive its constructive program. The following year
Julian wrote, for the *International Review,* "Some Political Notes and Queries," in which he predicted that
either Grant or Blaine was certain to be the Republican
candidate in 1880. The article also contained some criticism of the Democratic party, but the implication was
unmistakable that independent voters should use their
power to defeat the Republicans.[24]

Other articles revealed Julian's attitudes toward prevailing social and economic philosophies and conditions.
He had read Charles Darwin's *Origin of Species,* and
the works of Herbert Spencer and Walter Bagehot who
sought to apply Darwin's scientific theories to social
evolution. Julian found much of this "Social Darwin-
ism" repulsive. He could not accept the concept of the
"survival of the fittest," and he believed that the Dar-
winists' laissez-faire theory of progress made for social
lethargy and moral indifference. But he could accept

24 George W. Julian, "The Death-Struggle of the Republican Party,"
in *North American Review,* 126 (January-June, 1878):262-92; "Some Political Notes and Queries," in *International Review,* 7 (July-December,
1879):164-82; Julian's Journal, February 10, 1878; Julian to Laura Julian,
January 13, February 14, 15, 1878, Laura Julian to Julian, February 16,
1878, Julian Papers.

that part of the theory embracing a concept of universal progress. His problem was, therefore, to reconcile this with the need for reformers in society. His neat reconciliation of seemingly conflicting ideas appeared in an article in the *North American Review* entitled, "Is the Reformer Any Longer Needed?" Here Julian stated that there was, indeed, a law of progress, but that its existence did not permit men to wait patiently for it to operate. This patient role belonged to God alone, since only He had a long-range view of universal progress. But the strivings of every generation of men against social evil were essential to the whole evolution. "If progress has been evolved," said Julian, "it has also quite as certainly been propagated. It is not simply the product of law, but the fruit of human trial and sacrifice, voluntarily embraced for the improvement and regeneration of mankind."

In search of a crusade that would be as satisfying to him as the antislavery movement had been, Julian turned again to the currency question. With that remarkable ingenuousness of which he was capable, he apparently convinced himself that currency reform was as significant and far-reaching as the antislavery movement. Included among the books he read on financial matters was William Graham Sumner's *History of American Currency*, which brought authoritative support to Julian's belief that a nonmetallic currency had been a "curse to every country that [had] tried it, and that every scheme for relieving indebtedness of individuals or nations without payments [was] a violation of the command, 'Thou shalt not steal.' "[25]

[25] George W. Julian, "Is the Reformer Any Longer Needed?" in *North American Review*, 127 (July-December, 1878):337-60. From Julian's changing views about society it might be inferred that he also read some of Sumner's sociological writings.

Julian found another evil in the growth of cities and in the concomitant abuse of labor. "Labor is not a commodity, like cotton or corn," he wrote. "The rights of the laborer are the rights of humanity. The power of his employer to fix his compensation is the power over his life." Wages ought to be determined by mutual conference. But how in Julian's view, was the laborer to gain the necessary power to bargain successfully? Apparently not through the intervention of the Federal government whose tendency "toward usurpation and . . . centralization of power" he listed as another of the great dangers facing the nation. As a solution for labor troubles Julian could only suggest: "The people must snatch freedom itself from the perilous activities quickened into life by its own spirit. They must search out new defenses of Democracy in the new trials of its life."[26] Julian still argued that real democracy must have its roots in the soil, and he still seemed to believe that if land monopoly could only be destroyed all would be well. But while forcefully rejecting any "scheme of 'agrarianism,' " he virtually admitted that he could propose no solution for the "unrestricted monopoly of the soil . . . [so] repugnant to republican government."[27]

Missing from all of Julian's writings are specific references to many of the disruptions and developments of the post-Civil War era. There is no mention, for example, of the railroad strike of 1877 that was finally quelled by Federal troops. His professed interest in the laboring man did not lead him to mention the Knights of Labor or the efforts to establish Socialist parties in America in the 1870's. Considering Julian's concern about

[26] George W. Julian, "The Pending Ordeals of Democracy," in *International Review*, 5 (1878):734-53.
[27] George W. Julian, "Our Land Policy," in *Atlantic Monthly*, 43 (1879):336-37; Smith, *Virgin Land*, 192, 195.

currency and railroad monopoly, there is an incongruous absence of any reference to the Granger movement or the Greenback party, whose rise in 1878 seemed to threaten the "stable" economy of "sound" money advocates. How could a man overlook these significant developments while persisting in a cry for reform? Part of the answer is perhaps psychological; another part might be found in his social and intellectual milieu.

Among the reformers of the post-Civil War era Julian was not alone in his concentration on corruption in government, land monopoly, and a declining morality, at the expense of more flagrant and basic social maladjustments. Carl Schurz, the old German-American reformer, sat now in the Cabinet of President Hayes still transfixed with the idea that all of America's ills could be cured if only honest men were elected and appointed to public office. And "Old Zach" Chandler, once so eager to free the Negro and to destroy the slavocracy even at the cost of some blood, suffered from no apparent qualms of conscience in furthering the compromise with southern "Redeemers" that kept the Republican party in power as it sacrificed the Negro. Nor was Julian's enchantment with reform in political parties by any means inexplicable. From the time he had joined the abolitionists Julian had always seen political channels as the only practical means of effecting reforms. Since the Free Soil days he had always found a political party that he believed was dedicated to the specific reforms that he championed. Hence he probably reasoned that in the post-Civil War era the parties must be cleansed of corruption before other reforms could be achieved.

If Julian was inconsistent, it was not so much in his castigation of Republicans as in his espousal of Democrats. It required a considerable rationalization to convince himself that his break with the Republicans and his attachment to the Democrats was a repetition of his break with the Whigs in 1848 and his joining the Free Soilers. Yet this was an analogy that Julian drew repeatedly after 1872. If it seemed spurious to others, to him it was apparently genuine enough.

After 1877 Julian spent much time in Washington where he tried to build up his dwindling financial resources. The sale of his bank stock had continued, and he found it necessary to keep up the contributions to his brother Isaac. He sold some of his land in Iowa, but had difficulty collecting for it. He was almost constantly under the care of a physician. In short, Julian was feeling the effects of the depression in a very personal way. He preferred to devote his time to writing; but he could not make a living from it, and he was forced to turn to other activities. For a time it appeared that he might be appointed a swamplands agent for either Arkansas or Florida, but again he was disappointed. He continued to act as counsel for land claimants in cases in the Interior Department and before the Supreme Court, and in 1879 he formed a law partnership, specializing in land cases, with William A. Meloy in Washington.

Laura remained in Indiana where she wrestled with the difficulties of running the home and with many of the financial problems. For the most part, her letters were motherly and kind—she was greatly concerned about George's health—but occasionally she spurred him on to more lucrative endeavors. "Don't be afraid of your *dignity*," she once wrote. "You have put the democrats under obligations and may ask their attention with confidence I should think."[28]

---

[28] Laura Julian to Julian, March 3, 1878, and Julian to Laura Julian, March 5, April 20, 24, 27, 1878, Julian Papers; Clarke, *Julian*, 381. Julian also had an arrangement with Col. Robert Ingersoll, the famous agnostic

IV

If Julian expected Grant to be the Republican standard-bearer in 1880, against whom he could vent his wrath, he was disappointed. For, although Grant was the choice of the "Stalwart" wing of the party, the "Half-breeds" under the command of James G. Blaine succeeded in stalling the Grant forces, permitting the nomination of the Ohio "dark horse," James A. Garfield.

Even so, Julian entered the lists again in behalf of the Democracy. Still declaiming his independence—and this was the role in which the Democrats liked him—he made his most important address of the campaign at the Indianapolis Wigwam on August 24. After reviewing his whole political career to prove his independence, he launched into a philippic against the Republican party very similar to his famous Indianapolis speech of the 1876 campaign. After repeating the party's record of corruption, Julian brought his listeners up to date on the "fraud of 1876" and the perfidy of the Hayes administration in its failure to render promised civil service reform. There was little that Julian could say about the politically inconspicuous Gen. W. S. Hancock, nominee of the Democratic party, except that he was an honorable and incorruptible man. Garfield he depicted as a man incapable of rising above party considerations and tainted with the Crédit Mobilier scandal and with the fraudulent election of 1876. He denounced the spineless platforms of both parties, but reiterated his plea that the Demo-

lecturer, whereby the two men co-operated in several cases. Apparently the arrangement was very informal and of brief duration. In their most important case they had difficulty collecting their fee. Ingersoll Papers, April 12, October 19, 1878, Manuscript Division, Library of Congress. Julian also appealed to Samuel J. Tilden in his search for clients and received from him a promise that he would help whenever possible. Tilden to Julian, January 29, 1880, Giddings-Julian Papers.

crats were better equipped to foster "patience and good-will in both sections" without which the continuing bitterness between North and South could never be eased. For this and other speeches Julian received $1,500 from the Democratic National Committee.[29]

In 1884 Julian again took the stump for the Democrats, but by then he had dropped his mantle of independence. Perhaps he had finally decided to accept Laura's advice and to put away his dignity, for Julian was about to become surveyor general of New Mexico, the last public office of his life. It came in the first administration of Grover Cleveland as a well-earned reward for service to the Democratic party during the past decade.

There is something ironical and pathetic about the former abolitionist and Free Soiler begging at the Democratic patronage trough, and Julian's rather grossly distorted version of his appointment as surveyor general elicits more sympathy than contempt for him. Julian's account appeared in an article by him, published in the *North American Review* in 1887, in which he stated that Cleveland had given him the choice of governor or surveyor general of the territory. He had chosen the latter, said Julian, because it was more in accord with his qualifications and tastes. But his letters to President Cleveland, written shortly before the appointment, tell a far different story: He apparently wished and expected to be made Commissioner of the General Land Office in Washington. When news came that another man had been appointed, Julian wrote, "My defeat was very vexatious and humiliating, and nothing but financial necessity could have induced me, at my time of life, to join the

---

[29] Julian, *Later Speeches*, 176-214; William H. Barnum, chairman of executive committee, National Democratic Committee, to Julian, August 27, 1880, Julian Papers; Barnum to William H. English, August 19, 1880, English Papers, Indiana Historical Society Library, Indianapolis.

army of office-beggers in Washington." Next came the offer from the President for the post of governor or of surveyor general of New Mexico to which Julian, still hoping for a Washington appointment, replied, "As to New Mexico I had no thought of any position so far out on our frontiers and among so rough and miscellaneous population. It would have more attractions for a younger man with a future ahead of him which he might hope to mold in this way." At this point Julian began to fear that he had successfully talked himself out of an office, and subsequent letters had a conciliatory tone. He had now reconsidered, and, anticipating appointment as governor, he wrote, "I think I could make myself useful in checking the . . . land monopoly in the territory, and especially so if the Surveyor General should be the right sort of man." Julian's next letter was written just after the governorship had also eluded him, in the appointment of Edmund G. Ross of Kansas, the former Senator who had voted in 1868 against the conviction of Andrew Johnson. Julian now apologized profusely for the hastiness of his first letter, which he believed had prevented him from becoming governor; and he expressed the hope that his "impolitic diffidence and self-disparagement" would not exclude him from consideration for other appointments.[30] When the offer of the surveyor generalship did finally come, Julian did not deliberate but grasped it.

[30] Julian to Grover Cleveland, May 12, 19, 27, 1885, Cleveland Papers, Manuscript Division, Library of Congress; George W. Julian, "Land-Stealing in New Mexico," in *North American Review*, 145 (July-December, 1887):17-31. In seeking the appointment as Commissioner of the General Land Office Julian solicited aid from men in both the Democratic and Republican parties. Both Tilden and George F. Hoar recommended his appointment. Abram Hewitt also urged Cleveland to find a place for Julian.

To be sure, Julian's improvidence had aroused the sympathies of his friends and was in part accountable for his appointment as surveyor general. But he ought not be thought of merely as an office seeker looking for a pittance. His appointment fits logically into Cleveland's plans for reform in the Land Office and his efforts to check speculation in public lands and to end the depredations by the railroads of lands claimed by settlers under the Homestead Act or still maintained by the Federal government as public lands. Cleveland certainly had these reforms in mind when he appointed L. Q. C. Lamar to the Cabinet as Secretary of the Interior and William A. J. Sparks as Commissioner of the General Land Office, in the Interior Department.[31]

Of the several articles which Julian wrote attacking the Republican party after 1876 none was so authoritative or demonstrated so clearly Julian's knowledge of land matters as one entitled, "Railway Influence in the Land Office," which appeared in the *North American Review* in 1883. In attempting to show that the Land Office had become the servant of the railroads, Julian pointed to several practices that had become common there. Many illegal indemnities had been made to the railroads for lands to which they were not entitled. After 1880, the Secretary of the Interior had given a new interpretation to a ruling that had been in effect since 1859, when Attorney General Black had ruled that the railroads might receive, merely for their information, a certified list of lands due to come into their hands, but not yet earned by construction. Under the new interpretation, these certified lists became valid and conclusive and had the force of patents. In this way, 10,000,000

---

31 Allan Nevins, *Grover Cleveland, A Study in Courage* (New York, 1932), 207, 216, 223-28.

acres of illegal indemnity lands had been awarded to the railroads. Grants had been made to many railroads and these lands reserved from settlement without the railroads having earned them. In some cases, only part of the railroad had been built (North Louisiana and Texas Railroad); in others, nothing had been done (Pensacola and Georgia Railroad). The overworked Commissioner of the General Land Office was forced to sign decisions that he had never examined. Clerks with no legal training and with little acquaintance with rules of evidence frequently had the power to decide intricate cases. Worst of all, Julian argued, the settler was placed in a difficult position. Unable to employ competent counsel, he had to contend with the best legal talent money could buy employed on behalf of the railroads. There were no formal hearings in cases between railroads and settlers, and railroad lawyers "have access to the chiefs of divisions, and their constructions of law are generally impressed upon the minds of clerks having the cases in charge, notwithstanding the regulations of the department prohibiting conferences between attorneys and clerks, except upon permission."[32]

This article brought forth an immediate, indignant response from Carl Schurz. He was particularly annoyed with Julian's charge that he, as Secretary of the Interior, had been instrumental in securing for the railroads legal title to lands which they had not earned.[33] On this particular point Schurz may have been right and Julian wrong. However, subsequent scholarship on the subject substantiates Julian's thesis as to the power and influ-

[32] George W. Julian, "Railway Influence in the Land Office," in *North American Review*, 136 (January-June, 1883):240-55.

[33] Bancroft (ed.), *Speeches, Correspondence and Political Papers of Carl Schurz*, 4:184-94.

ence of the railroads in the implementation of public land policy.

V

Laura Julian had died suddenly of heart disease on March 31, 1884, and as Julian entered upon his duties as surveyor general of New Mexico he probably recalled his return to Congress after the election of 1860. On that occasion he had grieved for Anne, his first wife. Now he journeyed to New Mexico without Laura. He also suffered from a malady of the lungs, probably tuberculosis, which had afflicted him for nearly a decade. Still he undertook his new duties with great enthusiasm.

Almost immediately Julian became a controversial figure, and there was much opposition to his confirmation by the Senate. A Santa Fé citizen wrote to a Senator describing Julian as a "monomaniac as to Spanish and Mexican land titles" and accusing him of being "exceedingly injurious to the Territory." Annoyed with the opposition to his confirmation, Julian wrote a rather ungrateful letter to Cleveland, expressing his indifference as to the action of the Senate:

To me the question is of little moment. The labor and responsibility of my position are so great, and the salary so utterly inadequate, that I scarcely have any motive at all, financially, for desiring to hold it; but I like my work better than I anticipated, and find I can be exceedingly useful, if allowed to remain. On this account, and because I am anxious to see your action vindicated, I should dislike to be rejected by the Senate.[34]

To be sure, Julian's task, involving the settlement of innumerable Mexican and Spanish land grants, was a

[34] Julian to Benjamin Harrison, July 15, 1886, quoting letter from Senator Plumb, Benjamin Harrison Papers, Manuscript Division, Library of Congress; Julian to Cleveland, December 3, 1885, Cleveland Papers.

very difficult one. New Mexican officials had wrestled with the problem since the Mexican War. The Treaty of Guadalupe Hidalgo had guaranteed legal claimants the protection of the American government, but the ill-defined boundaries and the frequent lack of written documents proving ownership fostered a situation that was bound to attract land speculators. In 1854, the office of surveyor general had been created to help Congress in its herculean task of settling each claim by legislative enactment. But when Julian arrived on the scene he found in the hands of speculators 9,000,000 acres of land that he believed ought to have been included in the public domain. He attributed this condition to the ineptness of Congress and, particularly, to the fraudulent practices of his predecessors in the surveyor general's office.

Immediately Julian began an examination of claims approved by his predecessors, and of the thirty-five examined before the end of his term, he rejected thirty-three. As an enemy of the land monopolist operating under Spanish or Mexican claims, Julian had the unwavering support of Commissioner Sparks. In 1887, Julian wrote another article for the *North American Review* accusing Stephen W. Dorsey, among others, of stealing land in New Mexico under a forged grant. When the nature of the grant was discovered, Julian claimed, Dorsey had turned to the homestead and pre-emption laws for protection and had used his influence with the General Land Office to have reserved lands illegally opened for settlement. Julian's claims had been materially substantiated by Sparks, who wrote to him that he had searched the records of the Land Office but had "fail[ed] to find any instructions giving the Surveyor General . . . authority to extend the lines of the public land surveys over the area embraced in the original instructions for the survey of the Uña de Gato [Dorsey] Grant." Yet it appeared that the surveyor general had proceeded in 1879, 1880, and 1881, to let contracts that had not been approved and accepted by the Land Office.[35]

Another case, which occurred toward the end of Julian's term as surveyor general, involved the Mora grant. This case brought Julian into sharp conflict with S. M. Stockslager, Sparks's successor in the Commissioner's office. The disagreement was over the northern boundary of the grant, which Stockslager insisted was Ocate Creek, and he repeatedly ordered Julian to change the plat so as to show the stream as the boundary. This Julian refused to do, even after the Commissioner cited as legal precedent the case of *New Orleans* v. *U.S.*, purporting to show that under common law a stream once established as a boundary remained so in spite of a future change in its course. Julian replied that he could not comply with the Commissioner's order for to do so would completely reverse past decisions and policy. Instead, he was placing the whole matter again before the Commissioner "in the hope that general instructions may be issued by you for the guidance of this office in this and future cases." In reply to Stockslager's legal argument, Julian pointed out that the decision in *New Orleans* v. *U.S.* was not applicable to the Mora grant. The former case involved a corporation, the City of New Orleans, holding title to land "formed by the alluvial deposits on a navigable stream." The corporation owned the land to which the alluvium clung. This was an accretion, and

---

35 Julian, "Land-Stealing in New Mexico," in *North American Review*, 145:17-31; Stephen W. Dorsey, " 'Land-Stealing in New Mexico,' a Rejoinder," in *ibid.*, 145:396-409; Sparks to Julian, March 14, 1887, Land Office Records, National Archives.

GEORGE W. JULIAN, AGE EIGHTY

the general principle of the common law on that subject was perfectly applicable to it. But the Mora case, Julian argued, involved a tract of land two or three hundred acres in extent not created or moved by the action of the water. Then he cited a decision by Justice Miller wherein it was stated that lands claimed under Mexican or Spanish grants *"but not found within the limits of the final survey when made . . . are restored to the public domain by the survey."* The principle of riparian ownership, said Julian (citing Gould on Waters), did not always extend to the stream. Certainly it could not be applied in New Mexico where streams could not be depended on to be in the same location twice within twenty-four hours. What Julian wanted, he told the Commissioner, was a policy "that would give no countenance to the theory that the boundaries of a patented grant are floating in the air like clouds, instead of being fixed and determined lines on the earth's surface."[36]

It is apparent that Julian was well fitted by temperament and training to deal with the Spanish and Mexican land grant cases, but another part of the job that he regarded as equally important was to bring about the confirmation of the claims of small settlers under the pre-emption laws. Here he came into conflict with Commissioner Sparks. One of Julian's first acts after taking office was to approve and to forward to the Commissioner the applications of a number of settlers to have surveyed the lands they occupied. Sparks's rejection of many of these applications emanated from a desire for land reform that was certainly equal to Julian's in its intensity. But Sparks, while not forgetting the small settler, had become concerned with the need to conserve

[36] S. M. Stockslager to Julian, April 26, 1889, and Julian to Stockslager, May 3, 1889, Land Office Records, National Archives.

the country's natural resources. His policy was to approve no applications for surveys in mountain or timber areas. He returned many applications that Julian had approved, frequently requesting more information as to the nature of the land. This policy brought delays that annoyed Julian. Sometimes he complained to Sparks that he could not get more information without making personal examinations in the field for which Congress had provided no money. He accused Sparks of not being forceful enough with Congress in setting forth the need of further appropriations. Sparks received this criticism, for the most part, in good grace. His replies were firm but tactful and often expressed appreciation of the difficulties under which Julian worked.[37]

Sparks belonged to a school of land reformers who were maintaining ever more vigorously that the preemption laws no longer served the settler but abetted speculators, monopolists, and cattle companies. For the same reasons, he called for repeal of the commutation clause of the Homestead Act. His strongest plea was for the preservation of the forests, whose depletion reduced the cultivable area of the soil, increased the danger of floods, and made rivers less navigable. He warned that calamity would follow the widespread destruction of the forests and that they could be renewed only at enormous cost.[38] Sparks demonstrated a greater awareness of many of the realities of his era than Julian, who successfully

[37] Julian to Sparks, October 17, 1885, February 6, 1886, and Sparks to Julian, December 25, 1885, February 12, December 22, 1886, Land Office Records, National Archives.

[38] Report of the Commissioner of the General Land Office, 1885, in *Report of the Secretary of the Interior (House Executive Documents,* 49 Congress, 1 session, No. 1, Pt. 5, in 5 vols.), 1:155-236; Harold H. Dunham, "Some Crucial Years of the General Land Office, 1875-1890," in *Agricultural History,* 11 (1937):136-39.

convinced himself, and persisted in the belief, that the establishment of the settler on 160 acres of land would solve the nation's post-Civil War problems. Yet Julian's thinking about the actual settler, whose champion he longed to be, involved him in some gross inconsistencies. Indeed, he seems to have known little about this actual settler. Greenbackers and Free Silverites were anathema to him, but he never searched very deeply for the causes of the farmer's distress. By protecting a few settlers in New Mexico or by taking the part of a Hutchings in the Yosemite Valley, Julian really believed that he was coming to grips with the agrarian problem. For the Populists and their demands for more protection by the national government, he had nothing but contempt.[39]

Henry Nash Smith, in his *Virgin Land,* gives Julian a prominent place among those land reformers who clung tenaciously to the myth of an agrarian utopia, a garden of the world, in the American West. Such men, says Smith, "were employing ideas that had little relevance to the conditions of Western agriculture or American society in general in the late nineteenth century. . . . The myth of the garden of the world is still so vivid for Julian that he seems to think it can be realized by incantation."[40]

Thus in his approach to agrarian and land problems in the post-Civil War decades, Julian was demonstrating one of the perplexing dilemmas of the era—the tendency to turn back to the values and credos of the ante-bellum period for solutions to problems intricately related to a new era dominated by the Industrial Revolution. This basic factor in part explains Julian's role as a land re-

[39] See also Patrick W. Riddleberger, "George W. Julian: Abolitionist Land Reformer," in *Agricultural History,* 29 (1955):113-15.

[40] Smith, *Virgin Land,* 192.

former, but determinants stemming from the man's personality, as reflected in his adolescent reaction to Commissioner Sparks, who was basically in sympathy with his ideas, must also be considered. Time and time again Julian seems to have narrowly missed rising to the level of statesmanship because of his compulsion for controversy. His consciousness of himself as a crusader frequently blinded him to the over-all significance of the problems he was trying so desperately to solve.

11 THE LAST DECADE

11 ◇◈◇◈◇◈◇◈◇◈◇◈◇◈◇

IN 1889 Julian returned to Irvington where he spent the remaining ten years of his life in relative peace and quiet. Now, with battles for political office inexorably behind him, Julian's illnesses mitigated to a marked extent; and even though some of the insomnia and anxiety still remained, he handled them more calmly than ever before. Hence, only as he looked forward to death and gave up the struggle for life did he gain some of the serenity that he had so long sought.

Laura's death in 1884 did not leave Julian without a woman's ministrations. His daughter, Grace, was delighted to be able to assume her mother's role. Twenty years old when Julian embarked on the New Mexican venture, Grace accompanied him to Santa Fé and remained there with him much of the time. Of the three children who survived Julian, Grace was undoubtedly his favorite. She presented none of the problems that Fred had created for the family; she was obedient and loyal and shared her father's interests. In school she did her work proficiently; she respected her parents, and she took responsibility readily. At an early age she was writing affectionate letters to her father, and by twelve she was composing poetry to express her esteem for him. In her room she kept his picture, which, she wrote, looked at her "all night long." Once when Julian was absent in Washington the picture evoked this little poem:

Oft' do I miss thee
But think it may be
Because I oft' see
The picture of thee.[1]

Now in his old age it was Grace, well tutored by Laura, who was at Julian's side whenever he needed her. Although she was married by this time, she lived in her father's house, and the presence of a husband apparently did not interfere with the constant attention Julian liked.

But Grace was more than a servant to her father; she was his alter ego. After his death she began writing articles about him, and she edited some of his letters and speeches for publication. In 1923 her biography of Julian appeared in print. In this completely uncritical work, which is more of a memoir than a biography, Grace accepted without question Julian's opinion of himself and of his role as a public figure. The book is interspersed with long passages from his speeches and quotations from his diary, and the historical background as well as the interpretation of Julian's political career is lifted, sometimes almost word for word, from his *Political Recollections.*[2]

During that last decade of his life there was a stately air about old Julian. Still slim and erect and always carrying a cane, he took his daily walk about the town. Sometimes he stopped to talk with children along the

[1] Grace Julian to Julian, January 13, 1878, Julian Papers. Frederick Julian pursued his acting career, though achieving little renown. He died in 1911. Paul, Julian's son by his second marriage, became a civil engineer. He died in 1929.

[2] Grace Julian married Charles B. Clarke. She was active in the Democratic party and in various women's clubs in Indiana. Her devotion to her father and his memory sometimes became misguided; for example, when she tried to protect his name by destroying a portion of his manuscript collection, including, as mentioned above, the invaluable unpublished autobiography and his journals before 1869.

way. Visitors frequented his house, and Julian met with friends in the library to discuss current and past politics. Sometimes he autographed copies of his Congressional speeches and gave them to admiring visitors. One newspaper described him as the "Nestor of the community." On his birthday friends came from far and wide—many of them from the Whitewater country—to honor him and to celebrate with him. Julian continued to correspond with some of his acquaintances of his more active years. He kept a list of old antislavery friends on which he crossed out the names as death took them, one by one. There were also letters to and from new friends as well as old. Edward L. Pierce, writing his biography of Charles Sumner, consulted with Julian concerning various aspects of his work. The two became close friends, so much so that in 1894 Julian was invited to attend a dinner in Boston to honor the memory of Sumner and his biographer. "Advancing years and ailing health" prevented his going, but Senator George F. Hoar read a letter from Julian to the assembled guests. Theodore Clarke Smith, preparing the manuscript of his *Liberty and Free-Soil Parties in the Northwest,* came to Julian as one of the few remaining survivors of those prewar days. There were also friendly letters exchanged with James Ford Rhodes, whose *History of the United States from the Compromise of 1850* was in the process of publication from 1893 until after Julian's death.[3]

II

Thus Julian was not merely a doddering old man awaiting death. For one of his age his energy remained

3 Clippings in Grace Julian Clarke's Scrapbooks, Indiana Division, Indiana State Library; Clarke, *Julian,* 413; Edward L. Pierce to Julian, December 31, 1894, and Theodore Clarke Smith to Julian, October 3, 1897, Gid-

prodigious. He continued his reading on a wide range of subjects, but now he was probably more interested in the political news in the daily newspaper than in anything else. At the age of seventy-five he published his full-length biography of Joshua R. Giddings. He also continued to write articles for magazines on politics and other related subjects. One of the last of these was a review of John W. Burgess' *The Middle Period,* which appeared in *The Dial* for May, 1897.[4] Here Julian took Burgess to task for his unfriendliness to the abolitionists and for catering to the slavocracy. He also held that Burgess' interpretation of the Mexican War as a defensive war against an aggressor was completely fallacious.

The election of 1896 and its attendant elaboration of the free silver issue brought forth Julian's last significant statements on politics and on other public questions. To Julian the free silver movement was the latest evil, the most recent obstacle standing in the way of progress, that reformers must fight to overcome. The last significant speech of Julian's life was deliverd to the Sound Money League of Indianapolis in October, in which he attacked the advocates of free silver. The cause of the financial crisis and of the current depression, said Julian, could be traced to the legal tender acts of the Civil War and to the cheap money craze that had persisted since that time. These acts, he argued, "gave birth to the delusion that under the power to coin money and regulate the value thereof, Congress could create money, although the power to do this belongs exclusively to the Almighty." The quantity of money, asserted Julian, had nothing to do with the downward trend of prices

dings-Julian Papers. There are also letters from Pierce and Smith in the Julian Papers.

4 Pages 274-77.

over the last two decades, the cause of which could be found in the increasing supply brought about by improved technological processes.

Julian again asserted his political independence and raised the question as to which party men like himself ought to support. Why not support the Republicans, who so staunchly opposed the free silver appeal of Bryan? But the Republicans, Julian argued, had vitiated their position as the true gold party by a qualifying phrase in their platform indicating that bimetallism might be established under international agreement. The only course left to men who stood firmly opposed to bimetallism and who would not forsake their principles was to vote for the Gold Democrats, who refused to accept Bryan as the Democratic candidate, left the party, and founded their own party favoring the gold standard. This was the course that Free Soilers had taken in 1848; it was still the proper action for courageous men in 1896.[5]

Julian's analogy between the Gold Democrats and the Free Soilers was hardly valid. For the Sound Money League, which he addressed, was the creation of Henry Villard and of William Rockefeller, and the splinter party known as the Gold Democrats was the brain child of William C. Whitney. It was organized to preserve the Cleveland wing of the Democracy after its overthrow by the silverites, and many men believed that its real reason for being was to divert strength from Bryan so as to insure the election of William McKinley.

During the campaign two young men visited Julian to discuss the current political situation with him. They heard from the old man that the campaign was part of a great contest between capital and labor that would

[5] Indianapolis *News*, October 16, 1896.

end, eventually, in another civil war. Bryan and his followers, said Julian, were trying "to bring capital to its
knees." This was "revolutionary," and Julian was contemptuous of it.[6] In his diary Julian wrote further reflections on the Democratic candidate:

> Bryan's campaign . . . is unprecedented in the multitudes who
> flock to hear him everywhere and in the unbounded enthusi-
> asm of his followers. . . . If he can succeed, with all the busi-
> ness interests of the country against him solidly, and nearly
> all the newspapers, and all the colleges and educational in-
> fluences, it can only be accounted for on the theory of a
> stupendous retrogression in the work of civilization, which
> would be at war with the philosophy of evolution and irrecon-
> cilable with the belief of a Divine providence. I am therefore
> perfectly convinced that no such calamity is in store for us.[7]

In 1898, Julian wrote an article for the *Arena* in which
he restated his views on the money question. It was
the Greenback movement, he asserted, that had "brought
upon the country the frightful panic of 1873, and
[had] ever since exercised its malign influence over both
political parties." Silver dollars were merely "metallic
greenbacks." Politicians, Julian concluded, were completely incapable of solving these monetary problems.
Although Congress would have to enact appropriate legislation, it ought to follow the advice and the "deliberate judgment of a large body of well-informed and dis-
interested businessmen representing every interest of the
people and constantly striving for their welfare."[8]

Inevitably, letters came to Julian expressing incredu-
lity at his utterances. An old antislavery friend wrote that

6 Indianapolis *Sentinel*, November 2, 1901.

7 Julian's Journal, October 20, 1896, Indiana Division, Indiana State
Library.

8 George W. Julian, "Our Party Leaders and the Finances," in *The
Arena*, 19 (January-June, 1898):145-56.

he would not have been more astounded and grieved if Garrison and Phillips and Lucretia Mott had undertaken to re-establish slavery after its overthrow. But Julian remained "entirely satisfied" with the soundness of his article, and such letters only convinced him that he had "done his duty in publishing it."[9]

John Clark Ridpath, editor of the *Arena,* wrote an article in reply to Julian's. Recalling an earlier part of Julian's career, especially the Free Soil years, Ridpath lamented: "That he [Julian] should now . . . renounce his better self, abandon the cause of humanity, join the enemies of mankind, and attempt with a fallacious, misleading, pessimistic, and soulless argument to lead his countrymen into the brazen jaws of a slave-trap more deadly than that which held the African race in bondage,—is one of the most pitiable spectacles in the personal history of our times."[10]

Ridpath's lament was understandable in that he was a critic of American society and edited one of the early muckraking journals. Julian's ideas about reforms and reformers had changed radically as he approached the end of his life. He now believed President Cleveland —the plodding conservative opponent of Populist "paternalism"—to be the greatest living reformer. This view was in tune with Julian's latest ideas about reformers in general: "The order and well-being of society must at all events be entrusted to the care of the sane. If one man is accorded the right to undertake the work of reform as the chosen instrument of the Almighty, and to set aside the commands of the Decalogue, any other man might claim

9 Julian's Journal, March 4, 1898.
10 John Clark Ridpath, "The Finances and Our Party Leaders," in *The Arena,* 19 (1898):157-86. For quotation see pages 157-58.

the same right, and the multiplication of these saviors of society would turn the world upside down."[11]

Julian's writings and speeches during the last decade of his life indicate some interesting changes in his thinking about public matters. No longer, for instance, is there the glorification of the independent farmer whose secure place in America Julian had fought for through his efforts to bring about land reform. His concentration on currency and his strictures of cheap money suggest a narrowing of his interests and an atrophy of his humanitarianism and his vision of a democratic society. In 1896, Julian was approaching his eightieth year, so that there might indeed have been a withering away of his mental powers; perhaps there was a loss of nerve from normal deterioration. Yet this is not an entirely satisfying explanation of the inconsistencies which made him a pathetic spectacle to men like Ridpath. Nor are the inconsistencies as real as they seem at first glance.

In his animus against cheap money Julian was in the role of a genteel reformer of the latter years of the nineteenth century, and in it he was identifying with eastern rather than western reform. In looking back into Julian's life for those persons who were most influential with him we find that they were most frequently patricians, men and women regarded as intellectuals—Lucretia Mott, Lydia Maria Child, William Ellery Channing, Harriet Martineau—and that they were from the eastern United States or from Euorpe. Nor was Julian's rejection of Populism and Bryanism necessarily a rejection of the agrarian ideal, for the agrarian ideal was always essentially an apotheosis of individualism. Populists were not abhorrent to him because they were western farmers but

11 Julian, "Some American History Rewritten," in *The Dial,* 22 (January-June, 1897):277.

because as he saw it they had turned paternalistic. Even at the zenith of his career, as chairman of the House Committee on Public Lands, Julian had rejected proposals for government control of the operations of railroads in ways other than curtailment of subsidies. Hence, if Julian had come around by the 1890's to looking to businessmen for leadership and wisdom, it was partly because businessmen were now the paragons of individualism.

In some ways, therefore, Julian's personal tragedy in the postwar years was the tragedy of his generation, its too ready acceptance of the shibboleth of *laissez faire* and its almost hysterical fear of the state at a time when the state was the only power that could contend with the new industrial behemoths. This legacy of Jeffersonianism was the basis of an anachronism, condoned or perhaps misunderstood by reformers like Julian, which made for much unnecessary suffering. For all its ineptitudes and its failures, its prejudices and zaniness, Populism was at least trying to come to grips with some of the realities of the era; in fact, it was much closer to reality than men like Julian, who were incapable of a rational judgment of it.

Julian shared many of the characteristics of that group of men in the late nineteenth century which Richard Hofstadter calls the Mugwump type. They appear first in the Liberal Republican movement and in the 1880's are found voting for Cleveland against Blaine. (As we have seen, Julian had already made his departure from the Republican party and joined the Democrats.) Although some of them were to be found in the midwestern cities, they "flourished . . . most conspicuously about Boston, a center of seasoned wealth and seasoned conscience," and among them were such men as Charles

Francis Adams, Jr., Edward Atkinson, Moorfield Storey, and Thomas Wentworth Higginson. These were the same men whom Julian admired and whose company he sought whenever possible, men whose "cultural ideals and traditions [were] of New England, and beyond these of old England." With such an orientation and such tastes, it is little wonder that Julian preferred Washington to New Mexico and accepted the appointment to that territory only as a last resort.

"As a rule," says Hofstadter, the Mugwump type "was dogmatically committed to the prevailing theoretical economics of *laissez-faire,* [and] his economic program did not go much beyond tariff reform and sound money. . . . His pre-eminent journalist and philosopher was E. L. Godkin. . . . His favorite statesman was Grover Cleveland. . . . If he was critical of the predatory capitalists and their political allies, he was even more contemptuously opposed to the 'radical' agrarian movements and the 'demagogues' who led them. . . . The Mugwump was shut off from the people as much by his social reserve and his amateurism as by his candidly conservative views. In so far as he sought popular support, he sought it on aristocratic terms."[12]

If Julian differed from the Mugwump type in certain particulars, the trend of his thought and action during the last twenty-five years of his life was clearly of that genre. By 1896 he was probably as close to the stereotype as most of the men Hofstadter had in mind.

In discovering that Julian can be classified as a member of an identifiable group, such as the Mugwumps, we are, I think, enhancing our understanding of him. But the biographer ought to be careful not to fall into the

[12] Richard Hofstadter, *The Age of Reform, From Bryan to F. D. R.* (New York, 1955), 139-43.

trap of too easy classification of his subject. In the case of Julian, at any rate, there is always a personal side that is more difficult to fathom. If there is any one trait that predominates throughout his mature life it is his difficulty to handle more than one idea at a time. By his own admission he was a "one idea" man who preferred one war at a time. In Julian's case the metaphorical war was apt, because he was rarely disengaged from either public or private controversy. Frequently the result was an intellectual myopia which prevented him from seeing the complexity of a political issue or a social problem; rather, he would see one facet of it and convince himself that he knew its quintessence. When the conflict in which he was habitually engaged was an all-pervading and dramatic movement like antislavery, Julian appeared prescient; some even saw greatness in him. From the conflict he took strength, and there were times when it may have been his salvation. It was when he equated such a crusade as that against free silver in 1896 with the earlier antislavery crusade that the flaws in personality and intellect began to show.

It seems altogether fitting that Julian's long life ended as the nineteenth century drew to a close. A son of its frontier, he was caught up in its romanticism, swept along by its humanitarian reform, brought to maturity in political participation under its democratic institutions, and influenced by both the liberalism and the obtuseness of the Victorian era. He was, indeed, a child of nineteenth-century America more significantly than in a mere chronological sense. He died on July 7, 1899, at eighty-two years of age.

BIBLIOGRAPHICAL ESSAY

Primary Sources

By far the most important primary sources are the writings of Julian himself, both published and unpublished. There are two manuscript collections in which much of the Julian story can be found. One is the Julian collection in the Indiana State Library in Indianapolis; the other is the Giddings-Julian collection in the Manuscript Division, Library of Congress. A second very small Giddings-Julian collection is in the library of the Ohio Historical Society in Columbus.

Among the items in the Indiana State Library is his Journal. This is a valuable source which tells us much about what happened in Julian's life but even more about how he felt about it. Unfortunately the portions of the Journal covering the years prior to 1869 were destroyed by Mrs. Grace Julian Clarke, Julian's daughter. Claude Bowers was able to use the collection while it was still intact, and he quotes rather freely from the Journal in his *The Tragic Era,* as does Mabel M. Engstrom in an unpublished M.A. thesis written at the University of Chicago in 1928.

Although the manuscript collections of other Radicals, such as Benjamin F. Wade, Lyman Trumbull, Zachariah Chandler, and Carl Schurz, are helpful for what they tell about the Radicals, surprisingly few Julian letters are in them. The Schurz papers are very useful for the Liberal Republican Movement. These collections are in the Manuscript Division of the Library of Congress, where the author also examined the Robert Todd Lincoln Papers, the Caleb B. Smith Papers, and the Grover Cleveland Papers. The last of these contained material on the appointment of Julian to the post of surveyor general of New Mexico Territory. Additional material on this phase of Julian's life can be found in the Land Office Records in the National Archives.

The author examined, with some benefit, other manuscript collections in the Indiana State Library and the Indiana Historical Society Library. Among these are the collections of Oliver P. Morton, Henry Charles, Hampden G. Finch, and Daniel D. Pratt in the State Library, and the William H. English and Mitten collections in the Historical Society Library.

A pleasant surprise was the discovery of a few letters in the Samuel S. Boyd Collection at the Bancroft Library, University of California, Berkeley, bearing on Julian's difficulties in getting launched on his legal career in Indiana.

The published works of Julian are extensive. The most important is his *Political Recollections, 1840 to 1872,* published in 1884. Other works are two volumes of his own speeches and biographies of Charles Osborn and Joshua R. Giddings. He also published a number of articles: "The Death-Struggle of the Republican Party," in *North American Review,* 126 (January-June, 1878):262-92; "The First Republican National Convention," in *American Historical Review,* 4 (1898-99):313-21; "Land-Stealing in New Mexico," in *North American Review,* 145 (July-December, 1887):17-31; "Our Land Policy," in *Atlantic Monthly,* 43 (1879) :325-37; "Our Party Leaders and the Finances," in *The Arena,* 19 (January-June, 1898):145-56; "The Pending Ordeals of Democracy," in *International Review,* 5 (1878) :734-53; "Railway Influence in the Land Office," in *North American Review,* 136 (January-June, 1883) :237-56; "A Search After Truth," in *Unitarian Review,* 29 (1888) :48-57, reprinted in *Indiana Magazine of History,* 32 (1936) :250-60; "Some American History Rewritten," in *The Dial,* 22 (January-June, 1897):274-77; "Some Ante-bellum Politics," in *North American Review,* 163 (July-December, 1896):195-206; "Some Political Notes and Queries," in *International Review,* 7 (July-December, 1879) :164-82.

Of the government documents consulted the *Congressional Globe* was the most useful. Also helpful were the *Reports* of the Committee on the Conduct of the War; *House Miscellaneous Documents,* No. 15, 41 Congress, 1 Session, for Julian's contested election of 1868; and 15 Wallace 77-94 and 9 Wallace 187-97 for the California land cases.

The Report of the Commissioner of the General Land Office for 1885 (*House Executive Documents,* No. 1, 49 Congress, 1 Session) bears significantly on land matters in New Mexico while Julian was there as surveyor general.

The Indiana *House Journal,* 1845-46, sheds some light on Julian as a state legislator; *Indiana Election Returns, 1816-1851 (Indiana Historical Collections,* Vol. 40, Indianapolis, 1960) gives the results of the elections for the General Assembly and Thirty-first and Thirty-second Congresses in which Julian was a candidate.

It would be difficult to write a biography of Julian without resort to newspapers. The missing portions of the manuscript collections make this all the more essential. The continuing feud between the Julian political organ and the opposition Richmond *Palladium* is interesting and informative on matters that go beyond Julian's life and career. The Julian organ was published under different names at different times and places. It was first published in Centreville as the *True Democrat* and then as the *True Republican*. Later in Richmond, it bore the name *Julian's Radical*. The Indiana *Free Democrat*, published for a brief time in Indianapolis, might also qualify as a Julian organ. Files of the Centreville and Richmond papers are to be found in the Indiana State Library. The extant numbers of the *Palladium* are deposited in the office of the Richmond *Palladium-Item*. Also used extensively were the Indianapolis *Journal* (Morton, conservative Republican) and the Indianapolis *Sentinel* (Democratic). Other Indianapolis papers consulted were the *Gazette*, the *Herald*, and the *News*.

The Washington *National Era* was the spokesman of the Free Soil party during its active years. Occasionally Julian wrote letters to this paper which were published.

Some pertinent items were found in the New York *Times*, but Greeley's New York *Tribune* was more rewarding. For an Indiana Congressman Julian got a surprisingly thorough coverage in the *Tribune*, not always favorable.

In addition to Julian's own *Political Recollections*, other published reminiscences and letters are pertinent. The *Reminiscences* of Levi Coffin are informative as to the early antislavery movement in the Whitewater Valley. Henry C. Fox, *Memoirs of Wayne County and the City of Richmond* is useful for local history, as are David Turpie's *Sketches of my Own Times* and Lew Wallace's *Autobiography* for Indiana as a whole.

Josiah B. Grinnell, *Men and Events of Forty Years* (1891) is somewhat revealing on the Washington scene at mid-century. More rewarding for a later period and on national finances is Hugh McCulloch, *Men and Measures of Half a Century* (1889).

Mrs. Grace Julian Clarke's biography of her father, *George W. Julian,* qualifies in some respects as a primary source, and it contains portions of Julian's Journal and letters not available elsewhere. Mrs. Clarke also wrote several articles for the *Indiana Magazine of History* which, it seems might be properly listed among the primary sources: "Burnt District," 27 (1931):119-24; "George W. Julian: Some Impressions," 2 (1906):57-69; "Home Letters of George W. Julian, 1850-51," 29 (1933): 130-63; "Isaac Hoover Julian," 28 (1932):9-20; "A Letter of Daniel Worth to George W. Julian and other Documents," 26 (1930):152-65. Mrs. Clarke also kept scrapbooks containing newspaper clippings pertaining to Julian's political career, of which there are five volumes in the Indiana State Library.

The *Speeches, Correspondence and Political Papers of Carl Schurz* (6 vols. New York, 1913) contains material relevant to Julian's public life after the Civil War. These volumes are also very informative on the Liberal Republican Movement.

Secondary Sources

Although the author has relied for the most part on primary sources, there are a number of secondary sources which have had either a direct or indirect bearing on the book. What follows is an annotated list of those which appear most important.

For the settlement and early development of the Whitewater Valley the author read with great benefit six articles in the *Indiana Magazine of History* by Chelsea Lawlis: "Changes in the Whitewater Valley, 1840-1850," 44 (1948):69-82; "The Great Migration and the Whitewater Valley," 43 (1947):125-39; "Migration to the Whitewater Valley, 1820-1830," 43 (1947):225-39; "Population of the Whitewater Valley, 1850-1860," 44 (1948) :161-74; "Prosperity and Hard Times in the Whitewater Valley, 1830-1840," 43 (1947) :363-78; "Settlement of the Whitewater Valley, 1790-1810," 43 (1947):23-40. See also two articles by George S. Cottman in the *Indiana Magazine of History*: "A Hoosier Arcadia," 28 (1932) :96-113, and "The Whitewater Valley," 1 (1905) :204-8.

On the Old Northwest see R. C. Buley, *The Old Northwest, Pioneer Period, 1815-1840* (Indiana Historical Society, 1950) and Albert L. Kohlmeier, *The Old Northwest as the Keystone of the Arch of American Federal Union* (Bloomington, Ind., 1938). On Indiana history John D. Barnhart and Donald F. Carmony, *Indiana. From Frontier to Industrial Commonwealth* (4 vols. New York, 1954) is excellent. See also Logan Esarey, *A History of Indiana . . .* (2 vols. Fort Wayne, Ind., 1924).

On Indiana politics in the years spanning the Civil War, Kenneth M. Stampp, *Indiana Politics During the Civil War* (1949) covers a longer period than the title suggests, and is excellent. On the Republican party in Indiana see Roger H. Van Bolt, "The Rise of the Republican Party in Indiana, 1855-1856," in *Indiana Magazine of History*, 51 (1955) :185-220; Charles Zimmerman, "The Origin and Rise of the Republican Party in Indiana from 1854 to 1860," in *Indiana Magazine of History*, 13 (1917) :211-69, 348-412; Mildred C. Stoler, "The Democratic Element in the New Republican Party in Indiana," in *Indiana Magazine of History*, 26 (1940) :185-207. Two excellent articles on Hoosier Republican attitudes toward Lincoln are Winfred A. Harbison "Lincoln and the Indiana Republicans, 1861-1862," in *Indiana Magazine of History*, 33 (1937) :277-303, and "Indiana Republicans and the Reelection of President Lincoln," in *Indiana Magazine of*

History, 34 (1938) :42-64. See also Evarts B. Greene, *Some Aspects of Politics in the Middle West, 1860-72* (Madison, Wis., 1912) ; Edwin P. Harter, "Recollections of the Campaign of 1856," in *Indiana Magazine of History,* 16 (1920) :69-72; Henry C. Hubbart, "Pro-Southern Influences in the Free West, 1840-1865," in *Mississippi Valley Historical Review,* 20 (1933-34):45-62; and Charles Kettleborough, *Indiana on the Eve of the Civil War* (Indiana Historical Society *Publications,* Vol. 6, No. 1, Indianapolis, 1919).

There is no modern biography of Oliver P. Morton, but the two-volume work by William Dudley Foulke, *Life of Oliver P. Morton* (Indianapolis, 1899), contains a great deal of useful material on state and national politics. Additional biographies containing pertinent material are Charles B. Murphy, *The Political Career of Jesse D. Bright* (Indiana Historical Society *Publications,* Vol. 10, No. 3, Indianapolis, 1931), and Charles Roll, *Colonel Dick Thompson. The Persistent Whig (Indiana Historical Collections,* Vol. 30, Indianapolis, 1948).

On nativism in Indiana see Carl F. Brand, "History of the Know Nothing Party in Indiana," in *Indiana Magazine of History,* 18 (1922):47-81, 177-206, 266-306.

The best work on the Negro in the Hoosier state is Emma Lou Thornbrough, *The Negro in Indiana before 1900 (Indiana Historical Collections,* Vol. 37, Indianapolis, 1957). See also her article, "The Race Issue in Indiana Politics During the Civil War," in *Indiana Magazine of History,* 47 (1951) :165-88. Other works on the political antislavery movement and its leaders in Indiana and the Old Northwest are Helen M. Cavanagh, *Antislavery Sentiment and Politics in the Northwest, 1844-1860* (Chicago, 1940) ; Etta R. French, "Stephen S. Harding: A Hoosier Abolitionist," in *Indiana Magazine of History,* 27 (1931) : 209-29; Robert P. Ludlum, "Joshua R. Giddings, Radical," in *Mississippi Valley Historical Review*, 23 (1936-37) :49-60; Charles H. Money, "Fugitive Slave Law of 1850 in Indiana," in *Indiana Magazine of History*, 17 (1921) : 159-98, 257-97. William O. Lynch, "Antislavery Tendencies of the Democratic Party in the Northwest, 1848-50," in *Mississippi Valley Historical Review*, 11 (1924-25), is both informative and perceptive. Theodore C. Smith, *The Liberty and Free-Soil Parties in the Northwest* (New York, 1897), is still the best work on the subject. See also William H. Smith, *A Political History of Slavery . . .* (2 vols. New York, 1903). Julian's conversion to the Free Soil movement was treated by the author in "The Making of a Political Abolitionist: George W. Julian and the Free Soilers, 1848," in *Indiana Magazine of History*, 51 (1955): 221-36.

More general works on the antislavery movement are innumerable. One of the most recent, and perhaps the most authoritative, is Dwight L. Dumond, *Antislavery; the Crusade for Freedom in America* (Ann Arbor, Mich., 1961). Less detailed but valuable is Louis Filler, *The Crusade Against Slavery, 1830-1860* (New York, 1960). An earlier provocative work, emphasizing the religious aspects of the antislavery movement, is Gilbert H. Barnes, *The Antislavery Impulse 1830-1844* (New York, 1933). See also Alice D. Adams, *The Neglected Period of Anti-Slavery in America* (Boston, 1908); Dwight L. Dumond, *Antislavery Origins of the Civil War in the United States* (Ann Arbor, Mich., 1939); Stephen B. Weeks, *Southern Quakers and Slavery . . .* (Baltimore, 1896) ; Alto Lee Whitehurst, *Martin Van Buren and the Free Soil Movement* (Chicago, 1935). Henry Wilson, *History of the Rise and Fall of the Slave Power in America* (3 vols. Boston, 1872-77), is not without value even though it is the subjective account of a participant. Russel B. Nye examines the myth and the reality of a slave power conspiracy in his provocative *Fettered Freedom; Civil Liberties and the Slavery Controversy, 1830-1860* (East Lansing, Mich., 1947).

Two interesting interpretative works on the motivations of reformers which were found useful, are Eric Hoffer, *The True Believer* (New York, 1958), and Arthur M. Schlesinger, *The American As Reformer* (Cambridge, Mass., 1950).

On the Compromise of 1850 see Holman Hamilton, *Zachary Taylor* (2 vols. Indianapolis, 1941-51). More recent and with a new interpretation is his *Prologue to Conflict: the Crisis and the Compromise of 1850* (Lexington, Ky., 1964). Among the other works consulted on the decade of the 1850's are Allan Nevins, *Ordeal of the Union* (2 vols. New York, 1947) ; Roy F. Nichols, *The Disruption of American Democracy* (New York, 1948) ; Henry H. Simms, *A Decade of Sectional Controversy, 1851-1861* (Chapel Hill, N.C., 1942); and Avery O. Craven, *The Growth of Southern Nationalism, 1848-1861* (Baton Rouge, 1953) and *The Coming of the Civil War* (Chicago, 1957).

There are a number of differing interpretations of the causes of the Civil War with emphasis on the secession crisis of 1860-1861. Among the more important are David M. Potter, *Lincoln and his Party in the Secession Crisis* (New Haven, Conn. 1942) ; Kenneth M. Stampp, *And the War Came* (Baton Rouge, 1950) ; Arthur M. Schlesinger, Jr., "The Causes of the Civil War: A Note on Historical Sentimentalism," in *Partisan Review*, 16 (1949):969-81; James G. Randall, "The Blundering Generation," in *Mississippi Valley Historical Review*, 27 (1940-41):3-28.

Because the author has been primarily concerned with Julian as a Radical Republican during the Civil War years none of the innumerable works on military history is included here. The most valuable secondary source for the war years is T. Harry Williams, *Lincoln and the Radicals* (Madison, Wis., 1941), even though Professor Williams may be too harsh in his treatment of the Radicals. David Donald, *Lincoln Reconsidered* . . . (New York, 1956), is very helpful for suggestions as to the relationship between Lincoln and the Radicals. See also James G. Randall, *Lincoln, the Liberal Statesman* (New York, 1947); *Lincoln, the President* (4 vols. New York, 1944-55); and *Constitutional Problems under Lincoln* (New York, 1926).

An excellent essay on the historiography of the Reconstruction period is Bernard A. Weisberger, "The Dark and Bloody Ground of Reconstruction Historiography," in *Journal of Southern History*, 25 (1959) :427-47. The most recent new interpretation is Kenneth M. Stampp, *The Era of Reconstruction* (New York, 1965), which presents a more favorable view of the Radicals than the older histories, of which William A. Dunning, *Reconstruction, Political and Economic, 1865-1877* (New York, 1907), is the most definitive. For a briefer general account see John Hope Franklin, *Reconstruction after the Civil War* (Chicago, 1961). Two recent works on the Reconstruction policies of the Andrew Johnson administration are William R. Brock, *An American Crisis: Congress and Reconstruction* (New York, 1963), and Eric L. McKitrick, *Andrew Johnson and Reconstruction* (Chicago, 1960).

There is no recent study on the Liberal Republican Movement and the election of 1872, but the earlier work, Earle Dudley Ross, *The Liberal Republican Movement* (New York, 1919), is still useful. See also Eric Goldman, *Rendezvous with Destiny* (New York, 1952), which is excellent on reformers and reform movements after the Civil War. On the changing attitudes and roles of Radical Republicans in 1872 see the author's articles: "The Break in the Radical Ranks: Liberals vs Stalwarts in the Election of 1872," in *Journal of Negro History,* 44 (1959):136-57, and "The Radicals' Abandonment of the Negro," in *Journal of Negro History,* 45 (1960):88-102. The best study of the presidential election of 1876 is C. Vann Woodward, *Reunion and Reaction. The Compromise of 1877 and the End of Reconstruction* (Boston, 1951).

A good general work on the history of American public land policy is Roy M. Robbins, *Our Landed Heritage* (New York, 1950). Still useful also is the older work by Benjamin H. Hibbard, *A History of the Public Land Policies* (New York, 1939). Two excellent articles relevant to Julian's role in land reform are Paul W. Gates, "The Homestead Law in an Incongruous Land System," in *American Historical Review,* 41 (1936):652-81, and "Federal Land Policy in the South, 1866-1888," in *Journal of Southern History,* 6 (1940):303-30. Henry Nash Smith, *Virgin Land. The American West as Symbol and Myth* (1950), is important for intellectual history as it relates to the frontier and the West. On Julian as land reformer see also the author's article, "George W. Julian: Abolitionist Land Reformer," in *Agricultural History,* 29 (1955):108-15.

On American thought in the late nineteenth century Sidney Fine, *Laissez Faire and the General Welfare State* . . . (Ann Arbor, Mich., 1956) has been very informative. See also Volumes 2 and 3 of Joseph Dorfman, *The Economic Mind in American Civilization* (3 vols. New York, 1946-1959). For an interpretation of Populism and those who opposed it nothing has been so helpful as Richard Hofstadter, *The Age of Reform* . . . (New York, 1955).

INDEX

INDEX

Abolition of slavery, as aim of Civil War, 147, 153, 164, 165-67, 177, 201; in District of Columbia, 167; Emancipation Proclamation, 177-79; as military measure, 152, 164; Thirteenth Amendment, 203.

Adams, Charles Francis, 16, 38, 70, 287n; in Liberal Republican movement, 269, 270, 271.

Adams, John Quincy, 16, 18, 25, 41-42.

Allen, Charles, 52, 57, 70, 72.

Anderson, Maj. Robert, 146.

Anthony, Susan B., 270.

Antislavery movement, in Whitewater Valley, 6; in Congress, 16, 18, 45, 74-76; and politics, 16, 18-19, 33-34, 37-38, 41, 45-50, 91-104, 106-9, 111-16, 120-33; newspapers, 117, 122-23. See also Abolition of slavery; Fugitive slave law.

Bailey, Gamaliel, 52, 73.

Baker, Conrad, 28.

Baker, Col. Edward, 156.

Bickel, William, 134.

Bidwell, Andrew, 117.

Bidwell, Solomon, 117.

Birney, James G., 16, 18-19, 43.

Blair, Francis P., 110.

Bright, Jesse D., 81, 83.

Brown, B. Gratz, 271.

Brown, William J., 53-54, 81.

Bryan, William Jennings, 315-16.

Bryant, William Cullen, 182, 282.

Buchanan, James, 120, 136-37.

Buell, Gen. Don Carlos, 177.

Burgess, John W., 314.

Burnside, Gen. Ambrose, 176, 181.

"Burnt District," see Campaigns and elections, 4th and 5th Congressional districts.

Butler, Charles, 29-33.

Calhoun, John C., 49, 58.

California, admission of, 58-59; pre-emption of public lands in, 248-52.

Cameron, Simon, 161-62.

Campaigns and elections, *4th Congressional district* (1843), 19-20; (1845), 26, 27; (1849), 46-50; (1851), 78-83; (1852), 102-3; (1856), 116n; *5th Congressional district* (1858), 123-26; (1860), 132-34; (1862), 173-75; (1864), 195-201; (1866), 219-21; *4th Congressional district* (1868), 222-25; (1870), 257-61; *Congressman-at-large* (1872), 265-67, 271-72n; *General Assembly* (1843), 20; (1845), 26-27; (1847), 33-34; (1854), 102; (1856), 116n; *governor* (1843), 19-20; (1849), 46, 48; (1856), 115-16; *president* (1840), 16-18; (1844), 24-26; (1848), 37-40, 45, 47-48; (1852), 84-90; (1856), 114-15; (1860), 129-32; (1864), 198-200; (1872), 267-75; (1876), 284-92; (1880), 299-300; (1896), 314-16.

Capital punishment, bill for abolition of, 28.

Cass, Lewis, 37, 45, 47-48.

(335)

Seward, William, 58, 62, 71, 106; candidate for president, 131-32; secretary of state, 142, 144, 177, 179.

Sherman, John, 231n.

Sherman, Gen. William T., 209-10.

Slave trade, bill to abolish in District of Columbia, 45.

Slavery issue, raised by land acquisition after Mexican War, 58-59; attempt to settle by Compromise of 1850, 59-60, 62, 66-68, 71, 74-76; southern Congressmen sensitive on, 60, 63; reopened by Kansas-Nebraska bill, 91-93. *See also* Abolition of slavery; Antislavery movement; Fugitive slave law; Negroes.

Smith, Caleb B., candidate for Congress, 26; in Congress, 39n, 47, 48-49; in Lincoln's cabinet, 138, 139, 140, 141.

Smith, Gerrit, 182-83, 192.

Smith, Theodore Clarke, 313.

Southworth, Mrs. Emma, 73.

Sparks, William A. J., 302, 305, 306, 307-10.

Speed, James, 211.

Spiritualism, 135.

Stockslager, S. M., 306.

Spriggs, Mrs. ———, boarding house, 52.

Stanton, Edwin M., 161-62, 210.

Stevens, Stephen C., 85.

Stevens, Thaddeus, 154, 230.

Stone, Gen. Charles P., 156.

Stowe, Harriet Beecher, 91.

Suffrage, for Negroes, 193-94, 212-16, 226-28; for women, 229.

Sumner, Charles, 16, 43n-44n, 53, 65, 70, 142, 154, 270; death, 282; biographer, 313.

Swamplands, 240.

Taber, Stephen, 246.

Tariff, legislation, 150-51, 170; Julian advocate of free trade, 49, 263.

Taylor, Zachary, 209n, 239; candidate for president, 37, 40, 45; Julian's characterization of, 55-56n; opposes Compromise of 1850, pp. 59-60; death, 66, 68.

Terre Haute (Ind.), 87-88.

Test, Charles H., 22, 81, 107.

Thompson, Richard W., 118, 120.

Tilden, Samuel J., 299n, 301n; candidate for president, 286, 287, 288, 289, 290, 292.

Trumbull, Lyman, 267-68, 269, 287n.

Trusler, Nelson, 134.

Tuck, Amos, 52.

Uncle Tom's Cabin, 91.

Underground Railroad, 6.

Unitarianism, embraced by Julian, 11, 42-43.

United States Congress, antislavery petitions, 18, 74; *(31st)* speakership contest, 53-55; members, 52, 56, 57-58, 62; legislation, 59-68, 69-70, 74-78; *(37th)*, 146-51, 153-54, 164-70, 176-80; *(38th)*, 185-95, 201-6; *(39th and 40th)*, 219, 225-50; elections to and political alignment of, 19-20, 26, 27, 46-50, 78-83, 102-3, 116n, 123-26, 132-34, 173-75, 195-201, 219-21, 222-25, 257-61, 265-67, 271-72n, 274; investigation of patent office, 182; joint committee on conduct of war, membership, 154, 155-58, 209n; work of, 160, 181-82, 185-86, 203, 207-8, 209-10; reapportionment, 222-23n; election of senator (1867), 221-22.